ADVANCES IN
LIBRARY ADMINISTRATION
AND ORGANIZATION

Volume 9 • 1991

ADVANCES IN LIBRARY ADMINISTRATION AND ORGANIZATION

A Research Annual

Editors: GERARD B. McCABE
Director of Libraries
Clarion University of Pennsylvania

BERNARD KREISSMAN
University Librarian, Emeritus
University of California, Davis

VOLUME 9 • 1991

 JAI PRESS INC.

Greenwich, Connecticut   *London, England*

CONTENTS

THE I. T. LITTLETON
THIRD ANNUAL SEMINAR

INTRODUCTION

For Volume 9, Allen Veaner visits these pages once again with a chapter taken from his new book, Academic Librarianship in a Transformational Age. . . , G. K. Hall, 1989. It is revised and shortened somewhat for ALAO but should lead readers to seek out his book and read it thoroughly. For academic librarians and administrators it is must reading. Allen's ideas are incisive; he makes the reader think; what he has to say, we all need to consider.

Alice G. Smith returns also to these pages with a paper on Bibliotherapy. Librarians in the field and students in library science programs will want to read this paper about an important but little known area of librarianship. This is a subject to which some librarians made significant contributions, and Smith's report stirs pride in our profession.

Public library planning is the topic of the next paper by Annabel Stephens. She adds recommendations for others to follow as they begin the overall planning process for improving the service of their libraries.

In recent months, articles have appeared in various places on the subject of plagiarism. A recent new book on the subject received favorable reviews. Now the editors present a paper by Serena McGuire on the subject of book piracy. Why stop at a few paragraphs, why not take the entire work? She presents an historical overview and then brings the issue to modern times.

A detailed study of the motivational needs of corporate librarians follows. Written by Sohair Wastawy-Elbaz, this paper goes into the world of the special librarian.

Frederick Smith and George Messmer approach library planning from a state-wide basis with a report on current activities led by the State Library of New York. Their review of networking among various types of libraries should be of great interest to librarians in the field. This editor was intrigued by their discussion of the need to link various library networks around the state. This should be interesting to follow in news reports.

Following this paper, we present two short reports on libraries overseas. The first of these is about the Szechenyi Library, the great national library of Hungary. Elizabeth Rajec visited the library and prepared this report for our readers. Nahla Natour returns to our pages with a report on another library in her homeland of Jordan. It is most interesting how library developments are occurring in such countries as Jordan and we hope to present reports from other countries about their libraries in the future. Two bibliographies follow in keeping with our tradition of publishing what we believe are good, well prepared bibliographies. In one case, we are continuing to supplement Sitzman's "Bibliography of African Librarianship" which appeared in *African Libraries,* Scarecrow Press, 1988.

Lastly we welcome to our pages, the papers of the I. T. Littleton Seminar held at North Carolina State University. We plan to bring these papers to our readers each year. We welcome also Cynthia Levine as editor of the Littleton seminar papers. Her introduction precedes the papers.

ALAO continues the wish of its founding editor, the late Carl Jackson, that an eclectic annual be available for the longer paper that might not otherwise find its way into print. The present editors follow that desire, and so present Volume 9.

Gerard B. McCabe
Editor

ADMINISTRATIVE THEORIES, BUSINESS PARADIGMS AND WORK IN THE ACADEMIC LIBRARY

Allen B. Veaner

> A man is not idle because he is absorbed in thought. There is a visible labor and there is an invisible labor.
>
> —Victor Hugo, *Les Miserables*

SOURCES OF ADMINISTRATIVE THEORY

Like most service organizations and professions, librarianship depends upon researchers in behavioral science and organizational theory for its paradigms. Why the profession has evolved so little of its own administrative theory is not hard to understand. We are no different from other underfunded service agencies; perforce we all are natural borrowers and adapters. Besides, our fund allocators have given us, the practitioners, a mandate for action, not resources for organizational research. North American library administrators readily borrow any tech-

Advances in Library Administration and Organization,
Volume 9, pages 1–28.
Copyright © 1991 by JAI Press, Inc.
All rights of reproduction in any form reserved.
ISBN: 1-55938-066-7

niques they think will help their programs and clients.[1] But there are hazards in borrowing other people's ideas. Competing theories emerge in rapidly developing cycles and it is confusing to keep jumping from one to another. Also, it is easy to develop blind loyalty to one theory and believe it is *the* only sure fix. Despite the dislocations induced, constant movement between theories may not be bad in itself—as long as we recognize what we are doing, use current concepts to best advantage, keep looking for new ones, try not to impose someone else's "total package" onto librarianship and, respecting human judgment, intuition and experience, take the best ideas from each model and adjust them to reality. In the absence of perfect theory, situational responses and seasoned judgment have great validity, a point De Gennaro made colorfully and vigorously in a classic paper.[2]

The virtually hegemonic theories of Maslow, McGregor, Herzberg, and others of the behavioralist and human relations schools have enormously influenced modern administrative styles, just as the models of their predecessors—Frederick Taylor, Max Weber, and Henri Fayol—did in earlier times. But students and critics of administration, now some distance away from the behavioralist schools, are beginning to look upon the pioneering work of the human potential movement with some caution and skepticism.[3] In a survey of ten administrative and behavioral theories, Bottomley was highly critical. Etzioni, a structuralist and prominent scholar of organizational theory, was severely critical of the behavioralist approach, viewing some of its elements as overly simplistic. Hunt suggested that Maslow's hierarchy of needs enjoys popularity because it fits in well with organizational life, not because it can be verified empirically; in Hunt's opinion, some 60 percent of the work force are much more concerned with relationships outside the work environment than with work-focused achievement, power or self-fulfillment, as maintained by the behavioralists. Orne alleged that the behavioralists make unwarranted assumptions about the uniformity of motivation and other human attributes. Yankelovich viewed the Maslovian outlook as self-centeredness gone wild, the very peak of existentialist theory. In a devastating critique of the behavioralists, Maccoby characterized their views as misleading, mechanistic, unwittingly supportive of hierarchy, excessively bipolar, and failing to deal with the richness and ambiguities of human behavior. To these critiques we add our own view that the behavioralist doctrine is based upon ideas of universality, a presupposed uniformity of human character, and continuous economic progress—all concepts now open to serious question.

In 1987 Rehman exhaustively analyzed how management theory was being communicated in programs of graduate education in librarianship.[4] His study pointed out that research in management is moving towards theories of far greater complexity than those of the behavioralist school. Yet Rehman also showed that classical and behaviorist theories were taught the most and that graduate schools were giving comparatively little notice to new developments. Rehman's inventory of management topics excluded—*not* extensively covered or minimally treated in library school—is striking and would seem to demand immediate examination.[5] Evidence that the schools are beginning to reexamine education for administration and management is the 1986 desiderata list of curriculum changes foreseen by major library school deans.[6] One dean observed that curricular goals were demonstrating a consistent "shift of emphasis from how to why, from techniques to philosophy, from doing to thinking, from accepting to questioning. . . . "[7]

In practical librarianship the yawning gap between administrative theory and the real world of work remains irritatingly visible. In my experience of fifteen accreditation visits over a period of twenty years to graduate schools of library and information science, I heard a continuous refrain whenever the visiting team interviewed alumni: The schools ought to have given us a sounder foundation in administration and management. Although curricula in the graduate schools are slowly and continuously improving, modern administrators cannot wait for the next generation of better educated students nor for the latest administrative theories. They have to do their work today—*this* month, *this* week, *this* moment. They must do it with the resources at hand including, of course, all the staff they have, regardless of when they were hired or what may be their personal histories, outlooks, attitudes, skills and abilities.

REACHING FOR DEFINITIONS OF ADMINISTRATION

The voluminous folklore of academic administration obscures the true character of administration in high education. Popular axioms include claims that colleges and universities cannot be managed, that power is dysfunctional in a collegial organization, that organization charts are vital instruments of program implementation, and that administrations do not support change.

A generation ago it was comparatively easy to define administration. Whatever the environment, administration meant *control*. But even in control-intensive business and industry, consensus is emerging rapidly and nearly universally as a principal method for moving programs forward. In comparison with business management, academic administration, because it deals with a very large professional population, has always tended less towards control and more towards a specific type of consensus, collegiality. While the move to consensus is constantly growing, the change does not mean democratic processes are at work in administration—far from it—but it does signify a substantive stylistic shift in how organizational power and authority are used, even in academe.

Handbooks of administrative science and dictionaries are good sources of formal definitions for administration. We prefer unconventional definitions based

on paradox, because *paradox is the kernel of administrative reality.* The following informal definitions lay out somewhat starkly the dissonance, contradiction,
and ambiguity that are an inherent part of any administrative career:

> Administration is the unequal allocation of insufficient resources in a consultative but not
> necessarily democratic style.
>
> Administration is an organizational mechanism for the simultaneous creation and maintenance
> of inequality and equity.
>
> Administration means having a powerful, enduring impact without exercising direct, man-
> agerial control.
>
> Administration is making decisions that are necessary but that not everyone will like.

When I taught workshops on academic library administration, students of
library science—even including some experienced administrators—usually
heard these concepts with stunned silence and dismay, occasional distaste and
disbelief, even shock and horror. Asked beforehand to articulate their own definitions of administration, most students composed noble and appealing statements, replete with platitudes and sentiments pointing to high intellectual duties
and a mission of elevated responsibilities. Their views revealed the deep sense of
justice and desire to achieve fairness and equity that characterize the philosophy
and motivation of many library science students and young librarians.

One of the main functions of administration is surely to achieve a kind of
justice and fairness, but one that is circumscribed more by institutional constraints than by constitutional principles or grand social axioms. New or junior
administrators typically experience difficulty with a bureaucracy's impersonality.
They may confound their immediate, personal views of justice with the mandates
of institutional necessity, wishing to impose the former upon the latter. As
institutional goals are usually founded upon quite different, long-range perspectives, the resulting conflict can lead to administrative impotence, mental confusion, constant clashes with superiors, and even emotional disturbance. In brief,
some incumbent and potential library managers fail to understand their role as
agents of institutional authority or program. Such internal, emotional struggles
and difficulties relate to what Litterer and Person call the "Third Culture." The
third culture—management—which lies between C. P. Snow's two cultures,
science and humanities.[8] Person asserts—correctly in my view—that librarianship lacks a formal method for adequately socializing its managers:

> There is no widely-accepted program of study for individuals who must assume managerial
> responsibility in libraries, nor are there clearly defined paths within library organizations that
> provide a structured means of socialization. Compounding this problem is the lack of a
> widely-accepted body of knowledge about what a library manager actually *does*. Most li-
> brarians who assume a managerial role have received little structured preparation or guidance
> for that role.[9]

Person's statement helps explain demonstrable weaknesses in library management: the persistent search for democracy and equality, the failure to distinguish the rhetoric of behavioral theory from administrative realpolitik, and the inability to be decisive in tough situations. In support of Person's claim is research by Swisher, Du Mont, and Boyer whose disturbing conclusion is that most people who choose librarianship as a career do so because they wish to avoid administrative responsibility.[10]

That administrative decisions derive from processes that are essentially undemocratic and rarely deal in fairness tears at the fabric of much of our education and tradition, and is accepted only reluctantly or grudgingly by those whose orientation and traditions are strongly liberal. Some members of the profession can never submit themselves to a concept that seems to strike at the heart of democratic process; they are unlikely to be successful administrators.

As for equity, the several parts of any organization always receive differing degrees of support from the resource allocation authorities. Each does not get its fair share of space, staffing, money, equipment, or other resources. Of course, when an administration allocates resources, it rationalizes its decisions to accord with the organization's putative mission, goals, objectives. But invariably, the allocations follow the organization's *real* priorities. Inevitably such decisions invoke judgments that spell inequity. Consider the example of a business that installs a computerized data management system. It is much more likely that the system's first use will serve the information flow that directly affects the manufacture and sale of the company's products rather than some internal function, say, control of personnel records. This does not mean that personnel records are unimportant, merely that management has decided that external functions are more economically and politically sensitive. Similar decisions govern academic library resource allocation decisions. Historically, this is why circulation was automated long before cataloging—despite the obviously logical argument that an ideal circulation system should be based upon a master record containing the full bibliographic data that follow-on systems would need.

It is in procedures affecting employees' working conditions that an administration must be especially careful to maintain equity. Because library work reflects employment duality—an exempt professional staff and a nonexempt support staff—libraries must maintain both equity and inequality concurrently. They must administer different job classification and pay plans for exempt and nonexempt staff. The two plans must provide different work assignments to each category, in observance of the federally prescribed separation between exempt and nonexempt employees.

KANTER'S DUAL CONSTRUCTS: SEGMENTALISM
AND INTEGRATION

Analysis of business structures and leadership styles by Kanter and others urges
corporate America to adopt a new organizational paradigm: an "integrative"
rather than "segmental" approach to structure and function.[11] Kanter's distinctions between traditional and new organizational structures emerge dramatically
and forcefully in her tabulation of the assumptions behind the two styles as seen
in Table 1 below.[12]

For industry, Kanter's model is well founded. Indeed, much of the renaissance
of manufacturing in the United States is directly or indirectly attributable to its
implementation; but does it have anything to do with academic librarianship? In
criticizing the application to business of a social experiment conducted at a
summer camp, Kanter properly rejoined: "But that was summer camp, not a
corporation."[13] In attempting to borrow again from industry, as we have consistently done in the past, our considered response to our own question should be:
"But that is manufacturing; this is the academic world."

Funders in the public sector persist in regarding higher education as a business
and expect administrators to run colleges and universities—and their libraries—
as if they were just that. This forces library leaders to talk in one way to obtain
resources and in another to administer the funds they receive—a dichotomy that
will strike no library administrator as unusual. Translating the unique characteris-

Table 1.

Traditional Organization Design Factors (1890s–1920s)	Emerging Organization Design Factors (1960s–1980s)
Uneducated, unskilled temporary workers	Educated, sophisticated career employees
Simple and physical tasks	Complex and intellectual tasks
Mechanical technology	Electronic and biological technologies
Mechanistic views, direct cause and effect	Organic views, multiple causes and effects
Stable markets and supplies	Fluid markets and supplies
Sharp distinction between workers and managers	Overlap between workers and managers

tics of academic life into the world of work requires administrators to reconcile the two conflicting approaches, understanding where business and academe are conjoint and where they are disjoint. Table 2, on the following page, will assist in understanding why it is so difficult to graft business paradigms onto the problems of academic administration.

It is clear from Table 2 that managers and personnel experts who universalize their approach to human resources by applying office, factory or industrial management methods to academic libraries fail to understand that the academic workplace is far more complex than any business. *Productivity models, performance criteria, and management styles drawn from business and industry have very little relevance to the world of scholarship, and it is essential that academic librarians not be seduced by their mechanical, deterministic attractiveness.* In devastating critiques of business management methods in librarianship, De Gennaro warns against their uncritical adoption.[14] Colleges and universities cannot import wholesale every new technique and structure from the business world; were they to do so, higher education as we know it would cease to exist. Certainly the leaders of academe want their institutions to evolve, adapt, and change, but in a controlled manner—at least as controlled as is possible within the framework of what Cohen and March designate the "organized anarchy" of higher education.[15]

Many of the anecdotes in Kanter's work relate to new companies whose employees are comparatively young, for example, the fictional Chipco, where everyone is under 30, an age distribution impossible to imagine in academe.[16] It is equally impossible for higher education to surrender an organizational structure based on specialization, differentiation, and status differences and become a "parallel organization" where ". . . workers and mangers are involved in more egalitarian teams, where status distinctions are leveled and all struggle together for a joint solution."[17] Because academe intends to remain strongly "segmentalist," we have to distinguish carefully which views, attitudes, techniques, models and structures can and cannot be transferred to it from commerce. In reviewing eligible constructs, the first obvious principle is that academe is not going to give up its ancient social triad: faculty, students, everybody else. Correspondingly, academic librarianship as a major support arm of faculty and curriculum cannot give up its duality: librarians and everybody else. In personnel administration, the profession is forced to remain somewhat Janus-faced, looking simultaneously in opposite directions.

Despite the decision to remain "segmentalist," academic institutions and the people who work in them would still like to have all the benefits of integrative approaches: flexibility, opportunities for personal and organization development, empowerment, stimuli to innovation and creativity, enthusiastic teamwork, capacity to initiate and respond to change. How to accomplish this while maintaining the stratification of academic society is a major challenge.

Although Kanter was severely critical of hierarchy, it is important to note that

Table 2.

Business	Academe
Highly integrated processes.	Anarchic, highly personalized, jumbled processes; disorderly.
Strong attempts to rationalize not yet integrated processes.	Weak attempt to rationalize even conflicting processes.
Management provides central, strongly coordinated direction, with unified program.	Management provides vague direction, with little program unity; self-governance.
Tendency towards hierarchical organizational style; some experimentation with other styles.	Mixed organizational structure with islands of autonomy supported by a hierarchical infrastructure.
Outputs generally countable, with strong focus on bottom line or profits.	Main outputs intangible; quality and outcomes difficult to quantify; no profit.
Product and/or service orientation.	Service orientation.
Strong professional R&D component.	Weak R&D component but highly professionalized staff.
High-pressure environment.	High-pressure environment.
Few professionals; many operatives.	Vast number of professionals; large number of operatives.
Success measured in part by failure of competitors.	Success does not require competitors to fail.
Heavy use of deterministic, algorithmic processes; focus on the known, knowable, predictable.	Major emphasis on uncertain variables of human interactions; heuristics; many unknowns.
Wide age range of employees, with some young companies having very youthful staff.	Many older professionals; wide age range of other employees.
Highly specific job descriptions.	Vague statements for professionals
Work is highly specifiable; usually there is a best way.	Work uncertain, ill-defined; no two people do it alike; there is no best way.

she did *not* argue for dumping it. She concluded that a forward-looking organization really needs two administrative styles: a traditional hierarchy for doing what it must do in the way it already knows how, and a second aggressively entrepreneurial innovative structure—overlaid on the first—for coping with the unknown.[18] In short, new organizational paradigms do not necessarily invalidate or displace old ones; rather both paradigms co-exist with different mixes of responsibility, method, and attitude, plus altered distributions of power and interrelationships. This conclusion is highly constructive because it does not present an "either-or" choice for organizational renewal and reformation.

LIBRARY WORK COMPARED TO AND DISTINGUISHED FROM INDUSTRIAL WORK

In industry there are inputs, outputs, materials, a labor force, and energy sources to drive the engines of production. Traditionally, the production apparatus has been managed through a strongly hierarchical system. In relation to production itself, there are two major types of industrial work: factories and continuous processing plants.[19] The factory's assembly line aims to produce many of the same or similar objects, whether cheeseburgers, computer chips or underwear, with a maximum of efficiency. By definition, factory tasks are highly repetitive, procedures comparatively fixed, and routines firmly established. There is some room—but not much—for inventiveness, and there may be minor variations in routine, e.g., turning out different car models on the same line. Continuous processing (oil refining, pipeline transmission, chemical manufacture, electricity generation, bulk food processing)—is quite different in that rapid, independent judgment must frequently be invoked to keep the processes functioning safely or economically. Such plants are normally highly automated and employ only a small number of highly trained operators who understand the messages conveyed by meters, gauges or other signaling devices, and make the correct decisions immediately. Neither factory nor processing plant resembles the academic library.

A library too depends upon energy, facilities, materials, labor and administration—but its most significant output, the work of its professional staff, differs from an industrial product in two vital ways: First, it is as intangible as the bits and bytes that course through a computer's circuitry. Second, it is almost entirely customized for an ever changing clientele—people do not come back for "more" of the same information as they return to the supermarket for more fruits and vegetables. In essence, professional library work is a form of scholarly communication; the printed, displayed or spoken output is merely the codable, recordable and communicable result of cerebral processes. Catalogs and bibliographies are, in a manner of speaking, but side effects and by-products. Only a library's materials handling work (collating journals, labeling and pocketing books, reshelving, or keyboarding) is repetitive enough to warrant designation as "production" and hence require a staff of operatives. Even there, the operatives are frequently required to make judgments based on rules and procedures far more complex than those faced by their industrial counterparts.

In the preindustrial era and after the Industrial Revolution, when librarians performed huge amounts of clerical work, libraries might indeed have *looked* like bibliographic factories. But even then, there was never any mass production in libraries, nor is there any today. In the academic library almost no work is done twice. From the humblest stack maintenance job to the director's strategic planning work, almost every activity has some aspect of the creative or unique. In its work spectrum, the modern academic library is not a factory, job shop, or processing plant, but something quite different. Its intellectual work is customized: Collection development and cataloging are tailored to the clients' real or anticipated needs; reference and research assistance are specifically demand driven and call for the highest levels of ingenuity and inventiveness. Librarians are much more than mere gatekeepers; they are truly "information navigators" and "information transformers." They spend nearly all their time repackaging, reorganizing and reprocessing information and data, using their broad and varied knowledge, and their cerebral skills, to change one kind of information into another. The human animal is the information processing animal, and librarians are the most expert of all such animals.

LIBRARY WORK COMPARED TO R & D

The management literature of commerce, when not geared to the factory or office, sometimes points to the special problems of administering research and development establishments. Even Shapero, who is strongly focused on the general characteristics of professionals, places most of his emphasis on professionals working in R & D. While we hope that practicing librarians will always undertake research and publication, hardly any library funds a position that is exclusively research. The R & D paradigm for managing professionals is a poor fit simply because librarians must work in a highly structured environment; they cannot enjoy the loose or non-existent tether of a laboratory scientist. The following excerpt from an interview with Arno Penzias, Director of Research at AT&T Bell Labs is telling:

> The few competitors we have, who hire people as good as we do, and who fund them at least as well as we do, do not do as well as we do because they manage too closely. There is too much short-term management. One of the things that people are constantly amazed at in this place is just how little short-term management there really is, just how little short-term management I get. People don't believe that nobody tells me what to do on a daily, weekly, or even a monthly basis. Occasionally, I get a little bit of "fatherly" advice, but in the past year I do not think I have spent as much as four hours with my boss, discussing how I should be doing my job. Instead, we focus on our long-range objectives.[20]

One hopes that academic librarians also do not spend four hours each year talking with their bosses about *how* to do their work, but that they spend many hours throughout the year considering daily and short-range problems, and that they discuss long-range plans at appropriate intervals.

Basic researchers enjoy great freedom of choice in projects, rarely being told to go out and "invent" something, but librarians work under much tighter constraints. Their activities emerge from programs whose directions cannot be changed overnight, constructs with fairly specific educational and research goals and objectives set by a powerful external force, the faculty, whose demands must frequently be met on short notice. Even more demanding is the high volume traffic from students who also cannot be put off with the excuse that librarians are "busy" with other responsibilities.

WHO AND WHAT ARE ACADEMIC LIBRARIANS?

Understanding librarians' work as intellectual, abstract, developmental, experimental, and managerial is the key to establishing the professional character of their responsibilities. The forte of all librarians is not static, objective knowledge but *process knowledge,* the capacity to work out problems that are not neat, not well formed—exactly the type of problem faced by an administrator. Shapero has succinctly characterized why process knowledge is *the* critical characteristic of professionals:

> The information required on the job is never available in neat and ready form. The problems are messy, the deadlines are changeable and abrupt. Several problems must be dealt with simultaneously, and the criteria for evaluation are vague and changing.[21]

Kanter's inventory of the incentives for initiative showed a remarkable fit to Shapero's concept:

> . . . incentives for initiative derive from situations in which *job charters are broad; assignments are ambiguous, nonroutine, and change-directed; job territories are intersecting,* . . . and *local autonomy is strong* enough that actors can go ahead with large chunks of action without waiting for higher-level approval.[22]

In discussing how information technology enters the workplace successfully, Schement cited four aspects of professionalism closely related to those listed by Kanter and Shapero:[23]

1. the degree to which the members of an occupation control the content and scheduling of their own work;
2. the political consciousness and organization of the members of the occupation;

3. the attachment [that] members of the occupational group have to values of
    either innovation, or tradition, in the definition of their roles; and
4. the extent to which the occupation offers emotional or affective satisfac-
    tion to the members, or those that are served by it.

It would be impossible to administer any kind of academic library service
without a clear idea of who we are and what our mission is. Hence, it is essential
to articulate clearly to others—especially the funders—how the process knowledge described by Shapero, Kanter and Schement fits into a work scheme and
becomes translated into professional responsibilities. Professional associations in
both the United States and Canada have developed position statements outlining
the responsibilities and mandates of academic librarians. In the United States, the
Association of College and Research Libraries (ACRL) had for many years
striven to help academic librarians achieve faculty status. To that end ACRL, in
both 1971 and 1972, issued statements focusing primarily on faculty status but
only secondarily on who and what academic librarians might be if they lacked
that status. In 1988 the Canadian Association of College and University Libraries
(CACUL), a unit of the Canadian Library Association (CLA), released a wholly
generic statement that defines the role and responsibilities of academic librarians
independently of faculty status. Below are pertinent excerpts from ACRL statements and the entirety of the CACUL/CLA statement:[24]

The ACRL Statements of 1971 and 1972

The academic librarian makes a unique and important contribution to American higher education. He bears central responsibility for developing college and university library collections,
for extending bibliographical control over these collections, for instructing students (both
formally in the classroom and informally in the library), and advising faculty and scholars in
the use of these collections. He provides a variety of information services to the college or
university community, ranging from answers to specific questions to the compilation of
extensive bibliographies. He provides library and information services to the community at
large, including federal, state, and local government agencies, business firms and other
organizations, and private citizens. Through his own research into the information process
and through bibliographical and other studies, he adds to the sum of knowledge in the field of
library practice and information science. Through membership and participation in library and
scholarly organizations, he works to improve the practice of academic librarianship, bibliography, and information service.

Without the librarian, the quality of teaching, research, and public service in our colleges and
universities would deteriorate seriously and programs in many disciplines could no longer be
performed. His contribution is intellectual in nature and is the product of considerable formal
education, including professional training at the graduate level. . . .[25]

The following year (1972) the ACRL membership approved a Joint Statement on
Faculty Status of College and University Librarians, which included the following paragraph:

Librarians perform a teaching and research role inasmuch as they instruct students formally and informally and advise and assist faculty in their scholarly pursuits. Librarians are also themselves involved in the research function; many conduct research in their own professional interests and in the discharge of their duties.[26]

The CACUL/CLA Statement of 1988

The Role of College and University Librarians

College and university librarians play an integral role in the educational process of their institutions by their contributions to the pursuit, dissemination and structuring of knowledge and understanding. They combine specialized knowledge of the theoretical base of library and information science, management skills, and competence in subject disciplines in providing services which are central to the educational functions of their institutions.

College and university librarians deal on a day-to-day basis with a broad clientele, whose needs, age range and literacy skills vary considerably. The role of the librarians in non-degree-granting institutions emphasizes the instructional process and involvement with the varied user groups. The role of the librarian in degree-granting institutions may emphasize academic competence and involvement in the research processes. While the individual and institutional emphasis on these activities may vary, college and university librarians share a common role.

Library resources and library services have a direct impact on the quality and character of education in colleges and universities. Librarians contribute to the instructional and research functions of their institutions by the exercise of their professional knowledge and/or their competence in subject disciplines. They function as facilitators, instructors and communicators in making information available to the college and university community, and integrating library services with teaching and/or research programs and priorities.

Librarians' responsibilities are diverse and may include the development and evaluation of library resources collections, the provision of subject specialized reference services, the acquisition, bibliographic control, storage and preservation of library/resource collections, the management of human and material library resources, the development and implementation of a variety of library systems, and the provision of instruction in the exploitation of in-house resources or other resource networks. College and university librarians are administrators, scholars, teachers, bibliographic experts or a combination of the above.

Librarians share with faculty in the creative, intellectual and administrative goals of their institutions. They participate in the governance of their institutions as members of governing body committees, members of faculty and campus committees, and members of library committees. Librarians contribute to the intellectual, scholarly and community functions of their institutions by upholding intellectual freedom, by pursuing independent education and self-development activities, by undertaking research in library science or other disciplines, and by participating in college, university and professional associations.[27]

Other Views on Who and What Librarians Are

Both the ACRL and CLA/CACUL positions are congruent with a similar statement prepared by the author on commission from a major academic library:

An academic librarian is a professional who has selected the life of the mind as a career. An academic librarian is a creative partner to faculty, researchers, and students. Based upon the fact that "librarianship requires exacting preparation and that librarians perform functions vital to the well-being of the University," Paul H. Buck, University Librarian at Harvard, 1955–1964, unambiguously emphasized the intellectual focus of the profession in explaining Harvard's new library personnel program in 1958: ". . . the Library's professional staff is a group within the University fully as professional as the teaching faculty and entitled to comparable perquisites."[28] Academic librarians contribute to a university's intellectual work by linking their informational and organizational skills to all levels of the academic community. Fundamentally, academic librarians are problem solvers, system designers, service managers, and communicators; they create, build, maintain, manage and improve an information infrastructure that makes possible the conduct of effective teaching, learning and research.

As professionals, librarians contribute to the formation of their own goals and objectives within the constraints of a school's mission, goals and objectives and within the context of the library program determined by campus administration and head librarian.

Taylor formulated a broad definition for the "new" professional as a person responsible for "the design, operation, and management of systems and services for the creation, organization, movement, and use of messages relevant to the needs of any defined group of people."[29]

In summary, the work of academic librarians encompasses the widest range of professional goals, duties and responsibilities: faculty colleague in the educational process, manager, planner, system designer, leader and supervisor, mediator, contract negotiator, resource allocator, writer, speaker, fund raiser, researcher, teacher, research colleague of the client, subject expert, database searcher, collection builder, budget analyst, proposal writer, statistician, consultant, telecommunications expert, and entrepreneur.[30]

STRATA OF EMPLOYEES IN ACADEMIC LIBRARIES

The span of work in libraries, ranging from the highest intellectual challenges to workaday routine, naturally demands a spectrum of employment, a spectrum characterized more by discontinuities than smooth transitions. The continuity/discontinuity issue has a long and not very even developmental history that has held back librarians' status for many decades.[31] The bipolar division of work into professional and support levels, prevalent in almost all modern libraries is most acutely, and sometimes most uncomfortably, observed in academic libraries for three reasons: (1) higher education is inherently elitist and segmental; (2) librarians are usually faculty members or academic appointees; (3) many nonlibrarians in support staff positions are drawn from a labor pool that is the most highly educated in history, and the contrast between their educational achievements and their work responsibilities is painfully apparent. The result is a work environment of continuous unresolved conflict among all levels of library workers.

Owing to wide variations in personnel practice among privately and publicly supported institutions in the United States and Canada, the work force in academic libraries is not easily categorized. The most highly visible distinction in the United States is whether librarians are faculty members or non-faculty academic staff; the prevalence of faculty status is greater in state-supported than in private schools.[32] In discussing the work of librarians and support staff, we will deal only with the generic aspects of their activities, not specific details of assignments.

Another way of classifying employees is by legal status. Employees in academic libraries generally fall into one of four categories classed as exempt or nonexempt: professionals, support staff, students, and volunteers.[33] Full-time or part-time assistants, part-time students, and volunteers are nonexempt.[34] Depending upon jurisdiction, institution, and/or contract terms, professionals are designated variously, e.g., librarians, exempt staff, managerial/technical staff, professional/administrative, non-faculty academics, or faculty; support staff are typically called paraprofessionals, classified staff, library assistants, library associates, library technicians, clericals, or civil service employees. (The term "nonprofessional," now widely recognized as demeaning, is rapidly falling out of use to designate support staff.) Other than the designations "casual" or "hourly" there is not much specialized vocabulary to cover students and volunteers.

Wages, hours, working conditions, legal status, career development paths, and benefits for exempt and nonexempt personnel are vastly dissimilar. Nowhere in the academic world do law and contract make themselves felt more forcefully than in the recognition and implementation of differing rules and regulations for the several strata of campus employees. The legislative basis for distinguishing the work of librarians and support staff is Title VII of the Equal Pay Act of 1963, which requires payment of the same wages to all persons performing work that is the same or *almost* the same. To ensure observance of applicable labor laws, regulations, and collective agreements, as well as institutional policies, and to protect schools and themselves from lawsuits, administrators must understand, appreciate, and enforce all legal and contractual distinctions between these strata.[35] Persistent violation of the distinctions between librarians and support staff decidedly damages staff morale and may result in potentially serious legal challenges.

Except when new labor rules and fresh staff definitions are being formulated—an infrequent occurrence—librarians' opinions about employee classification are not normally sought. Other than at bargaining sessions connected with collective agreements, librarians generally have no voice at all in the formation of the laws, regulations, rules and agreements governing employment, unless they are asked by a legislative body to testify. But librarian-managers are agents of the institution and are required to accept and implement personnel regulations whether or not they personally approve of them.

DUALITY OF EMPLOYMENT IN LIBRARIES

Despite strong social shifts since the 1960s—movements away from control-centered management styles and a growing focus on individual motivation and teamwork—duality continues as the most visible and enduring structural aspect of employment in the academic library. Williamson, in his 1923 report, was the first to articulate clearly the distinction between librarians and support staff.[36] However, the distinction is probably a natural product of higher education's hierarchical traditions—an instance of a profession's maturing within the context of the established, elitist professoriate. Duality in librarianship, as an inherent aspect of academe, would probably have evolved without the Williamson report.

The concept of duality is so uncomfortable for some people that they prefer to reject it outright. Some writers even refuse to use the term "subordinate" in describing employer-employee relationships, on the ground that it is just as dehumanizing as "non-professional"—as if subordinacy implied intellectual or personal inferiority. We see little purpose in ignoring duality in a work environment where stratification is staring one in the face every moment of every working day. Pretending that it does not exist is like ignoring conflict: the pretense does not cause either to go away.[37] It is far better in academic librarianship to be up front about duality and accept it straightaway. White has put the matter neatly and succinctly: "We must distinguish between what paraprofessionals *can* do and what they must not be allowed to do."[38]

Duality is among the greatest challenges to academic library administration. It pits the two major personnel components against each other and makes cooperative enterprise difficult to establish or maintain. Library assistants tend to see librarians as remote from "real" operations. They resent the flexibility built into librarians' contracts; despite the Master in Library Science degree (MLS) as a bona fide occupational qualification, they resent the existence of a privileged employment enclave at a time when there are many more highly educated applicants than available openings.[39] Faculty status worsens the situation, as librarians are even farther removed from their service points, contributing to the work of faculty or schoolwide committees. Support staff often do not understand *why* librarians are attending planning sessions instead of "working at their desks"; they fail to see the developmental character of modern librarianship or appreciate the programmatic responsibilities of librarians. No wonder it is difficult to talk about establishing a unified library "team" along industrial or sports lines.

Kanter deplored the effects of hard-line stratification in industry because it promotes "segmentalism," an organizational style similar to departmentation.[40] But, as we have said several times, the academy is not a commercial enterprise and stratification is an inherent part of college and university structures. In the search for professionalism, Cline and Sinnott suggest that academic librarians may be squandering their energies arguing over their professional status vis-a-vis both faculty and support staff.[41] For the external world this claim may be valid, but because librarians are required to *manage* support staff, most of whom are highly educated, they *must* focus on their own status and professionalism.[42] It is impossible to ignore a duality that is *built into* the way all segments of staff interrelate in an academic library. One major library organization is so open about duality that it provides cash awards to incumbents who recruit new staff, the award for exempt personnel being *double* that for nonexempt! If the colleges and universities of the future ever do away with the centuries-old caste system, future administrations can deal with the challenge of creating new kinds of relationships between people, just as society has always done. We do not see duality weakening in higher education; in fact, the continuing evolution of bibliographic technology and the elitist character of higher education are likely to exacerbate the tensions between the two groups.

POSITION AND JOB

In library personnel practice, the main distinction between professionals (exempt) and support (nonexempt) staff centers on the difference between two terms that are often used interchangeably: position and job. Let us consider these two terms in some detail.

Position.   A position is a node of power and influence over the organization's program in that it represents the opportunity and the responsibility to make choices and decisions that influence the direction in which the organization moves. The occupant of a position, having the requisite graduate professional education, experience and potential, is privileged to decide whether and how to spend an institution's money and other resources in significant ways.

Position is a generic concept implying a developmental ladder where upward career advancement is the joint product of the incumbent's capacities/ achievements and the organization's requirements. Professional appointees have access to developmental opportunities quite different from those available to personnel in classified jobs. Through a dual track system they can advance independently of administrative responsibility and become eligible for promotion almost entirely on the basis of professional growth, expertise and achievement. In Bardwick's concept, those in professional positions by definition face early "structural plateauing" but need never worry about suffering from "content plateauing" or facing powerlessness.[43] The possibility for advancement is inherent *in the position;* progression up the ladder is naturally dependent on the actual achievement of the incumbent.

Additionally, line workers in a professional bureaucracy exercise substantial discretion in identifying and selecting the work to be done, help devise the system for appraisal of their own performance, assist in recruiting their own colleagues, and exert some limited influence on institutional program. Peer

judgment, mutual consultation, codetermination of the library program, plus a
capacity to deal with ambiguous forces or unexpected outcomes all define the
professional position.

Because the work of professionals is task indeterminate, unlike clerical and
support work, authority over these individuals is be definition diffuse: There is
no need for them to be subject to the highly directed, task-specific authority
structure characteristic of Fayol's machine bureaucracy or production-oriented
systems.[44]

A professional is not hired to "do a job" but to *be and become a certain kind of
person*. By definition and in accordance with United States labor law, a professional is an exempt employee.[45] Simply stated, an exempt employee is someone
hired to work *without regard to countable output and without regard to putting in
any specific number of hours*. Unlike nonexempts, exempt employees may work
any number of hours beyond the normal work week without receiving additional
monetary compensation. Normally, it is a condition of employment that exempt
personnel work on-site at least the institution's ordinary work week, usually from
35 to 40 hours.[46] But there is no compensation for overtime,[47] nor can the
salaries of exempt personnel be docked if they work less than forty hours. The
"working" characteristics of professional, exempt personnel might typically include long hours in attendance at professional conferences, evenings and weekends spent reading professional literature, staying late at the office to conclude an
important meeting with colleagues, travel time to and from business meetings,
time outside the office developing a proposal or refining a research project—all
without additional monetary compensation or equivalent time off. These activities make the professional that "certain kind of person" and emphasize that
professionalism is a life of commitment—not of hours counted or output units
produced.

Job.   "Job" is a construct altogether different from position, even though in
informal usage the two terms are frequently used interchangeably. "Job" is much
more specific than position, being tied to definite, usually assigned responsibilities. Within a job there is also a career ladder—but the ladder is within the
constraints of a specific set of tasks. For classified personnel the job ladder is
external to the person and is associated entirely with the character of the work to
be performed. This is why personnel professionals say that jobs, not people, are
classified.

In the United States jobs are almost always nonexempt, i.e., subject to compensation for authorized overtime.[48] Nonexempt personnel are hired as support
staff to carry out specific, well defined tasks whose extent, nature, and detail
have generally been determined (or approved) by the professional staff who
supervise them. Normally, an organization's job classification and pay plan will
rank nonexempt jobs from the simple to the complex, assigning to each a level

and a salary commensurate with the work's difficulty, complexity, or level of responsibility. The plan will also provide career development steps in recognition of service quality, longevity, and growth of expertise. The fact that an employee reaches the top of the salary scale for a given job, or has been employed for a very long time, however, is *not* generally a basis for promotion.[49] In addition, no matter how complex the assignment, no classified job ever carries with it programmatic responsibilities—the power to change the organization's direction. For classified staff, advancement up the career ladder is possible only by the employee's moving on to a different, more complex and better paid job. If professional staff in supervisory positions fail to accept these constraints, or are careless in the discharge of their administrative responsibilities, they destroy morale and establish grounds for support staff to file grievances—consequences that damage the library's program, consume disproportionate amounts of administrative time and, finally, invite costly litigation.

Many so-called "routine" tasks in an information organization are repetitive and boring yet at the same time require a very high degree of attention, alertness and perception. Examples of "routine" work calling for judgment abound. Applying property marks or spine labels raises questions and requires judgment: Do the end papers contain a unique map that must not be covered up by a book plate? Is there a volume number on the spine that must not be obscured? How should a compact disc be property-marked? Preservation microfilming or photocopying academic materials present perhaps the clearest examples of work that is at once routine and boring, but which requires the utmost attention to detail. Other attention-demanding routine work includes sorting and delivering mail, accurately reshelving library materials, keyboarding and proofing bibliographic or order entry data, updating files in transaction-oriented systems (e.g., serials check-in, charge out of library materials).

The need for personnel to perform some of these repetitive tasks will decline with continuing technological development. This is perhaps fortunate, as such work, although critical, offers little opportunity for job enrichment after the initial learning. The jobs are also characterized by both high stress and high turnover.

Few support staff in academic libraries, especially the highly educated, are content to carry out these kinds of responsibilities year after year. However, from time to time one finds employees who prefer closely limited work and are willing to stay in dead-ended jobs for a long time. Not only do some people resist job enrichment, but not all jobs can be enriched—a point conceded even by Herzberg, the assiduous proponent of job enrichment.[50] In such instances it is essential that management and labor reach a common understanding of the subsequences and consequences of choosing such a job. Management should carefully explain the nature of the job, articulate the risks of technological displacement, and offer options for future development, including retraining.

THE HEART OF THE DUALITY PROBLEM

The main deficiency in the administration of classified work in academic libraries is that the profession has failed to create or foster true career development
opportunities for the non-academic staff, especially those who are highly educated. Most of the focus is on librarians. We hire entry level librarians for their
potential and the bulk of our development effort is aimed at them. What do we do
for the growing cadre of workers on whose shoulders falls much of the genuine
labor in library work? Support staff also seek careers and they can be just as
committed as the best professionals. We remain ambivalent about support staff,
relying on their loyalty to support an indispensable element of our work but not
pushing them hard enough to look elsewhere for their own advancement. They,
in turn, resent the dualities and detest the snobbery inherent in the academic
workplace, perceiving that they are but cogs in a great machine and feeling
themselves to be "victims of paternalistic and authoritarian management."[51] It is
no wonder that in recent years support staff have become so discontent, many
joining unions in order to gain improved salaries, status, and working conditions.

There is another side to this vexing problem: some non-academic staff contribute equally, or possibly more, to their own predicament—the dead-endedness
of classified work—by refusing absolutely to look beyond the library. Whatever
the disadvantages of and complaints about the work, the comfort and stability of
library employment are powerful disincentives to change, inhibiting support staff
from ever looking anywhere else or undertaking self-improvement to build up
their qualifications for higher levels of employment. Like the librarians, many
support staff would like to have their "careers" (meaning unlimited promotion
opportunity) *in* the library environment. Unfortunately, this is rarely possible at
either level of work. Until administrations really grapple with this aspect of
duality, tensions between the non-academic staff and professionals will continue,
perhaps reaching a permanent adversarial stance, no matter how attractive the
working conditions.

A secondary deficiency relates to the impact of elitism itself on employees.
The academy is a world of widely varying privileges in which the tendency is to
value people differentially: the higher up you are in the hierarchy—the closer
you get to the professoriate—the better you are as human being. We may not
like—though we grudgingly accept—professorial arrogance. But when arrogance rubs off onto ourselves and we look down on support staff, imagining
that we are somehow "better" than they, we discredit ourselves and our profession. Such an unconscionable view is not only a gross violation of common
human decency but fails to acknowledge that while the library might function for
some weeks without librarians, it would collapse in an instant without support
staff.

Is duality a permanent condition? Perhaps not. The exempt/nonexempt duality
is an inheritance from an industrial society; it may no longer be appropriate to an

"information society." In the next century technology may drive a radical restructuring of work in the information field and eradicate the problem. But until that happens librarian/administrators are bound to observe all the legal distinctions duality imposes. Where there is no option, there is neither preference nor decision.

ANALYZING WORK IN THE ACADEMIC LIBRARY

In any environment the analysis of work is an extraordinarily complex subject. To sharpen the focus of our concept of duality in the academic library, we shall discuss briefly two major methods for analyzing work: functional job analysis (FJA) and factor analysis.

Job Analysis. Functional job analysis, pioneered in the 1950s by Sidney A. Fine when he directed research at the United State Employment Service, has been highly influential in the evolution of job classification and pay plans throughout North America. FJA eventually became the foundation of the third edition of *Dictionary of Occupational Titles* (Washington DC: 1965), as well as the *Canadian Classification and Dictionary of Occupations, 1971* (Ottawa: Employment and Immigration, 1974). Much of the methodology in the FJA system is derived from social welfare work, which involves a great deal of interviewing, filling out of forms, and counseling. The FJA method categorizes work in accordance with whether an employee is working with Data, People or Things; it is concerned only with what the worker *does,* not with the results achieved. The method explicitly and formally separates action from process:

> A task statement requires a concrete, explicit *action verb.* Verbs which point to a process (such as *develops, prepares, interviews, counsels, evaluates,* and *assesses*) should be avoided or used only to designate broad *processes, methods,* or *techniques* which are then broken down into explicit, discrete action verbs.[52]

An example cited refers to a social worker interviewing a client (People work: asking questions), taking down data (Data work: transcribing responses onto a form), and then typing the results onto a standard form (Thing work: using a typewriter in the capacity of an operative). It is immediately apparent that this separation of thinking from doing is totally inappropriate to academic librarianship where, we contend, all professional work activities come together as an *inseparable gestalt.*

The development of interactive computerized information systems, which did not exist in the 1950s, has totally changed the way professionals work with data, people, and equipment. Functional job analysis is surely an extraordinarily useful tool for understanding factory and office work, because it concentrates on *visible operations.* But it is completely inapposite to analysis of the professoriate, research and development work, or librarianship because a professional's "process work" cannot be disaggregated into convenient units, a point made over and over again by Shapero.[53] In short, job analysis may be a better tool for describing nonexempt work than for characterizing exempt work.

Campus personnel professionals rely upon job analysis as their prime tool, yet it is the very thing that often makes it hard for them to understand what goes on in an academic library and comprehend why librarians are different from support staff and why both differ from clerks and typists. This circumstance alone requires librarian administrators to maintain close peer relationships with campus personnel administrators.

Factor Analysis.   The well-known Hay System is an analytic compensation design tool that attempts to overcome the deficiencies of conventional work analysis systems. It is designed to evaluate work content (not adequacy of performance) in order to derive compensation levels that will be perceived as just throughout an organization. Expressly designed to analyze exempt work, chiefly that done by executives and professionals—but not making the distinction we postulate between position and job—the Hay System employs factor analysis. Four principles govern the Hay System:

1.   The most significant aspects of work are the knowledge required to do it, the type of thinking required for problem solving, responsibilities assigned, and the work environment.
2.   Jobs can be ranked in order of importance to the sponsoring organization and the "distances" between jobs can be determined.
3.   Factors appear in patterns that relate to certain types of work.
4.   Job evaluation relates to the requirements of the job itself—not to the skills, background or current pay of the incumbent.

To translate these principles into practical terms, the Hay System analyzes professional and executive work in accordance with three major factors:[54] (1) the know-how required to do the work, (2) the level of problem-solving responsibility, and (3) the extent of accountability for actions, decision, and consequences. An instrument, the Guide Chart-Profile, is used to assign points and develop a numerical score for each executive or professional slot in an organization.[55]

•   *Know-How.* Three dimensions comprise the total knowledge and skill needed (it does not matter how these skills are acquired): (1) knowledge of practical procedure and techniques appropriate to the work or occupation; (2) "planning, organizing, coordinating, integrating, staffing, directing and/or controlling the activities and resources associated with an organizational unit or function, in order to produce the results expected of that unit or function";[56] (3) face-to-face skills for interpersonal relationships.

• *Problem-Solving.* Problem solving has two dimensions: (1) the environment in which the problem-solving and thinking take place and (2) its degree of challenge or difficulty. It involves the nature of analysis, reasoning, evaluation, judgment, hypothesis formation, the drawing of inferences, and the reaching of conclusions.

• *Accountability.* One's answerability for actions: consequences. Its three dimensions, in rank order, are: (1) the executive or professional's freedom to act, (2) the extent and depth of an individual's direct impact on results, and (3) the magnitude and scope of the function or unit. This last dimension is sometimes expressed as the dollar value of revenues or expenses in the operations for which the professional is responsible.

To achieve the goal of compensation patterns that will be perceived as fair and reasonable, work is analyzed, benchmarks established and jobs ranked by a committee broadly representative of staff and line employees in the organization. This part of the work is typically a group effort, the aim being for the organization to "own" the results, believe in them and thus assure wide acceptance.

A "Guide Chart-Profile" method is used to implement the Hay System. A typical chart might postulate many different intensity levels for each category. For example, know-how could be illustrated by postulating seven levels of expertise, ranked in descending order: technical-specialized mastery; seasoned technical-specialized; basic technical-specialized; advanced vocational; vocational, elementary vocational; basic. The lowest rank of know-how would involve work at a strictly operational level governed by fixed guidelines; the highest rank would be associated with in-depth knowledge, expertise that is both industry-wide and internationally renowned. For problem-solving, levels might be: abstractly defined; generally defined; broadly defined; clearly defined; standardized; semi-routine; strict routine. In accountability, eight work levels might be ranked in descending order; strategic guidance; broad guidance; oriented direction; directed; generally regulated; standardized; controlled; prescribed.

A complex system of numerical weights and points is used to derive a total score, which might run from a low of 20 to a high in the mid-300s. The Hay point system is claimed to be independent of extraneous factors, such as gender, personality, and job tenure. One obvious benefit is that it gets away from oral tradition or emotional investment for ranking positions. However, there is disagreement about the impact of the Hay and similar point systems if administered confidentially. If the system's criteria are made public, some personnel officers fear that employees will attempt to structure their own responsibilities to "make points." If details of the system are kept secret, staff morale may suffer as employees perceive that their work—and the consequent job classification—is being measured by an invisible hand.

The Hay System functions very well in large organizations and has withstood critical review in judicial proceedings, administrative hearings, and arbitration cases. One of its doubtful aspects—perhaps important for the small college library or small branch in a large system—is that it tends not to acknowledge the full scope of the complexity factor in one-person operations. The Hay System apportions greater credit to those who do a greater absolute amount of specialized work and thus, seemingly, puts managers of one-person libraries at a disadvantage.

Factor analysis and point systems may be especially useful instruments for analyzing executive work in large, bureaucratic service organizations, such as insurance companies or government agencies. They are surely superior to industrial-style job analysis. Whether they are applicable to professionals in academe, especially those who operate in a collegial system, is controversial. Point systems inevitably create perceptions that some jobs are more important than others, a concept that is already rampant in the elitist academic environment. Yet who is more "important" when the college heating system breaks down: the professor or the steamfitter? It is fruitful to suggest that professional librarians are "more important" than those who check in journals or maintain the stacks? As stated earlier, the probability is high that a library could function without librarians for quite a while—but would collapse at once if the support staff quit or went on strike.

It is enough that we must contend with the stresses of employment duality; point systems may worsen existing antagonisms. As with many aspects of administration, there is no perfect method of analyzing library work. In general, broad and flexible guidelines are superior to closely detailed, prescriptive approaches.

SUMMARY

Employment duality closely follows the stratified social structures of higher education and is a permanent feature of this fundamentally elistist system. This duality cannot be wished away. Federal legislation contains specific tests to determine whether employees are exempt or nonexempt, although some judgment is always involved. Employment in academic libraries is governed by federal legislation in much the same way as other sectors of the economy; no special treatment is accorded to libraries because they are a "social good" or involve mental work. The chief determinant of exempt/nonexempt status is *work content and actual duties*—not job or position title and not even job description or position description. The duties under consideration must actually be performed, not merely assigned. Hence, it is vital that library administrators and supervisors know precisely what work their employees are actually doing, be certain that it conforms to the contents of the description and that it is congruent with the library program. Regardless of their personal views and opinions, managers and supervisors are charged with protecting a school's interests by fulfilling all legal requirements of the employer/employee relationship.

Librarianship is mental work done by professionals; as true information work, its output is chiefly intangible. Because there is almost no "production" work and little pure research, personnel management systems derived from business, manufacturing, or research and development have little relevance to the profession. But both administrative theory and practice in academic librarianship have been too slavishly imitative of styles derived from business, too uncritically accepting of apparel tailored for a quite different body. We have searched for techniques rather than principles. The academic world is not the world of commerce and is not the world of democratic politics. We must be more original and less imitative, less trendy and more oriented towards the long range. In short, we must tailor our garments to fit the body academic.

NOTES

1.   By contrast, in their *An Introduction to University Library Administration*, 4th ed., (London, Bingley, 1987), p. 63, James Thompson and Reg Carr rather pointedly state: "The application to library staff management of the principles of business theory—especially of American origin—has so far, mercifully, been quite limited in United Kingdom universities."

2.   Richard De Gennaro, "Theory vs Practice in Library Management," *Library Journal* 108(13):1318–1321 (July 1983).

 3.   Specific critiques of behavioralist theory and the human potential movement may be found in the following: (a) Michael H. Bottomley, *Personnel Management* (Plymouth: Macdonald and Evans, 1983); see esp. chapter 2, pp. 12–23, "Job Satisfaction and Motivation," which briefly surveys ten theories, ranging from F. W. Taylor to E. E. Lawler and L. W. Porter. (b) Amitai Etzioni, *Modern Organizations*, (Englewood Cliffs NJ: Prentice-Hall, 1964); see esp. chapter 4, "From Human Relations to the Structuralists." (c) John W. Hunt, *Managing People at Work: A Manager's Guide to Behaviour in Organizations* (London: McGraw-Hill, 1979), p. 5ff. (d) Jerrold Orne, "Future Academic Library Administration: Whither or Whether", in Evan Ira Farber and Ruth Walling, *The Academic Library: Essays in Honor of Guy R. Lyle* (Metuchen NJ: Scarecrow, 1974), pp. 82–95, esp. pp. 86–87. (e) Michael Maccoby, *The Gamesman: The New Corporate Leaders*, (New York: Simon and Schuster, 1976); see esp. chapter 8, "The Psychology of Development," pp. 210–233. (f) James Michalko, "Management by Objectives and the Academic Library: A Critical Overview," *Library Quarterly* 45:235–252 (July 1975). (g) Henri Savall, *Work and People: An Economic Evaluation of Job-Enrichment* (Oxford: Oxford University, 1981), esp. chapter 1, "The Problem of Job Design," pp. 13–59. (h) Daniel Yankelovich, *New Rules: Searching for Self-Fulfillment in a World Turned Upside Down* (New York: Random House, 1981), esp. chapter 23, "Getting Off Maslow's Escalator," pp. 234–243. (i) Frances FitzGerald, *Cities on a Hill: A Journey Through Contemporary American Cultures* (New York: Simon and Schuster, 1986), esp. pp. 280–286.

4.   Sajjad ur Rehman, *Management Theory and Library Education* (New York: Greenwood, 1987). See esp. pp. 86–87, 117–118.

5.   Rehman, *op. cit.*, esp. pp. 86ff.

6.   "Changes in Library Education: The Deans Reply," *Special Libraries* 77:217–25 (Fall 1986).

7.   Ann Schabas, in "Changes in Library Education: The Deans Reply," *Special Libraries* 77:224 (Fall 1986).

8.   Joseph A. Litterer, *An Introduction to Management* (New York: Wiley, 1978), page 9.

9.   Ruth J. Person, "The Third Culture: Managerial Socialization in the Library Setting," *Advances in Library Administration and Organization* 4:1–24 (1985). See esp. p. 3.

10.   Robert Swisher, Rosemary Ruhig Du Mont, and Calvin J. Boyer, "The Motivation to

Manage: A Study of Academic Librarians and Library Science Students," *Library Trends* 34 (Fall 1985):219–234, esp. pp. 230–32.

11.   Rosabeth M. Kanter, *The Change Masters: Innovation and Entrepreneurship in the American Corporation* (New York: Simon and Schuster, 1984).

12.   Kanter, *The Change Masters,* pp. 42–43.

13.   Kanter, *The Change Masters,* p. 261.

14.   See Richard De Gennaro's "Library Administration and New Management Systems," *Library Journal* 103(22):2477–2482, December 15, 1978, and his "Theory vs Practice in Library Management," *Library Journal* 108(13):1318–1321 (July 1983).

15.   Michael D. Cohen and James G. March, *Leadership and Ambiguity: The American College President,* 2d ed., (Boston: Harvard Business School, 1986).

16.   Kanter, *The Change Masters,* p. 133.

17.   Kanter, *The Change Masters,* p. 203.

18.   Kanter, *The Change Masters,* p. 205.

19.   There are, of course, other types of industrial work, e.g., mining and farming, which at various stages involve neither factories nor continuous processing plants, but these additional categories are not essential to the point we are making.

20.   Jeremy Bernstein, *Three Degrees Above Zero: Bell Labs in the Information Age* (New York: Charles Scribner's Sons, 1984), 232. Published originally in *The New Yorker* 60:42–70 (August 20, 1984), pp. 68, 70.

21.   Albert Shapero, *Managing Professional People* (New York: Free Press, 1985), p. 28.

22.   Kanter, *The Change Masters,* 143, emphasis in the original.

23.   Jorge Reina Schement, et al., "Social Forces Affecting the Success of Introducing Information Technology into the Workplace," in *Proceedings of the 48th ASIS Annual Meeting* 22:278–283 (1985).

24.   Excerpts include only those statements explicitly outlining the role of academic librarians; omitted are the arguments aimed at justifying faculty status.

25.   "Standards for Faculty Status for College and University Librarians," adopted by ACRL, June 26, 1971, *College & Research Libraries News 35(3):112–113* (May 1974). Reprinted in *Academic Status: Statements and Resources* (Chicago: Association of College and Research Libraries, 1988), p. 9.

26.   "Statement on Faculty Status of College and University Librarians," *College & Research Libraries News* 35(2):26 (February 1974). Reprinted in *Academic Status: Statements and Resources* (Chicago: ALA, 1988), p. 5.

27.   Prepared by the Canadian Association of College and University Libraries, Academic Status Committee. Published in *Feliciter* 34(10):8 October 1988.

28.   Paul H. Buck, *Libraries and Universities: Addresses and Reports* (Cambridge: Harvard University, 1964), pp. 95–96.

29.   Robert S. Taylor, "Reminiscing About the Future: Professional Education and the Information Environment," *Library Journal* 104:1871–1875 (September 15, 1979).

30.   Adapted from Allen B. Veaner, "Librarians: The Next Generation," *Library Journal,* 103(6):623 (April 1, 1984). The view of librarians as professionals and intellectuals developed powerfully after World War II. Much of the prior emphasis on education for library science focused on the concept that librarians were technicians who to some extent needed protection from the distractions of intellectual stimulation. See especially chapter 4, "The Professionalization of Academic Librarianship," in Orvin Lee Shiflett's *Origins of American Academic Librarianship* (Norwood NJ: Ablex, 1981).

31.   See the following two articles for further discussion on employment strata in libraries: Allen B. Veaner, "Continuity or Discontinuity: A Persistent Personnel Issue in Academic Librarianship," in *Advances in Library Administration and Organization* 1:1–20 (1982); Richard Rubin, "A Critical Examination of the 1927 *Proposed Classifications and Compensation Plan for Library Positions* by The American Library Association," *Library Quarterly* 57(4):400–425 (October 1987).

32. The history, specific advantages, disadvantages, and administrative aspects of faculty vs non-faculty status are thoroughly covered in the published literature. Current research and discussion on faculty status are amply covered in *The Journal of Academic Librarianship* and *College & Research Libraries,* while an historical overview is in Virgil Massman's *Faculty Status for Librarians* (Metuchen NJ: Scarecrow, 1972). A summary of ACRL positions, standards and guidelines on faculty status, as well as a literature review, are in *Academic Status: Statements and Resources* (Chicago: ACRL, 1988). A recent survey of the literature of faculty status is contained in Fred Batt's "Faculty Status for Academic Librarians: Justified or Just a Farce?" in Peter Spyers-Duran and Thomas W. Mann, Jr's *Issues in Academic Librarianship* (Westport CT: Greenwood, 1985), pp. 115– 188. Also available are sixteen articles of mainly historical interest in Robert B. Downs' ACRL monograph, *The Status of American College and University Librarians* (Chicago: ALA, 1958).

33. In some libraries there are three rather than two strata of employees: professional, supportive (or "library associate"), and clerical; education is sometimes the criterion for distinguishing these three, with graduate degrees a prerequisite for the first, college for the second and high school for the third. Whether there are two or three levels, however, does not change the distribution of programmatic responsibilities, which remain the exclusive prerogative of librarians.

34. Strictly speaking, volunteers are not employees, as they commonly receive neither wages nor benefits.

35. See especially 29 USC 152(12)(a) 1976, which defines the distinction between exempt and nonexempt staff.

36. Charles C. Williamson, *Training for Library Service* (New York: Carnegie Corporation, 1923), p. 136.

37. In his critique of a human-relations-school training film, Amitai Etzioni makes the similar point that differences in economic interests and power positions cannot "be communicated away" by clever media presentations. See his *Modern Organizations* (Englewood Cliffs NJ: Prentice-Hall, 1964), pp. 43–44.

38. Herbert S. White, remarks at the ASIS Conference, Las Vegas, 1985. (Cited with the author's permission.)

39. Richard M. Dougherty, "Personnel Needs for Librarianship's Uncertain Future," in Herbert Poole, ed., *Academic Libraries by the Year 2000: Essays Honoring Jerrold Orne* (New York: Bowker, 1977), p. 112–113. See also Veaner, "Continuity or Discontinuity."

40. Rosabeth M. Kanter, *The Change Masters,* chapter 7.

41. Hugh F. Cline and Loraine T. Sinnott, *The Electronic Library: The Impact of Automation in Academic Libraries* (Lexington MA: Lexington, 1983), p. 157.

42. William Joseph Reeves, in his *Librarians as Professionals: The Occupation's Impact on Library Work Arrangements* (Lexington MA: Heath, 1980), concluded that librarianship remains an "occupation" that has been unable to establish itself as a true profession. His argument was directed to the external world, however, and for our purposes is irrelevant for the same reason that Cline and Sinnott's is: librarians must *manage* resources, whether they wish to or not, and that requirement establishes a professional status within the work environment.

43. Judith Bardwick, *The Plateauing Trap* (New York: Bantam: 1988), p. 82.

44. Henri Fayol, *General and Industrial Management.* Translated by Constance Storrs. London: Pitman, 1949.

45. The term "exempt" means that the so-designated employee is exempted from government regulations requiring that others, i.e., nonexempt personnel, be paid for all work in excess of 40 hours weekly. The exempt/nonexempt distinction does not arise (in a legal sense) when the work week is less than forty hours. See 29 USC 152(12)(a) 1976; see also section 213a which lists eleven categories of personnel exempt from the requirement of overtime pay. Canada implements a similar, legislatively based distinction.

46. Correspondingly, in most institutions, exempt employees cannot "bank" time (by working a fictitious "overtime") to accumulate additional time for extended vacations. In short, overtime does not exist for exempt employees.

47. Overtime is not to be confounded with compensatory time, which is merely a rearrangement of schedule for personnel who work evenings or weekends.

48. In large libraries, some very high level technical positions may be filled by non-librarians, for example, the head of circulation in a major branch. If the position meets established criteria, the school may designate the position as exempt.

49. There could be exceptions to this principle if a collective bargaining agreement so provides.

50. Frederick Herzberg, "One More Time: How Do You Motivate Employees?" *Harvard Business Review* 46(1):53–62 (January-February 1968). Holley, in "The Magic of Library Administration," *Texas Library Journal,* 52:60 (May 1976), reports that one of his graduate students concludes that "a dull, boring job is still likely to be a dull, boring job. . . ."

51. James M. Kusack, *Unions for Academic Library Support Staff* (New York: Greenwood, 1986), page 86. See also Hugh F. Cline and Loraine T. Sinnott, *The Electronic Library: The Impact of Automation in Academic Libraries* (Lexington MA: Lexington, 1983), pp. 156–157.

52. Sidney A. Fine and Wretha W. Wiley, *An Introduction to Functional Job Analysis* (Kalamazoo MI: W. E. Upjohn Institute for Employment Research, 1971), pp. 10–11.

53. Albert Shapero, *Managing Professional People,* pp. xii–xviii, 28, and elsewhere. For a completely different view of the value of job analysis and the Fine/Wiley methodology in academic librarianship, see Forest C. Benedict and Paul M. Gherman, "Implementing an Integrated Personnel System," *Journal of Academic Librarianship* 6(4):210–214 (September 1980). See also Virginia S. Hill and Tom G. Watson's "Job Analysis: Process and Benefits" in *Advances in Library Administration and Organization* 3:209–219 (1984). Hill and Watson concede that job analysis is better suited to routine work having a tangible outcome than to professional service work.

54. There is a fourth factor, relating to work under physically hazardous or unpleasant conditions, that is normally not included when the system is used to analyze work that is strictly white collar.

55. For a full explication of the Hay method see Alvin O. Bellak, "The Hay Guide Chart-Profile Method of Job Evaluation," *Handbook of Wage and Salary Administration,* 2d ed. (New York: McGraw-Hill, 1984), and the earlier presentation by Charles W. G. Van Horn, "The Hay Guide Chart-Profile Method," in *Handbook of Wage and Salary Administration,* 1st ed., Milton L. Rock, ed. (New York: McGraw-Hill, 1972), pp. 286–297.

56. Adapted from "Job Evaluation Using The Hay Method," a booklet issued by Hay Management Consultants (n.p., n.d.)

WHATEVER HAPPENED TO LIBRARY EDUCATION FOR BIBLIOTHERAPY:

A STATE OF THE ART

Alice Gullen Smith

INTRODUCTION

In 1902 William K. Beatty, Librarian and Professor of Medical Bibliography at Northwestern University Medical School, Chicago, wrote the lead article in a landmark library science publication that stated the case for bibliotherapy. Beatty wrote:

> This paper will survey the major currents that make up the present river of bibliotherapeutic practice and philosophy. In addition, it will touch lightly upon some pertinent tributaries.[1]

These words were written almost a half century after the term "bibliotherapy" had become widely known to many doctors, nurses, librarians and educators.

Advances in Library Administration and Organization,
Volume 9, pages 29–56.
Copyright © 1991 by JAI Press, Inc.
All rights of reproduction in any form reserved.
ISBN: 1-55938-066-7

The scope of Beatty's paper is identical with the scope of this paper. It reflects the importance of the information that librarians and library educators need to know about the enduring fascination which bibliotherapy continues to hold for librarians and professional workers in many other disciplines.

The questions to be answered are:

1. **When** and where did the concept of bibliotherapy begin?
2. **Why** is bibliotherapy connected with librarianship?
3. **Where** has bibliotherapy been conducted?
4. **What** is an accurate definition of the term bibliotherapy?
5. **Who** is responsible for the education of bibliotherapists?
6. **How** effective is bibliotherapy?

This paper will answer these questions by presenting:

1. Definitions of bibliotherapy as it has evolved together with identification of some of the people responsible for the evolution.
2. A brief history and the present status of bibliotherapy as an emerging discipline.
3. The triad of literature, facilitator, and peer group which is essential to the interaction which is the heart of successful bibliotherapy.
4. The relationship of bibliotherapy to librarianship and the interdisciplinary aspects of bibliotherapy.
5. Research in bibliotherapy.
6. Education for bibliotherapy and the credentialing of bibliotherapists.

DEFINITIONS

Bibliotherapy

The first dictionary inclusion of the word bibliotherapy in 1941 reflected the practice used in the clinical world of medicine and psychiatry as it existed at that time.

> . . . the employment of books and the reading of them in the treatment of nervous disorders.[2]

By 1961 two definitions of bibliotherapy appeared in authoritative dictionaries.

> . . . the use of selected reading materials as therapeutic adjuvants in medicine and psychiatry: also guidance in the solution of personal problems through directed reading (*Webster's Third New International Dictionary*).

> . . . the use of reading as an ameliorative adjunct to therapy (*Random House Dictionary*).[3]

Some time later the American Library Association adopted the Webster's entry as the official definition.

As the practice of bibliotherapy spread the definitions used by practitioners in the field enlarged to reflect the change in clientele, purposes and practice.

Today there are three major types of bibliotherapy:

1. Prescriptive (or Reading Bibliotherapy)
2. Clinical
3. Developmental[4]

TYPES OF BIBLIOTHERAPY

Prescriptive Bibliotherapy

In prescriptive bibliotherapy a doctor, some other clinician, a librarian who may or may not be under the direction of a clinical professional prescribes didactic readings of one or more books or articles for a patient to read concerning his/her medical or emotional problem. The purposes are educational and sometimes pleasurable.

Clinical Bibliotherapy

In clinical bibliotherapy although a doctor or other clinician is in charge, a librarian selects the material and often presents it. The materials used are primarily literature with a possible emphasis on fiction and/or poetry. The goals are set in terms of problem solving or resolution and better understanding of emotional difficulties.

The material may be read by or read to the client(s) with discussion following the reading. Although the sessions may be on a one to one basis (one client/ therapist and/or facilitator) it is more often a group session with emphasis put upon the importance of group insights and perceptions. The librarian works closely with and under the guidance of the doctor or clinician.

Developmental Bibliotherapy

Developmental bibliotherapy is based upon the developmental stages and tasks of Erickson, Havighurst and other developmental psychologists. It is primarily undertaken to help normal individuals through the stages, tasks and crises which occur in the lives of all people from early childhood through old age. This is a group process led by a facilitator who can be a librarian working on his/her own or in conjunction with a guidance counselor, a social worker or some other clinically trained professional. The emphasis here is upon normal problems occurring to individuals who are not under treatment for psychological or emotional disorders. This form of bibliotherapy is closely related to the reading guidance carried out by librarians in public and school libraries and by many teachers.[5]

Arleen Hynes offers a descriptive series of definitions based on her many years of service with the hospital-based training program at St. Elizabeth's in Washington, D.C.

> Bibliotherapy [is a process] which uses literature to bring about a therapeutic interaction between participant and facilitator . . . it is not an umbrella term for all activities in which books are used for self-improvement.[6]

Hynes calls this "interactive bibliotherapy." She subsumes both clinical and developmental under her more inclusive term.

Reading (prescriptive) and the developmental form of interactive bibliotherapy are the two types of bibliotherapy which are of continued interest to the service-oriented librarian. Interactive developmental bibliotherapy is intended to

> help all kinds of people in their normal growth and . . . development . . . The basic techniques are the same as those used in clinical bibliotherapy but the depth is less probing . . . [This] is typically practiced in groups that have formed and meet in the context of the library, school, community center, church, or synagogue.[7]

HISTORICAL BACKGROUND

The term "bibliotherapy" is derived from the Greek words *biblios* 'books' and *therapia* 'healing.'[8] In simple terms the word means healing from books. The idea of such healing is as old as the Alexandrian Library in which the reading room of Rameses was called the hospital of the soul.[9] Although there has been some emphasis upon physical healing the primary accent is upon change of emotion, problem solving and learning the art of living. From Petrarch[10] in Rome to Dr. Samuel Johnson[11] in London to Oliver Wendell Holmes in Boston,[12] to the Menningers in Topeka, Kansas,[13] scholars, writers, doctors have affirmed the solace, the learning and the life giving qualities of books.

There is a long and documented history in Western civilization as evidenced in "Genesis," The Old Testament, of this strong belief in the power of the word or the book.

The actual term "bibliotherapy" was first used by Samuel McChord Crothers in an article which he had published in a 1916 edition of the *Atlantic Monthly*. Psychiatrists, in private practice and in hospitals, had been using the term in their employment of books, their reading and discussion, as therapy for their patients for many years.[14] As early as 1812 Dr. Benjamin Rush in his treatment of mental patients recommended reading as a diversionary tactic to keep the patients' minds off their troubles. He suggested that if patients could not be diverted by simple Bible stories they might be reached by the contemporary novels of the day. Later he extended the range of materials to include newspapers, and scholarly or scientific books according to the tastes and needs of the reader. Through his published works and his success with patients Rush had a tremendous influence upon the practice of psychiatry as it developed in the United States. Through his influence library service to mental patients in the late nineteenth century had became surprisingly sophisticated.[15]

By 1904 bibliotherapy was accepted as an aspect of librarianship. This was made evident when the job description for a librarian to be employed as the head of the library at the McLean Hospital in Waverly, Massachusetts, requested that the applicant be skillful in the selection and utilization of appropriate books for the patients and in the utilization of those books in discussions with the patients.[16]

Therapeutic use of books with patients was furthered by work done with books and patients in World War I hospitals. This work was enhanced through the availability of the war-time libraries supplied by the American Library Association. Library service in the veterans' hospitals which mushroomed following the war surged ahead in work with bibliotherapy. One outstanding example can be found in the work of Sadie P. Delaney. In the 1900s Delaney was recruited from the New York Public Library to organize the Veterans' Administration Hospital Library at Tuskegee, Alabama. She became such a successful bibliotherapist that students were sent from the library training schools to study her methods. She based her programs on the use of techniques which had been successful in her New York library work with delinquent children and in helping the foreign born in their adjustment to life in the United States.[17]

At that time Karl and William Menninger were becoming known through their publications and their successful psychiatric practices. These included work at the Menninger Clinic and their much publicized five-year project. The project was of special significance for bibliotherapy. Much of the work with patients was based upon the use of carefully selected pieces of great literature. The patients were assigned specific titles to read which they would then discuss in relation to their own problems, with their psychiatrist.[18]

By 1939 the Hospital Division of the American Library Association had established a Bibliotherapy Committee for the purpose of studying bibliotherapy, its implications for education of librarians and its multidisciplinary ramifications. At that time the greatest use of bibliotherapy was in hospitals. The ages of the clientele had spread. During war years armed service people of relatively young ages were the primary clients. As interest spread the work was beginning to be used with children in pediatric sections of hospitals (In 1953 Flandorf offered successful methods of bibliotherapy with hospitalized children),[19] with young male juvenile delinquents as reported by Flock in 1958 on the use of bibliotherapy with prisoners at the Detroit House of Correction (DeHoco),[20] and was beginning to be of intrigue to people in disciplines other than medicine, psychiatry, and librarianship. Psychodrama (Moreno), the precursor of drama therapy began to be used along with the reading of plays and the reading and writing of poetry.[21] Art, music, and dance therapy also came into play.

NATIONAL ORGANIZATIONS INVOLVED WITH BIBLIOTHERAPY AND KINDRED THERAPIES

A number of national organizations have been involved in the use and development of varying aspects of bibliotherapy. Because of the constant dependence upon librarians with their knowledge of books (as well as other materials) and their work with people, The American Library Association is one of the two most currently influential organizations which will be discussed here.

The American Library Association

The charge made to the Bibliotherapy Committee was to explore the possibility of using books to reshape attitudes. One outcome of this study was the realization that an interdisciplinary approach was needed for undertaking this task. Bibliotherapy was beginning to have more widespread ramifications than anyone had realized. Because of this a widely diversified group of librarians, physicians, psychologists, social scientists, chaplains, and educators were asked to prepare a small invitational bibliotherapy workshop to be held at the ALA's annual conference in June, 1964. This was financed by the U.S. Public Health Service through the National Institute of Mental Health.[22]

In preparation for the workshop, Ruth M. Tews, who was the current chairperson of the ALA's Bibliotherapy Committee was asked to conduct a survey to gather information concerning the status of bibliotherapy at that time. In connection with this she became the editor of an issue of *Library Trends* devoted to the topic of bibliotherapy.[23]

From this publication came many of the directives for education and research in bibliotherapy. Several of the papers lay much of the groundwork for the start, the continued interest and practice of developmental bibliotherapy.

Although the American Library Association grew in size and the divisions within the organization were reshaped to fit the changing needs of libraries, librarians and their patrons, the bibliotherapy committee continued to exist. Today it is a part of ASCLA (Association of Specialized and Cooperative Library Agencies). It, too, has reflected changes. The leadership has been held in turn by librarians who worked with inmates of prison libraries, with patrons of public libraries, and by library school educators who have taught about work with all kinds of patrons.[24]

The interest was so great that an organization which would fit the needs of a larger more eclectically oriented group was needed. In 1973 a bibliotherapy discussion group was founded under the wing of the bibliotherapy committee. The first chairperson of the discussion group was Rhea Rubin, a Ph.D. graduate of the Library School at the University of Wisconsin.[25]

The bibliotherapy discussion group meets at both the winter and annual meetings of the American Library Association. It is open to membership to anyone joining the ALA who is interested in bibliotherapy. It puts out a quarterly newsletter for which subscribers are charged a nominal fee to cover the expenses of duplication and mailing. This is a clearinghouse type of document which includes announcements of courses, workshops, and programs on bibliotherapy along with descriptive accounts of what is happening. in the bibliotherapeutic work of the members. It also includes bibliographies and a mailing list of the membership.

Two of the issues discussed both by the committee members and the discussion group has been the issue of education for bibliotherapy and national certification of bibliotherapists. The effort was spearheaded by Arleen Hynes who in addition to belonging to the American Library Association also belonged to the National Association of Poetry Therapists (NAPT). It was the consensus of the ALA group that Arleen Hynes be appointed as a representative to a federated board to be set up jointly by the interested members of the ALA bibliotherapy group and the interested members of the NAPT group. Alice Smith, who is also a member of both organizations, became the other member of ALA to serve on the Federation Board. The charge of the Federation has been to devise standards for two levels of accrediting professional biblio-poetry therapists (P.T.). The first level gives certification to developmental biblio-poetry therapists; the second (called registration) identifies the clinical biblio-poetry therapist.[26]

The National Association of Poetry Therapists

The NAPT was founded in 1969 by Jack Leidy, the first president and the author of two definitive texts on poetry therapy. In 1973 the Poetry Therapy Institute was founded by Arthur Lerner in California. Since then poetry therapy has flourished including the same varieties of people from other professions as the ALA bibliotherapy committee did in its first days. The organization is buttressed by several loci of specialized education such as Lerner's in California. Early in the work of the organization successful effort was put into designing and implementing a certification process for poetry therapists.[27]

Poetry therapy is akin to bibliotherapy in that while it concentrates on the use of poetry as its major literary modality it also uses all genres and forms of literature in its practice.

Although poetry therapy is based on theory similar to bibliotherapy it was not developed through any relationship to librarianship and so has not had a dependence upon librarians nor has it normally included them as a part of its team. This began to change during the years that Arleen Hynes and Kenneth Gorelick worked together at St. Elizabeth's Hospital. During the intervening years poetry therapists have begun to use other forms of literature in addition to poetry. A poem, however, is still considered to be "the shortest emotional distance between two points, the points representing the writer and the reader."[28]

Many poetry therapists are social workers, public health professionals, ministers, etc. who use the poetry modality in their work with clients. Others, however, as credentialed poetry therapists practice entirely as poetry therapists.

The organization publishes a scholarly journal, the *Journal of Poetry Therapy: The International Journal of Practice, Theory, Research and Education*. The journal is indexed or abstracted in *Psychological Abstracts, Social Science Citation Index, Social Work Research Abstracts, Sage Family Abstracts*, and others. It is a refereed journal which includes scholarly articles, poems, and other forms of relevant creative writing as well as discussion of therapeutic materials and sections devoted to recent and new poetic or literary publications. The editor of the journal is Nicholas Mazza, Ph.D., Florida State University, School of Social Work, Tallahassee.

NAPT also puts out a newsletter which offers assistance to people interested in poetry therapy. The information printed ranges from identifying speakers for groups interested in aspects of biblio-poetry therapy, association programs, workshops, and publications through information concerning the processes of national certification and registration of one's self as a biblio-poetry therapist. The certification requirements are of more immediate interest to librarians who are interested in receiving recognition as people who are considered qualified to be bibliotherapists.

For information about receiving the NAPT Newsletter write to:

> Alma Rolfs, LCSW, BCD
> Editor, NAPT Newsletter
> 420 N. Grove
> Oak Park, IL 60302 (subscription fee: $5)

The information packet describing poetry therapy as well as certification and registration may be received by sending $3 (a handling fee) to:

> NAPT
> 225 William Street
> Huron, OH 44839

For individuals joining the National Association of Poetry Therapy, the newsletter as well as the *Journal of Poetry Therapy*, are included in the cost of membership.[29]

RESEARCH IN BIBLIOTHERAPY

Once a procedure has acquired a technique it also acquires a name, a significance, and a need for research to validate its existence. This pattern can be seen in the continuous growth and wide reach of bibliotherapy as it spread rapidly during the first half of the twentieth century. The value of literature as an important element in augmenting the healing process as well as in directing human growth, the development of character, and emotional stability not to mention the motivation of changes in the direction of individual human lives was rooted centuries deep. It was found to be effective with children, teenagers, and senior citizens as well as with the ill who were recovering in hospitals.

As early as 1930, Alice Bryan strongly took the pulpit in favor of the value of reading books for the purpose of changing the attitudes and the values of readers at times of need in their lives. In view of this she felt that as many people as possible should be encouraged to use the library in ways that would provide enrichment of their own personal and social effectiveness.[30] Successful accomplishment of this goal would require study and work with psychologists and the inclusion of an appropriate course in the library school curriculum concerning the psychology of the reader. Such a study would open up the gate between research in psychology encouraging application of psychological findings in library advisory work with readers and books.

By the turn of the decade (1949–1951), several important scholarly works concerning bibliotherapy and its growing applications came out of a number of prestigious universities and library schools. Caroline Shrodes, from the University of California, gave a psychological framework for the dynamics of bibliotherapy.[31] Stein, from Western Reserve University, gave a discussion of practical bibliotherapy and an annotated list for librarians[32]; Hartman, at Stanford University, established a scientific base for the use of imaginative literature as a projective technique in therapy for emotional problems.[33] Shrodes introduced the use of Freudian terms and processes such as identification, abreaction, and catharsis and insight into the explanation of the importance of literature for the client.

Stein's paper which was concerned with the art of bibliotherapy was primarily devoted to works accomplished and materials used in those works from 1940–1949. Hartman, on the other hand, continued adding effective evidence for the science of bibliotherapy supporting the use of literature as a model for the dilemma of the reader in which a safe and possibly applicable solution could be found for the reader's own problem. Such effectiveness is the basic reason for the use of literature. Without this use there would be no bibliotherapy.

Other dissertations appeared at the rate of one approximately every year and a half from 1949 to 1975. Rubin gives a succinct analysis of their objective, design, accomplishments, and failures. She concludes that while progress has been made, research in the first half of the 1970s is confusing and conflicting.[34]

Hynes brings a fresh look to research by (1) redefining the emerging force of bibliotherapy, (2) dividing the trends into distinct categories, and (3) identifying ongoing research from the many disciplines which are intermeshed in bibliotherapy.[35] She identifies many authorities not directly concerned with research in the practice of bibliotherapy whose theories are important in the successful practice of bibliotherapy.[36] Among these are Abraham Maslow with his psychology of being, M. Maultsby and rationale behavior,[37] H. A. Otto on personality strengths,[38] Carl Rogers with personality theory and client centered therapy,[39] Rosenblatt with literature as an exploration,[40] Singer on creative uses of fantasy,[41] and many others. She also refers to more recent dissertations in bibliotherapy as well as the earlier research effort of Sister Miriam Schultheiss, an Ed.D. thesis at Ball State University in Muncie, Indiana.[42] This is the foundation of her Institute for the Study of Bibliotherapy in Fort Wayne, Indiana.

Students interested in obtaining authentic research information about bibliotherapy and its practice must go to a variety of resources. All of the indexes to research in the areas concerned with aiding the human quest for wholeness are available. These range from *Psychological Abstracts* through *Social Science Citation Index* and similar publications to the indexes of the wide variety of creative therapies such as art, drama, and music therapy. As an aid in such a search the *Journal of Poetry Therapy* presents two sections which identify research in biblio-poetry therapy. One section abstracts the information found in the indexes mentioned above; the other identifies relevant dissertations. For example, the 1989 spring issue of the *Journal of Poetry Therapy* annotates seven dissertations on poetry therapy and/or on bibliotherapy published from 1984 to 1987. None appear to have been carried out in library science doctoral programs. However, all are relevant to librarians who are interested in bibliotherapy.

The *Journal* also reports other research in bibliotherapy as well as gives reviews of new books. Eight research reports are abstracted. One of these is a review and analysis of the literature of bibliotherapy as it applies to special education. This review was also noted in ERIC. It should be noted that although there may be some of the same reports cited in various indexes, the duplication is of such a limited extent that it behooves the researcher to include more than one index to the literature for more effective research on the topic. Library science students are often directed to ERIC, a useful index of topics in education and in library science.

If a student uses bibliotherapy for a heading instead of several topical synonyms for the process which are a part of bibliotherapy, the search will locate very few reports of experimental research which will be of relevance to his or her needs. For example, a recent cursory search of ERIC using only the term "bibliotherapy" identified eighty-nine citations of journal articles published from October 1979 to spring of 1989. Of these articles, seven were published in library science publications. Three of the publications appeared in *Catholic Library World*, *School Library Journal*, and *Journal of Youth Services* (formerly *Top of the News*); the others in *Drexel Journal of Library Science* and *Florida School Media Quarterly*.

The other publications were primarily in divisional areas of education such as Reading, English, Guidance and Counseling, Special Education, Attitudinal Research, one from Gerontology with heavy emphasis upon children, teenagers, and some emphasis upon parents. They were primarily descriptive articles of programs ranging in time span from one session to several with heavy emphasis on lists of books and annotations of many titles. A few cited authoritative reference resources. Many purported to be reviews of research in bibliotherapy. Some of these were limited to (e.g.) research in bibliotherapy for children with specific types of handicaps. Few of them were global in their overview. The exception was *The Myth of Bibliography* by Lucy Werner.[43] Werner analyzed several of the early documents about bibliotherapy as well as a selected few published near the time of the author's investigation. Her reading was fairly extensive but not exhaustive. Several developments in bibliotherapy did not come within the parameters of her examination. However, her work is a good point of departure.

Students who are seriously interested in bibliotherapy must know enough about its interdisciplinary makeup that they are able to identify topics (and their synonyms) which are a part of the process. For example they may wish to examine research on the formation and guidance of discussion groups: optional size, importance of physical meeting place, modes of conduct, knowledge required of the leader, other aspects of group dynamics, and the effectiveness of learning in similar groups. These are only a few of the many important aspects to be investigated.

The paucity of citations retrieved from ERIC using only the term "bibliotherapy" does not mean that it is never advisable to use the term bibliotherapy in one's search. It does mean that such a use is only a beginning and that to analyze the effectiveness of the findings one must, also, be able to differentiate between descriptive articles and genuine research reports. This differentiation includes recognizing the authoritativeness of the author of each entry.

One way to begin identifying viable research is to subscribe to the NAPT (National Association of Poetry Therapy) Newsletter. The editors have prepared a list of authoritative readings for interested novices. The *Journal of Poetry Therapy* has a regular section in each issue on research abstracts. Other ways are to attend workshops and courses given by noted bibliotherapists, by universities, and by library science organizations. The winter and summer meetings of the ALA Bibliotherapy Discussion Group often are programmatic and always give information to the interested inquirer.

More specific information may be acquired in other ways. Inquiries may be made of Arleen Hynes at St. Benedict's College, St. Joseph, Minnesota concerning her program and consultantships. The School of Library and Information Science at the University of South Florida (Tampa) has been offering an introductory course in bibliotherapy in the January term of each academic year. Florida Library Association has a Bibliotherapy Caucus which has a programmatic meeting at each annual conference in May. Many other state library associations or state library departments offer similar opportunities. The avid seeker will find other opportunities as well.

Viable research is continuing to be carried out. As the recognition that such research exists increases, librarians can avail themselves of information which can aid them in their service to library patrons.

READING GUIDANCE AND BIBLIOTHERAPY

One of the confusing issues about bibliotherapy for librarians is the vast numbers of people in areas of education who write about and carry out a wide variety of programs which are labelled "bibliotherapy." Caroline Shrodes who devised the first psychological framework of a science of bibliotherapy is in part responsible for this confusion of roles. Shrodes cooperated with David Russell, a noted reading specialist, in writing a two part series of articles which exhorted classroom teachers to use bibliotherapy in their reading classes.[44]

A number of well respected educators used the views of Shrodes and Russell as a springboard in promoting developmental reading. The delights and hoped for successes described in these publications were exciting adjuncts to be used in a variety of educational situations. Writers of books on children's literature (as well as young adult literature) inserted descriptive mention of bibliotherapy as a technique to be considered in using books with pupils.[45] It is true that the writers inserted words of caution stating that such methods should not be used with children who had deep-seated emotional problems unless a guidance counselor or school psychiatrist was also involved in the process. Nevertheless everyone was eager to try the new techniques.

The educational atmosphere was ripe for urging teachers to use literature to change the behavior of children and youth. The same year that Shrodes's dissertation was published the revised and enlarged edition of *Reading Ladders for Human Relations* came out. The first publication was a pamphiet which grew out of a project of the American Council on Education to find materials and techniques for improving human relations.[46]

Hilda Taba, editor of the 1949 enlarged edition, believed that an important purpose of education was "to increase sensitivity toward people, their values and their ways of living."[47] She felt that fiction and drama deepened understanding. In this she was supported by the work on drama therapy which was in vogue as well as in role playing as described by the Shaftels[48] and creative dramatics for children and youth by Winifred Ward.[49] All of these efforts flowed together into the practice and theory of reading guidance or readers services as practiced in public libraries.

Evalene Jackson who was Director of the Division of Librarianship at Emory University, Atlanta, wrote strongly about the importance of reading guidance in public libraries. She felt that "bringing about effective encounters between people and books was an accepted part . . . "[50] of both the training for librarians and the role of those librarians as they administered educational programs in public libraries. An important element of librarianship in addition to the actual encounters of book introduction and book discussion was the skill of the librarian who knew books and was able to select and maintain an appropriate library collection.

In the public library the emphasis was upon providing reading guidance to persons who had not sought and might not need clinical help.[51] They were seeking relief from and solutions to the everyday problems of living. This might be found in "escape" reading or it could be found in the lives of fictional characters found in the books offered by the librarians. Harry Stack Sullivan's theories of dynamic psychology influenced Jackson who believed that not only were people influenced by significant other people but that a book could be, and often was, a significant other.[52] Through the reader's vicarious entering into the life of a book's protagonist, the reader was introduced to influential new ways of thinking about life's problems and solving them. This fit right into the thinking that was projected in *Reading Ladders*.

Ladders was (and is in its successive revisions) divided into themes of human relations which form ladders for raising readings from one level of understanding to another. The goals are changes of thought, attitude, and behavior. The first section in the most recent edition of *Ladders* is on understanding one's self. This is based on the premise that we must understand ourselves before we can understand others, an important concept for effective work in bibliotherapy.[53]

Reading guidance became an important issue for service in both the school libraries of the day as well as in public libraries. Library schools offered courses which were entirely or partially devoted to reading (or readers) guidance for children, for young adults, and for adults of all ages. One of the prominent reading guidance specialists who taught both librarians and classroom teachers in her classes was Florence Damon Cleary. Cleary wrote extensively and one of her most widely used texts which went into several editions was *Blueprints for Better Reading*.[54]

At the time of her publications Cleary was the head of the school library program at Wayne State University in Detroit. Cleary was widely known for her classes on reading guidance and her extensive publications in this area, in values, and the impact values in education for children had upon the equilibrium of democracy.[55] Although on many occasions she talked and wrote about bibliotherapy she was careful to state that the evidence was "not in" about the efficacy of bibliotherapy nor about the validity of it as a tool for librarians to use. Since Cleary headed a program preparing school librarians (at the time there were no media specialists) she was greatly influenced by the works of Russell and

Shrodes as well as by other noted educators who believed that the schools were
the proper arena in which to use bibliotherapy for the young.

Much of Cleary's work in reading guidance was based upon using fiction,
biography, poetry and other appropriate forms of good literature to match the
developmental stages and tasks of the young. She discussed storytelling, book
introductions (single book and multi-book "book talking") with appropriate
open-ended questions to use in facilitating group discussions. Discussion sometimes verged on the therapeutic. She felt the same concerns as a third library
educator, Margaret Monroe, did, "Where did reading guidance end and bibliotherapy begin?"

Monroe was Dean of the Library School at the University of Wisconsin,
Madison. She was influenced by the thinking of Ruth Tews, the editor of the
Library Trends issue on bibliotherapy and Evalene Jackson. Her belief, however,
differed in that she believed libraries more often served the human support
system of individuals than it served those systems of people who were experiencing personal crises. She believed that to be helpful in guidance the librarian must
know the client as a person, know about the problem, and know the library
resources and their potential for help. This was the point at which Monroe felt
readers' guidance came perilously close to being bibliotherapy. At such a crucial
point librarians then must know how to work in a team and have had long
experience in practicing these precepts before edging over into the still uncharted
land of bibliotherapy. Nevertheless she felt that the bibliotherapeutic process was
a natural outgrowth of the readers services provided by librarians.[56]

Monroe was responsible for several institutes on serving readers at the University of Wisconsin Library School. In 1971, through her instigation the School
issued "a mimeographed collection of papers presented at three Adult Services
Institutes held" in 1965, 1966, and 1968.[57] Six of the ten papers discussed
bibliotherapy. The other four discussed services in connection with reading guidance. Monroe stressed that terminology was not the important consideration but
that emphasis should be placed upon service.

Librarians in the 1990s are still baffled by the fine line of distinction which
separates readers' services (guidance) from bibliotherapy.

LIBRARY EDUCATION FOR BIBLIOTHERAPY[58]

From the first nineteenth century use of bibliotherapy in American hospitals the
search was on to obtain the services of adequately trained librarians. They were
needed to select appropriate materials and to maintain the collections ready for
use. They, also, were depended upon for guidance services in offering materials
in the ways that would attract the interests of the patients. The early literature is
full of references to such practices and to demands of adequate library education
of these librarians.

Among the other skills which were demanded were the abilities to work well as a team member and.to quickly learn and put into practice some of the therapeutic routines used by the clinical professionals. These requirements suggested a need for an in-service or a practical internship period.

At the time that Ruth Tews was gathering papers for the *Library Trends* issue on bibliotherapy several library schools were offering courses which were designed to be helpful to aspiring bibliotherapists. As the use of bibliotherapy spread into the areas of pediatric wards, prisons, schools, churches, and other institutions discussion as the pros and cons of bibliotherapy was rife among library educators. There was no total agreement that a specified track for bibliotherapy education should be offered. That meant a track involving courses which differed from the courses needed for selection and utilization of materials and services to a multiplexity of populations.

Library Education at a Crossroads

It must be remembered that library science itself was an emerging discipline and was undergoing a number of reforms. J. Periam Danton was instrumental in advocating the need for research courses as a part of the curriculum in every library school as well as the need for doctoral level programs to education library school faculty.[59]

Although the first doctoral program in library science had begun in 1932 only 173 doctorates had been awarded during the intervening thirty year period. Graduates of doctoral programs received far better salaries elsewhere than they did teaching in library schools. The schools found themselves in the predicament of employing professors who taught students with higher degrees of education than they themselves possessed. As the universities in which library schools were housed began to require an earned doctorate for all faculty members the practice of requiring a doctor's degree for appointment to a library school faculty became standard.[60]

At the same time a great deal of other healthy ferment occurred in library education. The push towards documentation and retrieval was in its infancy. The powerful explosions of population, knowledge, technology, and the probing of space were beginning to exert their forces. Education for school librarianship was changing. The magic power of multi-media hardware, software and their utilization was changing the quiet school librarian into the wizardry of a Madison Avenue styled media specialist.

Education for bibliotherapy was only one of many competing interests. It touched upon but was only a part of the mainstream of education. It was tinged with the faint aura of uneasiness which has always accompanied any hint of the mystery of healing. It was affected as well by the discomfort which arises with changes of thought in strong new schools of psychology. Freud was becoming less sacred. Was the conditioned reflex the prime factor in learning? Should purveyors of factual, higher education be concerned with such acts of leger-demain?

In spite of all these things there were a number of strong proponents for the establishment of library education for bibliotherapy. Among them were Ruth Tews, Margaret Kinney, Evalene Jackson, and Margaret Monroe, already discussed in the body of this work. Tews and Kinney were prominent librarians with administrative training and bibliotherapeutic duties. In addition they were active workers in the bibliotherapeutic movement in ALA. Tews was head librarian at the Mayo clinic. Kinney held a similar position at the Veteran's Administration Hospital, Bronx, New York.

Views from the Field

Both Tews and Kinney believed that while education of one's self for librarianship was an ongoing, life-time project, courses in library schools were needed to provide a foundation for self education. They agreed upon the importance of knowing the contents of books and how to select materials. They understood the need for skill in guiding patrons towards a choice of appropriate titles as well as the need for assistance in "how to read for meaning and understanding." They agreed with Alice Bryan[61] that it was as important to have as much knowledge about the psychology of reading and of the reader as it was to have knowledge about the books themselves.

Tews also agreed with Jesse Shera's statement that research is not just fact finding but is the application of accepted procedures which "seem most likely to produce truthful results."[62]

Kinney went into even greater detail. She felt that to be a successful bibliotherapist one must possess specific personal characteristics such as an inquiring intelligence and the ability to change, to perceive the points of view and the sufferings of others without being maudlin. In addition she felt the bibliotherapist must nurture the yen for self-discovery and wellness of spirit that is the core of every healthy individual. Only after this should the bibliotherapist study a variety of courses which she believed most library schools did not offer.

In Kinney's opinion library school courses were boringly didactic, more concerned with the what, where, and how of obtaining materials than in enjoying and encouraging the delight and usefulness "of their meaty contents."[63] She realized, along with Tews, that cataloging, classification, reference, and all kinds of bibliography (information sources) were important. And, although her work was in a hospital library she believed that the field practice of working in a public library assisting patrons of all ages and all kinds of backgrounds was invaluable training.

Above all, Kinney believed that a solid academic background should precede basic library training with as wide a reading background as possible. This could be abetted in library school by advanced courses which required analytic written annotations of current materials on a variety of topics. In addition she felt that all librarians should know literature for children, young adults, and older adults.

Kinney recognized the need for interdisciplinary education. Outside the realm of librarianship she felt bibliotherapists should have courses in the principles of clinical psychology and the evaluation of emotional responses. In addition the librarian should have an understanding of medical, psychological, and psychiatric terminology as well as the language of statistics with training in evaluation and report writing.

Finally, Kinney believed that there must be standards for training, accreditation of such a program of education on a national level, and a universally recognized certification of the bibliotherapists who had completed such a program.[64]

Two Library Educators

Jackson and Monroe, the library educators who were concerned about the faint line which separated reading guidance from bibliotherapy also had strong views about library education for bibliotherapy. Jackson who had done an experimental project on the influence of reading in changing attitudes toward racial minorities was interested in encouraging students to investigate current theories such as that of Harry Stack Sullivan and carry on research of their own in bibliotherapy. She was especially pleased with the work of Dewey Carroll who later went on to become the Dean of the Library School at the University of North Texas, Denton.

Jackson's educational credo included: (1) an assessment of the personality of the would-be bibliotherapist, and, then, (2) a listing of the courses which should be required in education for bibliotherapy.

Jackson felt that the bibliotherapist must:

1. Have a tremendous knowledge of books and a desire to continue adding to that knowledge.
2. Emulate the philosophy of Carl Rogers in understanding the characteristics of the helping situation. That includes willingness to help, warm feelings towards others, awareness of himself/herself in a non-judgmental fashion, extension of the non-judgmental attitude towards others.
3. In addition the bibliotherapist must be imaginative, intelligently inquisitive about the patrons, developing skills of interviewing, and be able to facilitate discussions which lead to growth.

Jackson listed a number of courses which she felt should not only be required but should also be substantial in content. These were:

- Reading guidance (a general course)
- Interpersonal relations

- Leading discussions in interpersonal problem situations
- Adult reading guidance
- Thorough and substantial courses in bibliography
- Advanced courses in both psychology and literature
- Field training in both clinical (explicit) and non-clinical (implicit) biblio-
  therapy
- Literature in multi-media formats (which medium appeals to which patron
  in what situations)[65]

Like Jackson, Monroe was a strong advocate concerning the importance of
research. First, know what has been done. Replicate it for validation. Then
branch out with fresh paths of inquiry.[66] She gave evidence of her beliefs in the
guidance of her doctoral students such as Rhea Rubin and Lesta Burt. Both of
these women did their doctoral studies on bibliotherapy in work with prison
inmates. Both continued to be active in ALA. Rubin has become an outstanding
freelance bibliotherapist, active in ALA, a consultant, the director of many
workshops on bibliotherapy as well as the writer of several important books
published in the field of bibliotherapy. Burt became director of the Sam Houston
State University Library Science program.[67]

As a result of her work and research in the field, Margaret Monroe set up a
basic bibliotherapeutic model for library service which merits intelligent consideration by librarians today. The six steps in Monroe's view of the bibliotherapeutic process are:

1. Read, view, or listen.
2. Identify with some element in the situation presented by the characters in
   the literature.
3. Experience the situation vicariously.
4. Experience catharsis.
5. Gain insight into the problems and one's self.
6. Change one's attitude and/or behavior.[68]

Monroe postulates her statements upon the premise that behavior and attitude
changes are measurable. Since such changes are associated with a reading-
discussion process the bibliotherapeutic model becomes a significant one for
librarians.

In addition to the model Monroe has created of guidance and caution for
librarians, she also sees distinctive uses of bibliotherapeutic materials and the
process for three groups of people: (1) those experiencing the personal crisis, (2)
those who are professional helpers in the crisis, and (3) those who form the
human support system to people with the personal crisis. In Monroe's opinion
libraries more often serve the human support system than those experiencing the

personal crisis. They may be involved in working with a client-in-crisis but primarily as a team member.[69]

Not everyone agrees with Monroe's perception. During the years which have followed Monroe's first presentation of her design, bibliotherapy as an increasingly complicated process has continued to evolve. Nevertheless Monroe's ultimate statement of what the librarian must know to support the bibliotherapeutic process is as true in the 1990s as it was thirty years ago.

The librarian must:

• Know the client (reader/viewer/listener) as a person
• Know the problem
• Know the library resources and their potential for therapy
• Know how to work in a team

Only after long experience in practicing these four precepts will a librarian be ready to make a "personal decision to move to further expertise."[70]

Monroe believed that emphasis for bibliotherapy should be placed more heavily upon education and research than on licensing. She felt that the real need was to establish a validity of the controlled use of books as therapy. She also believed that "truly adequate standards of education" could not be established until research proved the validity of the methods to be used. She urged librarians to undertake the research needed to move bibliotherapy to the status of a controlled science.[71]

Other Programs in Bibliotherapy Education

There are many dedicated people who are important in developing the potentials of bibliotherapy. However the librarian who has continuously taught, experimented, and studied in a fashion that has advanced the thinking and practice the most profoundly in the last twenty years is Arleen McCarty Hynes. As the patients' librarian at St. Elizabeth's Hospital in Washington, D.C., together with Kenneth Gorelick, Hynes trained a small number of people to learn the techniques used by her and Dr. Gorelick. Some of the trainees eventually stepped out as well trained bibliotherapists.[72] Barbara Allen and Clara Lack went to California. Rosalie Brown stayed in Washington and carried on the program after Hynes retired from St. Elizabeth's and joined the staff at St. Benedict's College in St. Joseph, Minnesota.

During Hynes's years in Washington a most rigorous program was set up which was instrumental in allowing Hynes to develop the idea of interactive bibliotherapy and to strengthen the role of the peer group facilitator as well as distinguish more clearly between the levels of bibliotherapy which have become known as clinical bibliotherapy and developmental bibliotherapy. The graduates of the Hynes-Gorelick program could function at either level. In spite of this, they recognized the need for bibliotherapists who would serve entirely in the setting of schools, public libraries, church, synagogue, and other non-clinical institutions.

A three hour credit course was, also, taught at the Catholic University of America's Graduate School of Librarianship. A practicum in group work with some bibliotherapy supervision was also available. When Hynes left St. Elizabeth's the connection with Catholic University was discontinued.[73] The St. Elizabeth's program, however, is still ongoing.

In Minnesota Hynes is teaching, doing workshops, continuing her research and her writing. She is active in the Poetry Therapy Association. Both she and her daughter, Mary Hynes-Berry, co-author of *Bibliotherapy, the Interactive Process: A Handbook*, participated in the program of the annual conference which was held in Minnesota in May, 1990.[74]

Other Influences on Bibliotherapy Education

Courses for bibliotherapy are also offered in the School of Library and Information Science at the University of South Florida, Tampa. For a number of years only an introductory course was offered.[75] When the School instigated its sixth year program one option was for further training in administration. The other was in services in libraries. As a part of the service track a program was planned with the Department of Counselor Education in which library science students could take guidance courses as well as other courses in psychology and relevant topics which would be accepted for their degree. In a similar fashion students in Counselor Education could take library science courses such as Selection of Materials, Reading Guidance, etc. and use them as appropriate courses for their degree. In addition to the basic course in bibliotherapy, two other courses were added: an advanced course in bibliotherapy and a practicum.[76]

The two courses in bibliotherapy are structured so that increasing numbers of peer group sessions are held in the last half of each semester. Peer group sessions are conducted in a circle or around a table. They may include as few as eight people or as many as twenty-four. An optimum number lies in the middle range. During the first course sessions are primarily planned and facilitated by the instructor. During the second course sessions are primarily planned and facilitated by the students. The first half of each session is lecture and textbook oriented with discussion of assignments and student planning. This planning is often augmented by independent work of further planning in preparation for the bibliotherapy practicum.

To register for the practicum students are required to have completed the first two courses in bibliotherapy and have an approved plan ready for implementation. At the time of the plan's approval arrangements are made for the site at which the program will be carried out, the on-site supervision, and the formation of the group with whom the bibliotherapist will be working. A limited number of students have completed their practicums.

One of the practicum students who came to the University of South Florida at the recommendation of Arleen Hynes had field experience in a mental health institute, as well as in an intergenerational program at a private school in Tampa. She, also, participated in planning a Reading Guidance Workshop which was held during two successive weekends. She co-operated in co-facilitating the sample facilitation session which was a part of the bibliotherapy presentation of the workshop.[77]

The bibliotherapy program has been designed and taught by Alice Smith. Smith had taken her master's degree in Library Science at Wayne State University under the direction of Florence Cleary.[78] She had become, first, an adjunct instructor and then, a full time member of the Library Science faculty. Two years after joining the faculty Smith entered the doctoral program in Teacher Education for Library Education.

Smith was impressed with Cleary's theories of reading guidance and bibliotherapy which shone effectively through so much of Cleary's teaching and writing. Smith patterned her own teaching on the ideas of "learning to learn," problem solving, and building coping skills. These have been especially effective in classes such as reading guidance, books and related materials for patrons of all ages, storytelling, and bibliotherapy.

Study in Smith's doctoral program also influenced her philosophy and acceptance of the psychological principles which undergird the bibliotherapy classes. This work included study of Carl Rogers and his philosophy of helping as well as study of the other personality theorists. The work of Bandura[79] on the importance of modelling as an aid to a child's growth and development was also influential along with the developmental theories of Erickson, Piaget, Havighurst, Maslow, etc. One of the most important factors was a year's independent study with Dr. Juanita Collier of the Psychology Department at Wayne State on the topic of literary imagery in Freudian and neo-Freudian psychology. This solidified the concepts of literature as the modality of importance in bibliotherapy. It deepened the value of using such techniques as creative dramatics, role-playing, and choral speaking as effective means of reinforcing the reader's identification with important aspects of the literature.

The bibliotherapy courses at the University of South Florida are purely instructional and are not taught in a setting in which the primary focus is on the day-by-day practice of bibliotherapy as was the case at St. Elizabeth's. Stress is laid primarily upon viable definitions of bibliotherapy and the feasibility of carrying out a program of bibliotherapy in non-clinical situations. Emphasis is put upon considering the possibility of defining bibliotherapy and facilitating the development of coping skills for solving some of life's developmental problems. Cautions are raised concerning possible emotional dangers which must be avoided. A knowledge of appropriate evaluation methods is also considered. Students are urged to keep careful records of classes and/or workshops taken, supervised practice and a log of actual bibliotherapeutic experiences suitable for evidence to be submitted to appropriate authorities for certification credit as a biblio-poetry therapist.

Courses Adaptable for Bibliotherapy: Based on a Random Sampling of Available Courses in Library Schools, 1988–1989

Among the fifteen library school catalogs (1988–89) examined in a random sample, the only courses headed "bibliotherapy" were offered by the School of Library and Information at the University of South Florida, Tampa. However, a number of courses similar to those recommended by Tews, Kinney, Jackson, Monroe, and others, as important in library education for bibliotherapy are being offered at the fifteen schools.

The available courses are in Children's Literature, Young Adult Literature, Materials for the Child and/or Young Adult, Materials for Adults, service courses at all levels (for children, for young adults, for adults of varying ages, for the indigent, for the incarcerated, etc.), Reading Guidance, Storytelling, Book and other Material Selection (Collection Development and Management). There are also a number of courses in Bibliography (Information Sources) as well as opportunity for directed study, research and/or reading. Arranged field work is also available.

Although several of the course descriptions talk about developmental tasks and meeting the needs of patrons or the importance of developing positive attitudes through books, no school specifically discusses bibliotherapy as a part of the content covered by a course.

Many of the library school course offerings are listed in the graduate catalog of the larger institution or university of which the library school is a part. Cited in many of these graduate catalogs are courses which are important to a study of bibliotherapy. Among these are courses in guidance and counseling. There are also relevant courses in Schools of Social Work as well as in departments of psychology, gerontology, specialized services to disabled people, etc.

The majority of the library science courses listed above are offered in almost all of the library schools which have a master's degree program accredited by the American Library Association. Interested persons should consult the most re- cently published catalogs of the schools in which they are interested to be certain of the availability of the courses. There is a trend in some schools which are placing the most heavy emphasis on information science to depend upon book courses for children and young adults that are offered by either Liberal Arts or the College of Education. In some isolated instances no provision is made for such courses. It may even be advisable for the would-be bibliotherapist to query the appropriate instructor of the preferred courses either in the School of Library

Science or in the College of Education to which these courses have been relegated.

SUMMARY

Bibliotherapy has been a slowly emerging discipline. Although its origins go as far back as the Alexandrian libraries in which there was a room called the hospital of the soul[80] it did not receive a name until the beginning of the twentieth century. In the early decades bibliotherapy became a much discussed therapy made known by the work of the Menninger brothers in their institutes and in Veterans Hospitals. Although several American hospitals depended upon libraries and librarians for assistance in the treatment of their patients the need was exacerbated by the influx of soldiers returning from the battle fields of World Wars I and II. Hospital journals carried many accounts of bibliotherapeutic practices.

The hospital division of the American Library Association included staff members of Veterans Hospitals. The ALA Bibliotherapy Committee was culled from their roster. The interest became so intense that a call was made for a national survey of the state of the art of bibliotherapy. Ruth Tews was appointed as the director of the survey. She also became the editor of the *Library Trends* issue on bibliotherapy which included the results of the survey. Noted people in the field also were contributors. Among the contributors were heads of library schools and other educators who were interested in readers' services in libraries who put forth their recommendations concerning bibliotherapy education as a part of library school education for librarianship. Specific courses were devised and new courses were recommended to be used in library education for bibliotherapy.

Several pieces of research contributed to the growth of interest such as the dissertation of Caroline Shrodes carried out at the University of California. Shrodes used her findings to cooperate with David Russell, a noted reading specialist, in a publication which exhorted classroom teachers to use bibliotherapy in their reading classes. This involved school librarians who in turn had been inspired by the reading guidance emphasis received in library schools. Several well known people in bibliotherapy today are graduates of those programs. They are instrumental in teaching, writing, giving workshops, and practicing bibliotherapy. The boundary between reading guidance and bibliotherapy became increasingly indistinguishable.

The definition of bibliotherapy expanded to include the strategies and goals of the practices of bibliotherapy. Bibliotherapy could be:

1.   Didactic or reading bibliotherapy—on a one to one educational base with a clinician in an institution prescribing informational materials for the client to read about his/her problems.

2. Clinical—primarily group work in an institution with emotionally dis-
   turbed patients with a clinical person such as a doctor or specially trained
   nurse of clinical therapist to head up a team of workers which would
   include a librarian.
3. Developmental—based upon the developmental stages and tasks of the
   psychologist Havighurst to be used with groups of people, usually in
   libraries. The librarian could head the group and be the only facilitator or
   the librarian could work as a team with a guidance counselor or some
   other professional person who had mental health and/or guidance education.[81]

Definitions two and three could be considered interactive bibliotherapy, a
distinction elaborated by Arleen Hynes. Specialists from other disciplines were
also developing their own strategies, methods, and requirements in the maturing
of their therapies. One of the organizations which has taken the most firm steps
forward in certifying therapists is the National Association of Poetry Therapists
(NAPT). Leaders from the NAPT together with Arleen Hynes representing the
American Library Association formed a federation to devise standards for the
education, certification, and registration of biblio-poetry therapists.

With the diminishing lack of formal education for bibliotherapy in library
schools, applying to the supervisory board of the certification/ registration examination for guidance on preparing for the examination is one way to help people
who are interested in becoming bibliotherapists. It offers a way for individuals to
plan an educational program for themselves which includes taking courses and
attending classes. There are many bibliotherapy workshops offered around the
country. State organizations of librarians interested in bibliotherapy are also in
existence. Bibliotherapy courses or courses related to bibliotherapy are offered in
some universities.

Hynes, the author of the most contemporary and authoritative textbook on the
subject continuously offers courses at St. Benedict's University in St. Joseph,
Minnesota. Alice Smith has offered courses in the School of Library and Information Science at the University of South Florida, Tampa. These opportunities
and others are advertised in professional journals and can also be located by
participating as a member of either the ALA bibliotherapy discussion group or
the National Association of Poetry Therapists or by querying individual state
libraries on the professional library organizations of each state.

RECOMMENDATIONS

If librarians continue to be interested in and involved in bibliotherapeutic activities, it behooves library educators to take some leadership in the education of
librarians for bibliotherapy. This has been debated by heads of library schools for

a number of years. While some library educators are not convinced of the importance of bibliotherapy, the practice is of special interest to librarians who are in the personal service areas of librarianship, that is in public libraries, school media centers, juvenile centers, hospitals, etc. Students interested in these types of service need guidance in curriculum choices and in opportunities for practice in group work. There are several ways in which this can be done.

Only one of these is to set up a joint degree at either the master's level or the sixth year level with a school guidance and counseling program in a college of education; or with some appropriate area in a school of social work; or with any other program of clinical education which would offer courses in psychology, human relationships, group counseling, etc.

If this is not feasible there are other ways of helping. The faculty members who teach courses in children's, young adult, or adult services could prepare themselves to act as advisors for the interested students. In preparation they could locate cognate courses at their universities which are appropriate for their students to take either during their degree work in library school or in continuing education. Such advising, to be effective, would involve making arrangements with instructors of the identified courses so that library school students are accepted in these courses. A variety of cooperative arrangements are possible.

The student organization, and its advisor, at the school of library science could be responsible for securing copies of information available from ALA, state library organizations, the National Association of Poetry Therapists, or any other educationally acceptable disseminator of information on this topic.

There are professional people at a national level who are available to come as short-term consultants, to lecture, to put on a workshop for interested faculty and students of any library school. Information about such people is available from national organizations such as ALA and the NAPT, or the *Journal of Poetry Therapy*. Computer searches of such data bases as ERIC, WILSON LINE, PSYCHOLOGICAL ABSTRACTS, and other indices mentioned in this paper, can also offer important information. The courses outlined in the body of this work considered by Margaret Monroe and others as important for bibliotherapy education in library schools are still viable offerings. Many of them are still available in the majority of library schools. Others can be devised. There is help available for this from ALA, NAPT, the state library associations, and individual consultants who belong to these organizations.

In addition, concerned library educators must find ways to become involved in the licensing process. This is a vital concern if the special needs of librarians are to be met. Somewhere there must be library educators who hear this call and set about instigating programs of preparation for work in bibliotherapy and becoming involved in making bibliotherapy a legitimate arm of library science. The librarian who is interested in the history of bibliotherapy should read both Rubin's *Source Book* and *Textbook*, the issue of *Library Trends* edited by Tews, as well as Brown's *Bibliotherapy and Its Widening Implications*. To understand bibliotherapy as it has evolved today, its applications, and how to plan to become a bibliotherapist, the librarian should study the handbook written by Hynes. Then, follow the "yellow brick road" to the amazing territory of bibliotherapy.

NOTES AND REFERENCES

1. William K. Beatty, "A Historical Review of Bibliotherapy." *Library Trends*, 14 (October, 1962), p. 106.
2. Rhea Joyce Rubin, ed. *Bibliotherapy Source Book*. Phoenix, AZ: Oryx Press, 1978. p. xi.
3. Ibid.
4. Alice G. Smith. "Will the Real Bibliotherapist Please Stand Up." *Journal of Youth Services*, 2 (Spring, 1989), pp. 241–249.
5. Ibid.
6. Arleen Hynes. "Bibliotherapy Defined." In *Proceedings of the Fourth Bibliotherapy Round Table Held in Washington, D.C. 28–29 January 1977*, Arleen Hynes, Kenneth Gorelick, editors. pp. 1–3.
7. Arleen Hynes and Mary Hynes-Berry. *Bibliotherapy, the Interactive Process: A Handbook.* Boulder, CO: Westview Press, 1986. pp. 10–18.
8. Rubin, op. cit., p. xi.
9. Holbrook Jackson. *The Anatomy of Bibliomania*. New York: Avenel Books, 1981. p. 337.
10. Ibid., pp. 166, 345.
11. Ibid., pp. 42, 44, 65, 277, 419, 425.
12. Ibid. Holbrook cites the "Autocrat," "Professor," and "Poet at the Breakfast Table," pp. 133, 290, 611–616, et al.
13. William C. Menninger. "Bibliotherapy." *Bulletin of the Menninger Clinic*, 1 (November, 1937), pp. 263–274.
14. Rhea Joyce Rubin. *Bibliotherapy: A Guide to Theory and Practice*. Phoenix, AZ: Oryx Press, 1978, p. 1.
15. Eleanor Frances Brown. *Bibliotherapy and Its Widening Applications*. Metuchen, NJ: Scarecrow Press, 1974, pp. 13, 14.
16. Ibid., pp. 280–281.
17. Ibid., pp. 125–127.
18. Menninger, op. cit.
19. Vera Flandorf. "Getting Well with Books." *Library Journal* (April 15, 1958), pp. 57–59.
20. M. M. Flock. "Bibliotherapy and the Library." *The Bookmark* (December, 1958), pp. 57–59.
21. L. J. Moreno. *Psychodrama* (Vol. 1). New York: Beacon House, 1964 (First published 1946).
22. Brown, op. cit., pp. 20–22.
23. Ruth M. Tews. "Introduction." *Library Trends*, 14 (October, 1962), pp. 97, 98.
24. Smith, "Real Bibliotherapist," op. cit.
25. Telephone conversation of May 10, 1990 between Alice Smith and Kathy Mayo, past chairperson, ALA Bibliotherapy Committee.
26. National Federation for Biblio/Poetry Therapy. Minutes from Annual Meeting 7 June 1989, Skidmore College, Saratoga Springs, N.Y. Sent to Alice Smith from Deborah Langosch, NFB/PT, Executive Director.
27. Rubin, *Source Book*, op. cit., p. 167–172.
28. Rubin, *Guide*, op. cit., p. 75.
29. *The NAPT Newsletter*, 10 (March, 1990).
30. Alice I. Bryan. "The Psychology of the Reader." *Library Journal*, 64 (January, 1939), pp. 7–12.

31. Rubin, op. cit., *Guide*, p. 36.
32. Beatty, op. cit., p. 111.
33. Ibid.
34. Rubin, *Source Book*, op. cit., p. 55.
35. Hynes, *Handbook*, op. cit., p. 59.
36. Abraham G. Maslow. "The Dynamics of Psychological Security-Insecurity." *Journal of General Psychology*, 33 (July, 1945), pp. 21–41.
37. M. Maultsby. *Rational Behavior Therapy*. Englewood Cliffs, NJ: Prentice-Hall, 1984.
38. H. A. Otto. *Group Methods to Actualize Human Potential: A Handbook*. 3rd limited ed. Beverly Hills, CA: 1973; *Dimensions in Holistic Healing*. Chicago: Nelson, 1979.
39. Carl Rogers. *A Way of Being*. Boston: Houghton-Mifflin, 1980.
40. L. M. Rosenblatt. *Literature as Exploration*. 3rd ed. New York: MLA, 1976.
41. J. L. Singer. *Mind Play: The Creative Uses of Fantasy*. New York: Harper, 1976.
42. Miriam Schultheiss. "A Study of the Effects of Selected Readings Upon Children's Academic Performances and Social Adjustments," Ed.D. Thesis, Ball State University, Muncie, Indiana, 1969.
43. Lucy Werner. "The Myth of Bibliotherapy." *School Library Journal* 17 (October, 1980), pp. 107–111.
44. David H. Russell and Caroline Shrodes. "Contributions of Research in Bibliotherapy to the Language Arts Program I." *School Review*, 58 (September, 1950), pp. 335–342; "Contributions of Research in Bibliotherapy to the Language Arts Program II." *School Review*, 58 (October, 1950), pp. 411–420.
45. Charlotte S. Huck and Doris Young Kuhn. *Children's Literature in the Elementary School*. 2nd ed. New York: Holt, 1968. This is just one example of many fine text books which suggested the use of bibliotherapy in the language arts program.
46. American Council on Education. Committee on Intergroup Education in Cooperating Schools. *Reading Ladders for Human Relations*. Washington, D.C., 1949.
47. American Council on Education. Committee on Intergroup Education in Cooperating Schools. *Reading Ladders for Human Relations*, Eileen Tway, editor. 6th ed. Washington, D.C., 1981. pp. 3–7.
48. Fannie and George Shaftel. *Role Playing for Social Values: Decision Making in the Social Studies*. Englewood Cliffs, NJ: Prentice-Hall, 1982.
49. Winifred Ward. *Stories to Dramatize*. Anchorache, KY: Children's Theatre Press, 1952.
50. Evalene Jackson. "Bibliotherapy and Reading Guidance: A Tentative Approach to Theory." *Library Trends*, 14 (October 1962), p. 118.
51. Idem.
52. Ibid., p. 119.
53. *Ladders*, 6th ed., op. cit., pp. 15–50.
54. Florence Cleary. *Blue Prints for Better Reading*. 2nd ed. New York: H. W. Wilson, 1972.
55. Florence Cleary, Alice M. Davis, and Arnold R. Meier. *Understanding Democracy*. Detroit: The Citizenship Education Study, 1948.
56. Brown, op. cit., pp. 11, 12.
57. Margaret E. Monroe, ed. *Reading Guidance and Bibliotherapy in Public, Hospital and Institution Libraries*. Madison, WI: Library School, The University of Wisconsin, 1970.
58. The programs discussed here are both selected from and in addition to those presented by Rubin in *Guide*. This discussion is primarily devoted to programs presented in graduate programs of library and information science which are or have been accredited by the Committee on Accreditation of the American Library Association. This selection is in accord with the purpose of presenting the status of library education for bibliotherapy.
59. Alice Gullen Smith. "A Survey of the Sixth-Year Program in Library Schools Offering the ALA Accredited Master's Degree." In *Advances in Library Administration and Organization*, Vol. 6, pp. 197–220. Greenwich, CT: JAI Press, 1986.

56   ALICE GULLEN SMITH

60. Ibid., p. 201.
61. See "Research in Bibliotherapy."
62. Tews, op. cit., p. 103.
63. Margaret M. Kinney. "The Bibliotherapy Program, Requirements for Training." *Library Trends*, 14 (October, 1962), pp. 127–135.
64. Ibid., p. 135.
65. Jackson, "Bibliotherapy and Reading Guidance," op. cit., pp. 123–125.
66. Monroe
67. Hynes
68. Rubin, *Source Book*, op. cit., pp. 257–260.
69. Ibid.
70. Ibid., pp. 263–265.
71. Rubin, *Guide*, op. cit., pp. xviii, ix.
72. Kenneth Gorelick. "Observations on a Training Program." In *Proceedings of the Fourth Bibliotherapy Round Table Held in Washington, D.C. 28–29 January 1977*, Arleen Hynes, Kenneth Gorelick, editors. pp. 60–66.
73. Arleen Hynes. "Certification and the St. Elizabeth's Hospital Bibliotherapy Training Program." In Rubin, *Guide*, op. cit., pp. 205–212.
74. *The NAPT Newsletter*, op. cit., pp. 11–15.
75. School of Library and Information Science. "A Self Study Prepared for the Committee on Accreditation of the American Library Association." Tampa, FL: University of South Florida, 1980. pp. 177, 178.
76. University of South Florida School of Library and Information Science. *Bulletin: Education Specialist*. "Education Specialist in Curriculum and Instruction with a Specialization in Library and Information Science with Concentration on Library Service to Special Groups." Tampa, Florida: University of South Florida, 1978.
77. Lois Porfiri who went to Minnesota upon graduating.
78. Alice Gullen Smith. "Alchemy: Five Steps in Reading Guidance: Creative Play, Creative Dramatics, Role Playing, Choral Speaking, and Creative Writing." Unpublished master's thesis. Wayne State University, Detroit, Michigan, 1957. The master's thesis was a series of case studies in reading guidance.
79. A. Bandura. *Social Learning Theory*. Englewood Cliffs, NJ: Prentice-Hall, 1977.
80. Jackson, op. cit., p. 337.
81. Hynes, *Handbook*, op. cit., pp. 12–17.

THREE LIBRARIES' USE OF THE PUBLIC LIBRARY PLANNING PROCESS:

AN ANALYSIS ACCOMPANIED BY RECOMMENDATIONS FOR FUTURE USERS

Annabel K. Stephens

INTRODUCTION

In 1980 the American Library Association (ALA) published an exciting new tool to assist public librarians desiring to engage in comprehensive planning. *A Planning Process for Public Libraries*[1] outlined a process by which librarians could work with trustees and lay citizens to plan programs of service based on the library-related needs of local communities, a radically different approach to public library planning.

In 1987 *Planning and Role Setting for Public Libraries: A Manual of Options and Procedures*,[2] a revised and expanded version of the ALA Planning Process,

Advances in Library Administration and Organization,
Volume 9, pages 57–82.
Copyright © 1991 by JAI Press, Inc.
All rights of reproduction in any form reserved.
ISBN: 1-55938-066-7

was developed to alleviate some of the problems libraries experienced with the earlier manual. The revised version of the Process emphasized the importance of role-setting and downplayed the attention paid to data collection by the previous edition.

In the interval between the publication of the two versions, hundreds of libraries used the earlier edition of the planning manual with varying degrees of success. The literature contains a limited number of articles[3] detailing the benefits and some of the problems encountered by individual libraries using the planning manual.

Research comparing three southeastern library systems' use (and misuse) of the original Process[4] provides additional insights, many of which are extremely relevant to a library's successful experience with the current version of the Planning Process. Substantive variations were observed in the three systems' preparation for the Process, in the information provided to and used by the planners, in their choice of a mission and goals and objectives and development of strategies and plans for implementation and evaluation, in their involvement of staff and community members, in the leadership provided, and in the benefits acquired by the library systems.

The following account summarizes the three systems' experiences with the Process and enumerates the tentative conclusions reached by the researcher. A checklist developed to assist librarians in their employment of the Process is appended.

BACKGROUND

Since the early 1950s a substantial increase in the planning efforts of American business and industry has been reflected in many books and articles, and the majority of large companies now have their own specialized planning staffs and elaborate long-range plans. These efforts were intended to prevent managers from

> uncritically extending present trends into the future, from assuming that today's products, services, markets and technologies will be the products, services, markets and technologies of tomorrow, and above all, from dedicating their resources and energies to the defense of yesterday.[5]

Theorists and administrators alike realized that the type of planning necessary to accomplish the above-mentioned purposes was a form of planning known as strategic planning. Strategic planning is concerned not only with defining an organizations's goals and objectives but also with designing policies, plans, and organizational structure and systems to achieve those objectives. Borrowed from the military, such planning has become increasingly important in the modern business world because of the growing difficulty of achieving corporate goals in a rapidly changing economic, social, political, ecological, and technological environment.[6]

Strategic Planning for Libraries

Public service agencies such as hospitals, schools and universities, and libraries are affected by many of the same rapidly changing environmental factors affecting business and industry. As a result some form of strategic planning is also becoming a more necessary facet of library administration. The need for such planning has been heightened by the present inflation coupled with shrinking library budgets, rising expectations of library users, advances in computer and communications technology, and the necessity of providing more essential services to meet the unique needs of changing and diverse clienteles.

Advocates of strategic planning for libraries assert that planning combats uncertainty and accommodates environmental change and is therefore required to maintain a stable organization.[7] Such planning gives direction to growth and minimizes complexity in today's environment of uncertainty, thus preventing ad hoc decisions or decisions that unnecessarily narrow tomorrow's choices.[8] Its advocates also warn that the absence of planning will result in a state of "crisis management" in which constant attempts to solve "yesterday's problems" will make planning for the future even more difficult.[9]

Early Planning Efforts for the Public Library

Prior to the 1980s much of the planning activity for local public libraries was directed toward individual operational aspects such as the development of new services or products, the opening of new facilities, and the acquisition of new technologies. This has led to little comprehensive or strategic planning,[10] terms which are often used synonymously in the library literature.

Until the 1980s, planning for individual public libraries was undertaken in the form of surveys conducted by consultants and professional research firms. Many of those surveys merely analyzed current library resources and services and paid little attention to the communities and individuals being served. An analysis of public library surveys conducted from the 1930s to the 1960s revealed that the chief method used during that period was to compare a library's activities and resources with the standards for public libraries formulated by ALA,[11] first issued in 1933 and in the subsequent years of 1943, 1956, and 1966.[12] Although examination of the standards documents may reveal "a progressive effort to add components of on-going planning," it has been surmised that the heavy emphasis on the use of national quantitative standards in planning actually exacerbated the lack of comprehensive planning in many local public libraries.[13]

The recognition of diversity and the increasing necessity for the services of public libraries to be tailored to the needs of various clienteles, whether situated in rural, urban or suburban communities, resulted in increasing dissatisfaction with the type of institutional standards devised by the ALA. The standards were criticized for being institution- rather than user-oriented, relying on the untested judgement of librarians rather than on research and input from citizens and political leaders, lacking relevance for current problems, and lacking a foundation of objectives indicating what standard services were meant to accomplish. They were also criticized for promoting sameness by applying the identical criteria to very different communities and resulting in mediocrity by stressing minimum standards.[14]

The necessity of reevaluating the programs and services of public libraries and basing them on carefully devised unique goals and objectives had long been advocated. By the mid 1970s only a few librarians, however, had reported formulating specific goals and objectives for their institutions.

A Planning Process for Public Libraries

The movement toward more comprehensive planning for local public libraries began in 1970, when the Public Library Association (PLA) of ALA charged its Standards Committee with revising the 1966 standards. The Committee, aware of the dissatisfaction with them, decided that a similar "traditional relatively minor, update" of the 1966 standards would not be appropriate and that library standards should start with the needs of community residents rather than with institutional needs, a radically different approach to standards development.

After much consideration the PLA Standards Committee, renamed in 1974 the Goals, Guidelines and Standards Committee, concluded that it would be inappropriate for a committee of public library leaders to set a single set of standards for all public libraries. The Committee proposed, instead, that a process by which individual public libraries could develop their own standards and plan and evaluate service programs appropriate for each community be designed.

The Committee requested research proposals for designing such a rational, comprehensive planning process and interviewed prospective researchers for the project. A contract was awarded in 1977 to King Research, Inc., to conduct "The Process of Standards Development for Community Library Service,"[15] with Vernon Palmour as principal investigator.

A manual describing the recommended process of planning was developed and field-tested by three American and two British library systems. Revisions were made to reflect the experiences of the field-test libraries and suggestions offered by a group of library leaders asked to critique the manual in draft form, and the revised manual, entitled *A Planning Process for Public Libraries,* was published by ALA in the Spring of 1980.

Description of *A Planning Process for Public Libraries*

A Planning Process for Public Libraries was designed to enable a public library to "plan effectively without spending large amounts of time deciding how to proceed," thus allowing the planners to focus on analyzing information and developing recommendations for change.[16] The planning manual instructed public library administrators in the formation of a planning committee of citizens and library board and staff members, in the compilation of information about the community and the library, and in the use of the resulting information to set goals, objectives, and priorities. Sample data-gathering instruments, tables for displaying data, and techniques to aid in group decision-making were included.

The manual emphasized the necessity of a period of careful preplanning before the actual planning process is begun. It stressed that the climate within the library must be hospitable to the changes and risks inherent in a process that requires reexamination and questioning of present assumptions about the library's community and its service priorities. Since the process also encouraged library staff to plan in conjunction with community members, the manual advised that the lay citizens on the committee would have to be carefully chosen. They would need to be educated about current philosophies concerning public library service and provided background on the role of their library in its particular community.

Explicit instructions for a seven-step process were outlined in the manual. These steps included (1) assessing community library needs; (2) evaluating current library services and resources; (3) determining the role of the public library in its community; (4) setting goals, objectives, and priorities; (5) developing and evaluating strategies for change; (6) implementing the strategies; and (7) monitoring and evaluating progress towards goals and objectives.

Step one, the assessment of community library needs, included the construction of a profile of the community derived from census data, community planning documents, and a survey of the community's citizens. Questions by which the planning committee could assess their community's needs for general information, specific information, and coping information were suggested.

Step two, the evaluation of current library services and resources, involved analyzing library statistics, performance measures, and the results of the citizen survey provided for the first step plus the results of two additional surveys, one for library users and another for library staff members. The purpose of this analysis was to ascertain the extent to which the library seemed capable of satisfying the information needs determined in step one.

Step three, the definition of the role of the public library in the community, was the selection of the actual role that the library would take in its community during the planning period. Since step three forms the basis for the remaining steps of the process, it is crucial. The manual provided a sample form on which the planners could rank possible activity areas, types of services, and user groups. The chosen role might be a verbalization of the library's present service philosophy or a new, more relevant role.

In step four, the development of goals, objectives, and priorities, the planners were to use the role statement developed in step three as a basis to define broad service goals specifying who should be served and how services are to be delivered, with specific objectives by which the service goals are to be realized. In addition, the planners were expected to develop resource management and administrative goals and objectives to support the service goals. The planners were then advised to establish priorities among objectives according to different funding contingencies and to take into consideration conflicting priorities of various interest groups.

Step five, the development and evaluation of strategies for change, involved examining the library's traditional services and operations and devising new methods to achieve the goals and objectives chosen by the planners. Step six, implementation of strategies, included devising specific plans for implementing the chosen strategies detailing who is to do what, when, and how. Step six also involved developing a system of management data and defining measurements necessary to establish baselines and measure progress toward achieving goals and objectives.

Step seven, monitor and evaluate strategies for change, was both the final step of a library's initial or primary planning cycle and the first step of its second cycle. The development of a system for monitoring, evaluating, and measuring begins the second planning cycle. Monitoring and evaluating progress was to be a continuing function of the planning committee; the manual stated that once the committee had determined the information needed to measure progress, it should periodically review specific objectives and revise the library's plan to reflect the changing conditions affecting the library.[17]

The key characteristics attributed to the Process by its supporters are that it was based on careful analysis of local conditions and needs, it was participative since librarians and community leaders plan together, it was based on acquiring and examining "solid information" about the library and its community, it was cyclical, and it was flexible. It was not meant to be a "blue-print to be followed slavishly" but a framework to be adapted to local needs by a local planning committee.[18] The Process combined tools and techniques previously used to some extent by library plannners with a new emphasis on output-related performance measures and concepts of management derived from MBO (management by objectives) and participatory management.

PURPOSE OF RESEARCH

Several libraries had begun using *A Planning Process for Public Libraries* at the time the present study was proposed. Because the Process had been formulated so recently, however, only a few had completed it at that time. Although the planning documents of some of those libraries were available, there had been no detailed report of the actual planning experiences of libraries following the Process. Little was known about why it was undertaken, how it had been adapted, what problems had been encountered, and what had worked well under what circumstances.

The purpose of this researcher's investigation was to examine the comprehensive planning experiences of libraries using *A Planning Process for Public Libraries* in a limited number of communities. The study focused on the past planning experiences of the libraries, the purposes for their undergoing the Process, their adaptation of the Process to fit local planning needs, the activities and contributions of the members of the Planning Committees, the involvement of other staff and community members, and the immediate recommendations resulting from the Process. The study attempted to evaluate the usefulness of the Process as a device for strategic or comprehensive planning in these particular libraries.

METHODOLOGY

The case study method, a form of qualitative analysis, was chosen for examining the libraries' planning experiences. This approach was selected because it allows a variety of data-gathering techniques to provide comprehensive information about a research problem, provides a wide range and great depth of experience by the breadth and added levels of data gathered and the analysis of interaction over time, and has been recognized as being especially useful in exploratory studies and in group and process analysis.[19] This method was especially suitable for the present research topic because so little was known about the usefulness of the Process to the libraries in which it has been employed. Through in-depth analysis of the planning experiences of three libraries, the researcher attempted to record the application of this new, very different, approach to library planning, to reveal problems in the manner in which the Process was being interpreted and conducted, to suggest techniques and methods to help libraries use the Process more effectively, to add to the limited knowledge of library goals and objectives formulation, and to provide insight concerning staff and citizen participation in library planning.

Three diverse methods were used to gather data on the libraries' planning experiences: (1) field observation, (2) document analysis, and (3) the use of interviews and a questionnaire. The data were collected in three phases: phase one was conducted prior to the libraries' first Planning Committee meetings; phase two during the libraries' planning periods; and phase three after the Planning Committees' final meetings.

In order to hear and record each group's planning deliberations and to observe the involvement and interactions of the representatives of the library and the lay citizens, the researcher attended twenty-seven Planning Committee meetings, four staff meetings, and five board meetings at the selected libraries. Observation allowed the researcher to know what was actually occurring, to collect data she would not have otherwise known to ask about or that would not have been reported, and to cross-check data acquired from other sources.

To obtain information on the history and development of the three libraries and to acquire insight into the administrative employment of the Process, the researcher examined all reports, memos, minutes, and documents generated by the libraries and Planning Committees for a period of ten years prior to the beginning of the Process, throughout the planning period, and for six months after the Process was completed. The document analysis provided a background and context for the study, helped to raise pertinent questions to be clarified during the interviews, and afforded opportunity for reflection and analysis.[20]

To verify evidence gathered through observation and document analysis and to ascertain the perceptions of those involved, six interviews were conducted with the libraries' directors, four with the chairmen of the boards of trustees, three with the libraries' data coordinators, nine with library staff members, and fourteen with citizen Planning Committee members. A questionnaire was developed to elicit the library staff members' opinions of their libraries' experience with the Process and the recommendations made by the Planning Committees.

SUMMARY OF LIBRARIES' PLANNING EXPERIENCES

Research on the use of *A Planning Process for Public Libraries* was conducted in three medium-sized consolidated library systems located in three states in the Southeast. One of the systems studied is a multi-county regional library; the other two are city-county libraries. The libraries' identities have been disguised to maintain their anonymity; pseudonyms have been used for both the libraries and their geographic locations.

There were striking differences in the three library systems studied. The largest has its headquarters in a large city and serves a population of approximately 348,000 living in two counties, of which one is 87 percent urban and the other predominantly rural. The system maintains a central library and five branches. The next in size of population served, approximately 197,000, has its headquarters in a slightly smaller but fast-growing city; its central library and four branches provide service for the city and its surrounding county, which is 78 percent urban. The smallest has only one service outlet and serves approximately 75,000 people living in a much smaller, medium-sized, city and the county around it, which although 67 percent urban contains five towns with populations under 4,000. The number of staff members and materials owned by these three systems ranged from 86 to 21 and from 566,802 to 114,486. Incomes ranged from $1,884,000 to $385,208, and annual circulations ranged from 721,897 to 224,634. (The land areas served and the systems' current per capita support and circulation are shown in the table below.)

	Library System A	Library System B	Library System C
Land area served in square miles	558	1,761	806
Per capita support	$5.17	$4.76	$9.57
Per capita circulation	3.01	2.08	3.87[21]

Despite their differences, the three library systems had in common one essential characteristic: each would begin using *A Planning Process for Public Libraries* during 1981 or 1982. A second commonality was that the three systems were located within the same geographic region, indicating possible similarities due to a common historical and economic background.

While all three systems began using the Planning Process within a seven-month period, the number of Planning Committee meetings held and the time-span during which the Process was conducted varied considerably. Library System A's full Planning Committee met nineteen times during a period of almost two years. Library System B's met only five times within a period of one year and three months; much of the Committee's work was conducted during meetings of the subcommittees to which each member of the Planning Committee was assigned. Library System C's Planning Process was prematurely ended after only three Planning Committee meetings had been held, the first two within two weeks of each other and the third and last meeting a year and five months later.

Considerable differences in several other aspects of the three systems' employment of the Planning Process were observed throughout the research involved in the study. The systems varied greatly in their preparation for the Process, provision and use of planning data, choice of a mission and goals and objectives, development of strategies and plans for implementation and evaluation, involvement of staff and community members in planning activities, leadership provided to the planners, and, consequently, in the benefits accruing from their use of the Process. The libraries' actions pertaining to each of the above-listed aspects are described in the following section, and the disparate benefits realized by the libraries are discussed.

Preparation for the Process

Little time or effort was expended in preparation for Library System A's use of the Planning Process. Few decisions were made concerning its conduct and little attempt was made to inform and involve the staff, Friends of the Library, city and county officials, and other citizens prior to the first Planning Committee meeting. Library System B's director and board, on the other hand, spent a year and a half in preparation. Funding was secured, and many important decisions were made by a Preliminary Planning Committee consisting of the director, assistant director, and members of the board and Friends. Considerable effort was devoted to informing the staff, Friends, city and county officials, and other citizens.

Library System C's director spent almost two years in preparation, securing a small grant and making tentative decisions concerning the Process. Neither the board nor the staff, however, were involved in the pre-planning decisions, although both were informed of the director's plans. Most of the Friends of the Library, city and county officials and other citizens were not informed that the system would be using the Process.

Provision and Use of Planning Data

Library System A's Planning Committee was not provided with an adequate community profile. The Committee was inundated with data revealing the library's current status, but the members were not encouraged to evaluate its services and programs or to consider additional services offered by other libraries. Because of inadequate design and flaws in the methods by which they were conducted, Library System A's five surveys did not obtain reliable, in-depth information on the citizens' information needs or their opinions of the library's current services. The individual surveys received little discussion; instead composite totals were formed, and the minimal analysis attempted was based on the aggregate figures.

New services suggested by write-in responses to open-ended survey questions received no consideration. In fact, little attempt was made to employ either the meager community profile or the survey results to analyze the citizens' information needs or the extent to which they were being met by the library. The survey results were used instead to support the library's needs, which were reiterated by its director throughout the Process.

Library System B's Planning Committee was supplied with a full and very detailed community profile and an abundance of statistical data about the library. The Committee members received little assistance in interpreting or assimilating the community information, but although no explanation of the library-related data was made to the Committee as a whole, staff members provided additional information during meetings of the three subcommittees.

Although all the surveys and performance measures were conducted in full accord with the planning manual's instructions, their results were given less than adequate explication. Library System B's Planning Committee was concerned with both the improvement of current services and the addition of new services, and attention was paid to the few new services written in as answers to open-ended survey questions.

The Committee's limited needs assessment was based less on the community profile or the needs assessment questions in the manual and more on the responses to the surveys, the comments and recommendations of the library's director and staff resource persons, and the personal opinions and experience of the Planning Committee members. Its evaluation of current services and resources was also based largely on the opinions of the administration, staff resource persons, and individual Committee members, but the results of the surveys and performance measures were heeded.

Library System C's Committee received extensive information about its community and about the library system's services and programs, but there was little discussion or analysis of the information. The two surveys that were employed were conducted after the Planning Committee's final meeting.

Choice of Mission and Goals and Objectives

Library System A's Planning Committee made no attempt to choose a role for its library. Influenced by the librarians' professional philosophy and Committee members' opinions supported by the survey results, Library System B's role statement both reflected the system's current philosophy and practice and indicated a new focus for its future. Library System C's Planning Process ended before its Committee had begun to discuss the library's role.

Library System A's Committee selected goals and objectives that reflected the specific library needs reported by the director. Although some of the goals were supported by the surveys, others either were not clearly substantiated or had no relation to the survey results.

Developed independently by three subcommittees, several of Library System B's goals and objectives specified a new focus or called for new services to be offered. Although the goals and objectives developed by the subcommittee on programs and services were certainly indicative of its members' professional positions, they were also supported by the survey results. Those developed by the subcommittee on facilities were based more on site visits, a local planning agency's report, and the opinions of subcommittee members and staff resource persons, but the survey results were consulted and did influence at least one of the subcommittee's choices. The subcommittee on collections relied heavily on the recommendations of its staff resource persons but also referred to the survey results, which corroborated several of its goals and objectives.

68 ANNABEL K. STEPHENS

Development of Strategies and Plans for Implementation and Evaluation

Strategies were developed by Library System A's Planning Committee. The library system's director reported having no plans for implementing or monitoring the goals, objectives, or strategies selected by the Committee. Library System B's Committee did not participate in a formal strategy formulation, but many of their goals and objectives included or suggested strategies. A checklist assigning categories of goals to Library System B's board members and department heads for their consideration and implementation was also intended for use as a monitoring device.

Involvement of Staff and Community Members

Involvement of Library System A's staff members and the majority of the community residents in the system's use of the Planning Process was quite cursory. There was no evidence that staff members were kept informed about the Process, and the citizens were not informed that their library was implementing the Process until after the Planning Committee's third meeting. Participation in Planning Process activities by Library System A's staff members was minimal, and citizens other than those chosen to attend Planning Committee meetings or assist with conducting surveys were also given little opportunity to participate.

In accord with the director's belief that education and public relations are the main strength of the Planning Process,[22] staff and community involvement were essential elements of Library System B's planning experience. Both staff and community were kept informed about and encouraged to participate in the system's planning experience.

Virtually no attempt was made to involve either the majority of the system's staff members or the residents of its service area in Library System C's short-lived planning activities. Few staff or community members were informed of the system's progress with the Process or encouraged to participate in its brief planning efforts.

Leadership

The lack of adequate leadership was evident throughout Library System A's planning experience. It was perhaps unfortunate that the system's director attempted to serve as both data coordinator and chairman of the Planning Committee. The problems created by his lack of knowledge of survey design and sampling techniques, his failure to motivate the subcommittees charged with designing and conducting the surveys, and his lack of success in conducting group discussions during Committee meetings were numerous.

More critical to the system's lack of success with the Planning Process, however, was the director's inability to lead the Committee members in an unbiased examination of the library's services and programs. His repetition of the system's needs as he and the board perceived them and his seeming lack of knowledge of (or unwillingness to discuss) innovative services then being offered by other public libraries unfortunately limited the Committee's consideration of services to those already offered by the library system or previously desired by the director and library board.

Library System B's planning efforts were characterized by leadership of the highest quality. Several of those interviewed by the researcher[23] acknowledged the expertise of both the chairman and the data coordinator, whose wise selection was instigated by the library system's director, who chose to attend the Committee meetings as an ex-officio member without voting power. The director was also responsible for the system's careful preplanning and the numerous efforts to interest and involve the library staff and area citizens in the system's planning activities.

Leadership for Library System C's short-lived planning efforts was provided by the system's director, who served as both data coordinator and Planning Committee chairman. Although she exhibited enthusiasm for the Planning Process both before its inception and during the Planning Committee's first two meetings, she waited for a year and four months before reconvening the Committee for a third meeting. The director then terminated the system's use of the Planning Process sometime after the Committee's third meeting.

Benefits Resulting from the Process

With such variance in preparation, provision and use of planning data, choice of mission and goals and objectives, development of strategies and plans for implementation and evaluation, involvement of staff and community members, and provision of leadership, the three library systems could not be expected to have received equal benefit from their use of the Planning Process. Library System A failed to take advantage of the full potential of the Process in any of its aspects. Library System B received considerable value from its use of the Process as a device for planning, staff development, and improved community relations. Library System C terminated its planning efforts too early to have profited much from its use of the Process.

With the possible exception of increased support by those few Planning Committee members who remained active, the only result discernible from Library System A's two-year planning efforts was a set of five goals, most of which called for incremental inputs to be awarded by the library's funding body. The absence of in-depth analysis of the library-related data as applicable to the information needs of the community combined with inattention to innovative services other than those desired by the director and board severely limited the Committee's planning efforts, causing the members to become unduly focused on the needs of the library as perceived by its director and board. Library System A's director stated that "the Process is supposed to have been a self-evaluation if you go by that book. . . . We don't know if we actually did that. . . ."[24] His statement was certainly indicative of the system's less than successful use of the Process as a planning device. Unfortunately, Library System A also failed to realize the Planning Process' potential as a mechanism for staff development and improved public relations.

Of considerable value to Library System B, its Planning Process resulted in a community-based, staff-approved plan calling for a revised mission and improved and new services. The system's conduct of the Process provided excellent opportunities for staff and board development, higher visibility in the community, increased rapport with local governing officials, and the possibility of increased support from citizen Planning Committee members. It also provided a vast collection of primary and secondary data already used for making collection development decisions, preparing grant proposals, and determining service reductions. Two of the citizen Planning Committee members and one of the system's department heads,[25] in fact, suggested that other libraries employ Library System B's use of the Planning Process as a model. The system might have benefited even further, however, from a more thorough examination and explication of the community profile and the data obtained from the surveys and performance measures.

The early termination of Library System C's use of the Planning Process made it unlikely that much benefit could have accrued. Results that can be ascertained include planning data acquired by two surveys; information on the system's service area, services, and programs assembled for the Committee; and, possibly, the Committee members' increased knowledge of the community and library. An unknown factor is the effect their brief involvement with the Process has had on the interest and support of the citizen Planning Committee members, three of whom were representatives of local governing bodies.

TENTATIVE CONCLUSIONS

Three medium-sized library systems employing the Process during 1981–84 in one geographic region certainly do not constitute a sample of all public library systems that have used *A Planning Process for Public Libraries* since its inception. Aspects have been revealed in this research, however, that allow tentative conclusions to be reached which may assist library planners and serve as hypotheses for further study of the Planning Process.

- Decisions made and actions taken during the preplanning phase can have an effect on the subsequent efforts of the Planning Commitee and can help ensure a climate hospitable to change.

Little prior consideration was given to the choice of a data coordinator or Planning Committee chairman, to funding or conducting the data collection, or to the number, timing, or scope of Library System A's Planning Committee meetings. As a result, the work of the Committee required nineteen meetings spread over almost two full years. With no additional funding or consulting assistance, the data collection became the responsibility of the system's director and the Planning Committee members, who spent over a year discussing methods of data collection and conducting surveys. The staff was not asked to suggest prospective Planning Committee members; in fact, little attempt was made to prepare either the staff or the public for the Planning Process.

The year and a half spent in preparation for Library System B's use of the Process facilitated their planning efforts in several ways. The committee charged with the preliminary planning was able to make carefully-considered decisions regarding the choice, timing, and conduct of data collection and the number, timing, and scope of Planning Committee meetings; to secure adequate funding to pay a data coordinator and to contract to have the Citizen Survey conducted; and to select a data coordinator, Planning Committee chairman, and Committee members recommended by board and staff members. Since decisions concerning data collection methods and arrangements for their conduct were made ahead of time, the data collection phase was completed in less than two months. Dedicating sufficient time to pre-planning also enabled the director to set the proper climate for the Process by educating the board of trustees and staff about the Process, allowing the department heads and other interested staff members to read the planning manual, and informing and involving the Friends of the Library, city and county officials, and other citizens.

Library System C's director secured a small grant and made a few tentative decisions about the Process. Little effort was devoted, however, to creating a climate hospitable to planning.

- The inclusion of lay people on a library's Planning Committee produces citizens who are more knowledgeable about the local library and its problems. These citizens may also become more willing and able to support the library as a result of their experience.

During Library System A's planning experience, lay people served on sub-committees which designed and conducted the five surveys used by the system and developed strategies to accompany its goals and objectives. Several of the lay people also attended the many meetings held to discuss the surveys and their results and to review the goals and objectives and strategies recommended by the Committee members. The lay people received extensive information, both oral and written, about the library system and its problems.

At Library System B, lay people were assigned to one of three subcommittees which focused on either the system's programs and services, its facilities, or its collections. To assist them in evaluating their areas and developing appropriate goals and objectives, subcommittee members were supplied with relevant information attained during the library data collection phase. Staff resource persons attending the subcommittee meetings provided additional information and explanations, as did the system's director and board chairman, who attended the five Planning Committee meetings.

Regardless of the differences in the manner in which they were involved in the planning activities, without exception those lay people who remained active throughout their libraries' planning periods indicated that serving as Planning Committee members had increased both their knowledge of their local libraries and their knowledge of the importance, and the problems, of public libraries in general. Perhaps even more importantly, the lay members of both Committees indicated that serving as Planning Committee members had increased both their desire and their ability to support their libraries.[26]

An additional benefit of having a group of citizens whose experience as Planning Committee members has stimulated their increased willingness to support the library is the establishment of a pool of potential library board members. Described by the system's director as "the absolute best training ground for Board of Trustee members,"[27] Library System B's Planning Committee provided three very knowledgeable and committed new board members for the system.

- If lay citizens are included, an orientation session should be provided to explain the Planning Process and their roles and responsibilities to the citizen Planning Committee members. The citizen members should also be educated about public library organization, services, and issues.

Although the Planning Process was described during both Library System A and B's initial Planning Committee meetings, citizen members from both Committees expressed the need for a fuller orientation. A member of Library System A's Committee suggested that "definite guidelines for the Committee should be spelled out more specifically for expediency and for the comfort of Committee members."

One of Library System B's citizen members objected that he "was really blank, had no idea where we were going, what our conclusions would be, what even our purpose was basically." Saying that she felt the Committee was "floundering for a long time in not knowing how far to reach," another member explained that she did not understand "what the purpose of the whole thing was for a long time" and was frustrated that the Committee had no "guidelines from the staff about what type objectives they wanted and what type of implementation."

A citizen member of Library System A's Committee suggested that staff members explain their particular jobs to a Planning Committee. One of Library System B's citizen members suggested an "incubation period" during which a staff would educate the lay people about library issues and about "how libraries need to be run."[28]

- It is crucial that the person who will serve as chair of the Planning Committee be someone skilled in planning and in group leadership. The possibility of having this position filled by someone other than the library's director or board chairman should be considered.

In addition to failing to motivate the subcommittees conducting data collection to proceed more rapidly, Library System A's director/Planning Committee chair devoted an inordinate amount of the Committee's time (most of twelve meetings) to discussion of the methods, rather than the results, of their data collection. Those few members still active then had to attend seven more monthly meetings to plan goals and objectives and strategies. He was also unable to elicit much input into discussions from the citizen members. Both the director's misuse of time and the lack of response from the citizen members were criticized by the board chairman and several of the Committee members.[29]

More relevant to this library system's lack of success with the Process, however, was the director/Committee chair's inability to lead the Committee members in an unbiased examination of his library's services and programs. One of the Committee members made the somewhat obvious point that a planning process should be led by someone who would not be so affected by its results.[30]

A planner by profession, Library System B's Planning Committee chairman was praised by the system's board chairman, staff, and several Committee members for making the best possible use of the members' time and for having a good mixture of input into Committee discussions from library representatives and citizen members. The system's director and board chair, who served as ex-officio members, and the staff who attended Committee meetings as Committee members or staff resource persons expressed satisfaction with the extent of their involvement in Committee discussions.[31]

Library System C could have benefited greatly from having someone other than the system's director chair its Planning Committee meetings. Perhaps having a citizen chair would have motivated the director to continue the Process after many of the results she had hoped to accomplish through the Process were obtained otherwise. At least having someone to share the work of conducting the Process could have allowed the director more time to devote to the planning and implementation of her other projects while continuing with the Planning Process.

Although it may not always be possible to have a professional planner as the Committee chairman, even smaller communities have persons with experience in leading church and civic groups. Nearby colleges might be called on to provide training in group leadership or a citizen could be sent to workshops or conferences to attain such skills. The important point is that the person chosen should be someone who can motivate the planners, elicit discussion during

Committee meetings from both library representatives and citizen members, and lead the Committee in an objective examination of the library's current resources and services and in realistic planning for its future.

- Careful consideration should be given to the amount and type of primary and secondary data that are collected. Once gathered, the meaning of that data and their implications should be explained adequately.

Because little or no consideration had been given to how any of the data were to be used, Library System A's Planning Committee was not supplied with an adequate community profile but was inundated with data concerning the system's current status and with results from five different surveys. The large number of surveys took such a long time to design and conduct that several Committee members lost interest and stopped attending meetings; they also produced more data than the director was able to analyze or interpret. There was little discussion or explanation of the meager community information or of the individual surveys, and little attempt was made to use either of these to identify or analyze the information needs of the citizens or the extent to which they were met by the library. In fact, the primary and secondary data appear to have been used mainly to support the library system's needs for additional funds, staff, and facilities.

Reflecting those needs pointed out by the system's director and board chairman throughout the Process, some of the goals and objectives chosen were corroborated by the planning data. Others either were not so clearly supported or had no relationship to the results.

Because it was feared that they might be easily overwhelmed, the citizens on Library System B's Planning Committee were assigned to focus on either the system's services and programs, its facilities, or its collections. The members were supplied with a full and very detailed community profile, an abundance of data on the system's current status, and the results of five surveys, but were given little assistance in interpreting or assimilating the information. The surveys and performance measures were given little explanation, a shortcoming that was pointed out by several staff and Committee members. Although the majority of the goals and objectives chosen were well-supported by the planning data, a more thorough presentation of the data might have resulted in a fuller attempt to identify potential community library needs and to evaluate current library resources with those needs in mind.

Planning Committees should limit their data collection to that information which can be collected, analyzed, interpreted, and understood by those involved. The data collected should also be limited to that which is necessary for planning and decision-making. A small body of relevant data adequately explained would obviously facilitate planning much more than a larger amount that is not used.

- If surveys are to be conducted, it is crucial that the person who will serve as data coordinator be competent in survey design and random sampling techniques. Data coordinators not already possessing these competencies should be trained prior to the inception of the Process and should be assisted by a competent researcher throughout the Process.

The lack of prior knowledge of survey design and sampling techniques combined with inattention to the data collection methods in the planning manual prevented Library System A's director/data coordinator from providing adequate assistance to the subcommittees designing and conducting the surveys and patron observations. As a result, both of these activities were poorly designed and the validity of their results was compromised by methodological flaws in the number and identification of survey respondents and patrons observed. The utility of the results for the Committee's planning efforts was questioned by the chairman of the board of trustees and by one of the Committee members. Their utility for future planning will also be minimal.

All surveys and performance measures used for Library System B's planning efforts were designed and conducted in full accord with the planning manual's instructions by a data coordinator trained in statistical research or by a professional research team. The board chairman, library personnel, and Planning Committee members expressed confidence that their efforts resulted in reliable data for the planners. The planning data have also been used in making collection development decisions, preparing grant proposals, and determining service reductions, and they will be instrumental in the library's planned employment of output measures.

Although it may not be possible for smaller, less well-funded libraries to obtain the services of a professionally trained data coordinator, attempts should be made either to secure funding for consulting assistance or to train a staff member who can be released from other duties to devote adequate time and attention to data collection. It would be totally impractical for a busy library director without adequate training or assistance to attempt such a time-consuming and crucial undertaking.

- The Planning Committee should at least make a tentative choice of roles and begin to develop a mission statement for the library prior to beginning its goals and objectives formulation phase. In choosing roles the Committee should examine the effectiveness of the library's current roles and services in meeting the information needs of the community's citizens.

After devoting twelve meetings to data collection, Library System A's Planning Committee immediately began formulating goals and objectives with no consideration of an appropriate role or roles for the library even though the director had previously said the Committee might choose to reconsider and revise the role statement issued by the board several years earlier. With no role or direction to guide their efforts all the goals and objectives suggested by the Committee members merely called for increases in either the library system's inputs or outputs. One of the citizen Planning Committee members criticized the outcome and suggested that the process be "done over again." She recommended that the Committee look more "not at what we need to increase so much as to what we need to keep the same or change." [32]

The goals and objectives concerning Library System B's services and programs were said by its members to have come directly from the role statement developed by the subcommittee on programs and services. The role statement reflected the system's present philosophy and practice and indicated a new focus for its future, and several of the goals and objectives the subcommittee chose also specified a new role or called for new services.

The point is not that a Planning Committee must choose new roles or services but that it should at least consider the appropriateness of the library's present roles (where such exist) and its current services. It must then plan appropriate roles and services for the library's future. Once a committee begins to formulate concrete goals and objectives without the philosophical context of a mission statement, it is very unlikely that it would go back in time to consider such an abstract assignment. If made to select roles after formulating goals and objectives, it is more likely that a committee would merely choose roles to fit the goals and objectives already selected.

- Library staff members' satisfaction with the goals and objectives chosen by the Planning Committee and with their library's overall experience with the Planning Process is related to their perceptions of involvement with the Planning Process. Involvement of staff can also help ensure a climate hospitable to change and can assist in staff development.

Library System A's staff members were afforded minimal involvement with their system's use of the Planning Process. The staff was understandably less than enthusiastic about both the goals and objectives chosen without their knowledge and their library's overall experience with the Process in which they were so little involved. Only 12.5 percent of the staff agreed, and 37.5 percent disagreed, that they were satisfied with the goals and objectives; 50 percent expressed uncertainty. As for their satisfaction with the system's overall planning experience, 14.2 percent agreed, and another 14.2 percent disagreed, that they would describe the experience as totally satisfactory; an overwhelming 71.4 percent were uncertain. [33]

Neglecting to fully explain the purpose of the patron observations to the staff created concern over how the results would be interpreted and used. The record of low library use induced, the first time by a local fair, and a second time by a local football game, alarmed members of the staff who believed the Planning Committee members would think the library was overstaffed.

Attention devoted to keeping the staff informed and encouraging them to participate in Planning Process activities was an important aspect of Library

System B's planning activities. A majority (77.5 percent) of the staff members indicated acceptance of the goals and objectives chosen by the planners, and a majority (64 percent) indicated satisfaction with their system's overall planning experience. Of those reasons given by staff who were not satisfied with the Process, most pertained to perceptions of non-involvement by these staff members.

Library System B's department and branch heads were more intimately involved with the Process than were the lower-level staff; those responding all agreed that they were satisfied with the goals and objectives and with the overall experience with the Planning Process.[34] Their director pointed out that as a result of their involvement with the Process the department and branch heads had become stronger middle managers and that most had become more professional and objective and were interacting with their staffs at a higher level.[35] Many of the suggestions offered by staff for other libraries using the Process related to involvement of staff in Planning Process activities.[36]

The relationship between a staff's perception of involvement with the Planning Process and its perceived satisfaction with the goals and objectives and the overall Process was examined using a statistical test (Chi Square). The two systems' responses to each of the statements used to examine perceptions of staff involvement (being kept informed, being encouraged to participate, being given sufficient opportunities to express their points of view, and having their points of view taken into consideration) were combined and compared to their combined responses to the statement regarding perceived satisfaction with the goals and objectives and the one regarding perceived satisfaction with the overall Planning Process.

The statistical test indicated that a staff's perceived satisfaction with both the goals and objectives chosen and with its system's overall use of the Planning Process is indeed related to the staff's perceptions of being kept informed about the Planning Process, being encouraged to participate in planning activities, and being given sufficient opportunities to express their points of view, respectively. A staff's perceived satisfaction with the overall use of the Planning Process was also found to be related to its perception that the staff members' points of view were taken into consideration.

- Efforts devoted to publicizing a library system's use of the Planning Process result in increased visibility which can in turn benefit the library system. Special attention directed to informing and involving local government officials can be of considerable benefit to a library system.

The higher visibility provided by seven articles in local newspapers publicizing its intended and actual use of the Planning Process and by additional special efforts to inform and involve local government officials provided several immediate benefits for Library System B. The system was asked to prepare a public service announcement to be televised during the city's promotional campaign; a local state senator volunteered for the first time to sponsor library legislation; and the system's previously-cut appropriation was restored. The system's director also reported that the city officials had become much easier to work with, that the system didn't have to fight as hard for funding as they had before, and that, in fact, the city mayor had told her that the Planning Process had increased the library system's credibility.[37]

GUIDELINES FOR PLANNING

The directors, board chairmen, citizen Planning Committee members, and staff members of Library Systems A and B offered over thirty recommendations for prospective users of the Planing Process. Although the essence of many of the recommendations is suggested in the conclusions discussed above, a more explicit listing was incorporated, along with additional suggestions based on the observations of the researcher, in the appended guidelines, entitled "Checklist of Steps for Successful Employment of the Planning Process." The researcher hopes that these guidelines will prove helpful to libraries using the Planning Process in the future.

CONCLUSION

The purpose of the researcher's investigation was to examine the use of the Process by three library systems. Substantive variations were observed in the three systems' preparation for the Process, in the information provided to and used by the planners, in their selection of a mission and goals and objectives and their development of strategies and plans for implementation and evaluation, in their involvement of staff and community members, in the leadership provided to the planners, and in the benefits accruing from their use of the Planning Process.

As a result of the study, tentative conclusions were reached and a checklist of guidelines was developed. A summary of the three libraries' planning experiences has been provided, along with the tentative conclusions and the checklist developed by the researcher, to assist librarians and library consultants in their future employment of the Planning Process. The tentative conclusions could also serve as hypotheses for other researchers studying the use of the Planning Process.

APPENDIX

"Checklist of Steps for Successful Employment of the Planning Process"

1.   The director and board chairman read the planning manual thoroughly and understood the concept of rational, participative planning intrinsic to the Process;

2. The director and board chairman considered the costs as well as the benefits of the Process;

3. The director and board chairman had prior experience in planning and/or requested assistance from PLA, their state library agency, or state, regional and local planning agencies;

4. The library's organizational climate was hospitable to planning, and a formal communication structure was in place;

5. The director and board chairman engaged in careful and extensive pre-planning which included

  a. informing all levels of the staff about the
     Process and its prospective use by the library,
  b. informing all board members about the Process and
     its prospective use by the library,
  c. informing the governing officials and the citizens-at-large about the
     Process and its prospective use by the library,
  d. asking staff and board members to suggest prospective Planning Committee members, particularly if lay citizens are to be included,
  e. acquiring funding and/or promises of volunteer assistance if needed,
  f. selecting people with skills in planning and group leadership (plus techniques of survey research, if surveys are to be conducted) to lead the planning efforts,
  g. making preliminary decisions about the scope and extent of the planning and data collection to be attempted (choosing levels-of-effort),
  h. planning methods for informing and involving
     staff and board members throughout the planning period, and
  i. planning methods of informing and involving governing officials and citizens-at-large throughout the planning period;

6. If surveys were used, the data coordinator was knowledgeable of survey research and sampling techniques and able to devote sufficient time (half- to full-time during the planning period) to data collection;

7. The chair of the Planning Committee was experienced in planning and in techniques of group leadership; consideration was given to having someone other than the director or board chairman assume this position;

8. If lay citizens were appointed to the Planning Committee, they were provided with an appropriate orientation to the Planning Process and to public library purpose and services and given explicit instructions concerning their responsibilities;

9. Only those data considered necessary to ascertain the library-related needs of the community and to evaluate the library's services and resources were collected;

10. If surveys were used, they were conducted according to proper research and sampling techniques;

11. The results obtained during the data collection phase were organized and interpreted for the Planning Committee;

12. The flexibility inherent in the Process was used to tailor the Process to the planning needs of the library but was not used in a way that violated the rational participative nature of the Process;

13. Knowledgeable staff members provided information and other assistance to the Planning Committee but attempted not to influence the members unduly;

14. The library's previous roles and services were examined in light of the planning data, and a limited number of roles to emphazize were selected by the planners;

15. Goals and objectives were selected to enable the library to progress toward fulfilling the roles chosen by the planners;

16. Alternate strategies for accomplishing the chosen goals and objectives were developed;

17. A plan was delineated designating how, when, and by whom the strategies would be implemented and how progress toward the goals and objectives would be monitored;

18. Means of informing staff, Planning Committee members, governing officials, and citizens-at-large of the library's progress were considered; and

19. The work of the Planning Committee was conducted in as short a time and with as few meetings of the overall Committee as was feasible; much of the preliminary work was done by the data coordinator, library staff and small subcommittees.

NOTES

1. Vernon E. Palmour, Marcia C. Bellassai, and Nancy V. DeWath, *A Planning Process for Public Libraries* (Chicago: American Library Association, 1980).

2. Charles McClure et al. *Planning and Role Setting for Public Libraries: A Manual of Options and Procedures* (Chicago: American Library Association, 1987).

3. See Sally Hunt, "The Participation Problem in Planning, *Public Libraries* 21 (Winter 1982):151–52; Kenneth Sertic, "Rural Public Libraries and the Planning Process," *Public Libraries* 22 (Spring 1982):29–20; Gordon Welles, "Public Relations and a Planning Process," *Illinois Libraries* 65 (March 1983):194–196; Rick Speer," "Guidelines for Pre-planning," *Public Libraries* 22 (Spring 1983):26–27; Donna Davoren, "A Planning Process for Public Libraries: One Library's Experience," *Arkansas Libraries* 40 (Summer 1983):19–24; Ann Friedman, "From Objectives to Strategies: Completing the First Cycle," *Public Libraries* 22 (Summer 1983):64–67; Pamela Chislett and Amy Soltys, "Planning Process—Grande Prairie," *Public Libraries* 23 (Spring 1984):19–20; John Halliday, "A Process for Planning getting: The real value of PLA's Planning Process is not in goal-setting," *American Libraries* 16(March 1985):177; Melissa Carr and Janice Wiese, "Long-range Planning—A Learning Process," Show-Me Libraries 38 (July 1987):9–12.

4. Annabel K. Stephens, "A Planning Process for Public Libraries: Its Use in Three Selected Libraries," D.L.S. dissertation, Columbia University, 1988.

5. Peter F. Drucker, *Management: Tasks, Responsibilities, Practices* (New York: Harper, 1974), pp. 121–122.

6. James Whittaker, *Strategic Planning in a Rapidly Changing Environment* (Lexington, Massachusetts: Lexington Books, 1978), pp. 3–4.

7. G. Edward Evans, *Management Techniques for Librarians* (New York: Academic Press, 1976), pp. 101–102.

8.   Robert Kemper, "Library Planning: The Challenge of Change," *Advances in Librarianship*, edited by Melvin Voight, vol. 1 (New York: Academic Press, 1970), pp. 207–239.

9.   Charles McClure, "The Planning Process: Strategies for Action," *College and Research Libraries* 39 (November 1978):456.

10.   Vernon E. Palmour, "Planning in Public Libraries: Role of Citizens and Library Staff," *Drexel Library Quarterly* 13 (July 1977):441.

11.   E.A. Wight, "The Contributions of the Library Survey," *Library Quarterly* 38 (October 1968):297–98.

12.   The standards promulgated by the ALA include: "Standards for Public Libraries," *Bulletin of the American Library Association* 27 (November 1933):513–14; ALA Committee on Post-War Planning, *Post-War Standards for Public Libraries* (Chicago: ALA, 1943); ALA Coordinating Committee on Revision of Public Library Standards, *Public Library Service: A Guide to Evaluation with Minimum Standards* (Chicago: ALA, 1956); and Public Library Association, *Minimum Standards for Public Library Systems, 1966* (Chicago: ALA, 1967).

13.   Palmour, *Planning Process*, p. 2.

14.   For these and other criticisms see PLA Goals, Guidelines and Standards Committee, *The Public Library Mission Statement And its Imperatives for Service* (Chicago: ALA, 1979), pp. iv–v; Peter Hiatt, "Traditional Standards," *Library Journal* 92 (December 1, 1967):4387–88; Lowell Martin, "Standards for Public libraries," *Library Trends* 21 (October 1972):164–177; Meredith Bloss, "Standards for Public Libraries-Quo Vadis?" *Library Journal* 101 (June 1, 1976):1259–60; and Lowell Martin, "Library Planning and Library Standards: Historical Perspective," *The Bookmark* 39 (Summer 1981):253–60.

15.   *Mission Statement*, p. vi.

16.   Mary Jo Lynch, "Public Library Planning: A New Approach," *Library Journal* 105 (May 15, 1980):1133.

17.   Planning Process, pp. 6–10,12,43–47, 52–53, 61–63, 77–78.

18.   Lynch, p. 1133.

19.   William J. Goode and Paul Hatt, *Methods in Social Research* (New York: McGraw-Hill, 1952), pp. 339–40.

20.   Jerome T. Murphy, *Getting the Facts: A Field Work Guide for Evaluators and Policy Analysts* (Santa Monica, California: Goodyear Publishing Co., 1980), pp. 71–113.

21.   *American Library Directory*, 41st ed (New York: Bowker, 1988), s.v.

22.   Interview with the director of Library System B, conducted October 6, 1983.

23.   Interviews with two of Library System B's department heads, conducted February 3,4, 1983, and with the chair of the board of trustees and two lay Planning Committee members, conducted February 17, 1983.

24.   Interview with the director of Library System A, conducted February 29, 1984.

25.   Interviews with one of Library System B's department heads, conducted February 3, 1983, and with two lay Planning Committee members, conducted February 16, 1983.

26.   Interviews with lay members of the Planning Committees of Library Systems A and B, conducted February 9, 10, 17, and 29, 1984; and February 16, 17, and May 6, 1983, respectively.

27.   Interview with the director of Library System B, conducted October 6, 1983.

28.   Interviews with lay members of the Planning Committees of Library Systems A and B, conducted February 10, 29, 1984; and February 16, 17, 1983, respectively.

29.   Interviews with the chair of the board of trustees of Library System A, conducted February 17, 1984, and with three lay Planning Committee members, conducted February 17, 22, and 29, 1984.

30.   Interview with a lay member of Library System A's Planning Committee, conducted February 22, 1984.

31.   Interviews with the chair of the board of trustees of Library System B; with a lay member of the Planning Committee; the department heads; and the director; conducted October 7, 1983; February 17, 1983; February 3, 4, 1983; and October 6, 1983, respectively.

32.   Interview with a lay member of Library System A's Planning Committee, conducted February 22, 1984.

33.   "Questionnaires [Library System A]," February 1984.

34.   "Questionnaires [Library System B]," May 1983.

35.   Interview with the director of Library System B, October 6, 1983.

36.   "Questionnaires [Library System B]," May 1983.

37.   Interview with the director of Library System B, conducted October 6, 1983.

BOOK PIRACY AND
INTERNATIONAL COPYRIGHT LAW

Serena Esther McGuire

THE PROBLEM: LITERARY PIRACY AND
AUTHOR'S RIGHTS

Authors and inventors are among the greatest benefactors of mankind. We should all be shocked if the law tolerated the least invasion of the rights of property in the case of merchandise; while those which justly belong to the works of authors are exposed to daily violation.

—Henry Clay and Daniel Webster
("American Book-Piracy," p. 670)

The Development of Copyright

The problem of plagiarism dates at least to Roman times. The term has been traced to Martial, who applied the legal plagium (for stealing a human being) to the act of stealing his "children"—his verses. At that time, and for many years thereafter, it was not recognized as a legal problem, and the only penalty was

Advances in Library Administration and Organization,
Volume 9, pages 83–104.
Copyright © 1991 by JAI Press, Inc.
All rights of reproduction in any form reserved.
ISBN: 1-55938-066-7

public opinion. Even in Martial's writings, his concern seems to have been for accuracy at least as much as for finances. The absence of control over foreign printing has occasionally even worked to the author's advantage in distribution, if not in compensation. This was the case when, after being banned by the French censors, Voltaire's works were printed in Holland and Switzerland and copies smuggled into France (Ladas, 1938, vol. 1, p. 13–17).

Perhaps it is necessary to pause at this point to clarify a few key terms. Ralph R. Shaw, in *Literary Property in the United States*, defines publish as "to offer or to make multiple copies available to the public, or to present the writing visually or orally or otherwise before a group, the members of which are not all personally selected by the author; to put the writing in a public place where members of the general public may see, hear, consult, or have access to it; i.e. to make any public use." General public is "construed as any group of persons not all of whom are personally selected by the author" (Shaw, 1950, p. 168). The United States International Trade Commission quotes the definition of copyright from *Ballentine's Law Dictionary*: "the exclusive privilege, by force of statute, of an author or proprietor to print or otherwise multiply, publish, and vend copies of his literary, artistic, or intellectual productions, and to license their production and sale by others during the term of its existence" (U.S. International Trade Commission [USITC], 1983, p. 1). Some argue that copyright law can exist only *within* a nation, and be extended by "*inter*-national conventions granting more or less reciprocal privileges to subjects or citizens of other nations." However, the words "international copyright act" can be found in the statute books as early as 1844, and the phrase clearly has legal meaning by the Berne Convention of 1887 (Nowell-Smith, 1968, 14–15). Piracy is a ". . . comprehensive term now in common and legal use to mean the stealing of an author's work by reprinting it in full or in substantial part without the authority of the copyright proprietor, and is in fact an infringement at wholesale or otherwise of the author's exclusive right" (Bowker, 1912, p. 251).

The first effective national control over printing and reprinting was the English Copyright Act of 1709, which became effective in 1710. The Statute of Anne, as it is generally known, specifically forbade importing foreign language books without recognition of author's rights. Since this Act preceded the American Revolution, nearly all authors of English-language books were protected as British subjects. It was not, however, enforceable throughout the Empire, much less the rest of the world. In fact, disregard for the Act seems to have been considered patriotic in Ireland until the Union of 1801, and in the United States well into the nineteenth century (Steinberg, 1959, p. 212; Patry, 1986, p. 4–5).

The basic philosophy of copyright was concisely summarized by Lord Mansfield, speaking in the legal case of Sayre *versus* Moore, 1785: "We must take care against two extremes equally prejudicial. The one that men of ability who have employed their time for the service of the community may not be deprived of their just merits and the reward of their ingenuity and labor, the other that the world may not be deprived of improvements nor the progress of the arts be retarded. . . " (Marke, 1977, p. 121–122). Although primarily concerned with the author's right to compensation, copyright also protects the author when delaying publication temporarily, as when finalizing a manuscript, or for the entire term of protection. This right of non-publication is often concerned with personal material, such as "letters of extreme affection." It clearly is not absolute, however, since these often have been used in court proceedings (Shaw, 1950, p. 107–108).

Copyright in the United States

In the United States, the first book known to carry a copyright imprint, Charles Henry Wharton's *Letter to the Roman Catholics of the City of Worcester*, appeared in 1784. Seven of the 13 states had some copyright protection by 1786 (Lehmann-Haupt, 1939, p. 91–93). The United States Constitution specifically grants to Congress the authority to make legislation "To promote the progress of Science and the useful arts by securing for limited times to authors and inventors, the exclusive right to their respective writings and discoveries." This clause was agreed to *nem. com.* on September 5, 1787, and appears in the final version as Article I, Section 8, Clause 8 (Benton, 1986, p. 829–830; 928–929). The first law under this authority was written in 1790 to cover books, charts and maps. Its coverage would gradually be expanded to include designs, engravings and other prints (1802); dramatic works (1856); photographs and negatives (1865); paintings, drawings, sculpture, models, designs for fine arts, dramatizations and translations (1870); and film (1912). Other modifications included mandatory deposit of one copy at the Library of Congress (1865) [later two copies]; mandatory notice of copyright in books (1874); and lengthening the term of protection to 28 years (1909) (Marke, 1977, p. 122). Works "prepared by an officer or employee of the United States Government as part of that person's official duties" are ineligible for U.S. copyright, but may be protected in other countries (Patry, 1986, p. 52).

Piracy of Foreign Authors

Treatment of foreign authors was defined by traditions known as "trade courtesy," which were, of course, entirely voluntary. Central to this system was the understanding that when one publisher issued a work ineligible for copyright, others would refrain from duplicating that work. Many questions arose, however, which did not have clear answers. If a publisher announced an *intention* of issuing a work, was it then unavailable to others permanently or for a period of time, or was actual publication necessary? If one publisher made an agreement for payment with the author of a work, but another put it into print first, whose claim was stronger? (Usually the second!) Did publication of one work give a publisher a claim on later works by the same author, an incentive to take the risks of publishing unknown but promising authors? What happened when two publishers announced simultaneously? These situations were handled inconsistently, and often to no one's satisfaction (Holt, 1888, p. 28–29; Tryon, 1963, p. 302).

As suggested by the second of these questions, publishers sometimes entered into voluntary agreements with foreign authors to share a portion of American sales. George Palmer Putnam is generally credited with beginning this practice shortly after his opening of the London branch of Wiley and Putnam in the early 1840s (Lehmann-Haupt, 1939, p. 127; Madison, 1966, p. 16–17). Putnam's son, however, cites Mr. Niles, of Roberts Brothers (later Little, Brown and Co.), as the first to make such an agreement (Putnam, 1915, p. 62).

James Ticknor Fields, of Ticknor and Fields, arranged a royalty of 10 percent of retail sales with Charles Dickens in 1866, apparently a frequent practice among several publishers by that time. Others, especially the Lippincotts of Philadelphia and the Harpers of New York, attacked the practice as "treachery, dishonesty, deceit, and shabby business methods." The basis for these attacks was that, since others had published Dickens previously (albeit in pirated editions), Fields was violating the basic tenet of trade courtesy. Overall, however, the trade courtesy system worked surprisingly well (especially considering its voluntary basis) up to the time of the War Between the States. It collapsed because of disagreements such as these, combined with the "get-rich-quick" attitudes prevalent in the Reconstruction era (Tryon, 1963, p. 302–307).

Publishers' Series

Most of the pirates published their books in series, called "libraries." The first seems to have been the "Lakeside Library," begun in Chicago in 1854 by Donnelly, Gassette and Lloyd. Five years later it had 270 titles selling for 10, 15 or 20 cents each. Lovell's "Lovell's Library," Beadle's "Fireside Library," Munro's "Seaside Library," Frank Leslie's "Home Library of Standard Works by the Most Celebrated Authors," and Fergus' "Popular Library" and "Globe Library" quickly entered the market. By 1877, 14 "libraries" were in the piracy business. Of these, Seaside was the most successful, reputedly amassing a fortune of at least seven million dollars for its publisher ("American Book-Piracy," p. 670–671; Madison, 1966, p. 52–53).

It may be difficult for people living in an era of copyright enforcement to imagine how openly books were pirated. A complaint by one British author quoted in 1885, "A remonstrance from Mr. Hamerton regarding a cheap reprint of his *Intellectual Life* has only led to his letter being printed as an advertisement," is just one illustration ("American Book-Piracy," p. 670).

Fiction was always more popular than non-fiction, but both were subject to piracy. Quality of content varied widely, with excellent works issued in the same "libraries" with very poor ones. Nearly all, however, were printed on cheap paper, usually in tiny, unleaded type, two or even three columns to a page. At first some were completely unbound. Even after most were covered, some in cloth, the pages were still difficult to read and unpleasant to the touch and sight. In spite of their similar format, the "dime novels," sometimes assumed to be pirated, were not (Holt, 1888, p. 33; Madison, p. 52–53; Holt, 1891, p. 440). Although one source includes Harper's "Franklin Square Library" among the pirates ("American Book-Piracy," p. 670), others state that this series, and their later non-fiction "Handy Series," were attempts to beat the pirates at their own game. The key difference is that the authors were paid, despite the low prices (usually 25 cents per copy) and the inexpensive paperback formats. (Madison, p. 54; Barnes, 1974, p. 16) Harper's "Library of Select Novels" was begun in 1831, preceding the pirated libraries, but in 1877 the price was lowered to meet the intense competition (Stern, 1980, p. 154; Madison, 1966, p. 54).

Nineteenth-century publishers sold most of their work locally, through their own stores; regionally, through travelling agents; or by exchange arrangements with publishers in other cities. Trade fairs increased in popularity during this period, making book exchange arrangements among publishers easier. Subscriptions by mail gave the widest possible distribution, obviously an advantage in the low-price, high-volume piracy market (Tryon, 1947, p. 212–214, 222–223). Since many pirated works were sold in "series" by mail, and originals were often mailed from England, low rates on domestic and international postage helped to make the business profitable, even with the low prices (Holt, 1888, p. 33; 1891, p. 440; Madison, 1966, p. 52–53).

In selling books from abroad, the first publisher on the market with a new title was in an advantageous position, and extreme measures were taken to assure that lead. For the sake of speed, sections of the same book were sometimes spread out to different printers, then reassembled into sets. Books are reported to have been on sale within 24 hours of the arrival of the first copy at the dock. The New York publishers had a clear advantage in this race, since most of the ships docked there before proceeding to other American ports (Lehmann-Haupt, 1939, p. 166).

Best Sellers

British authors were very popular in the United States. By 1934, 10 works (other than school or text books) first published in the late 1800s had been issued in editions totalling at least 500,000. Four of the nine authors were British, and therefore ineligible for copyright protection. These figures are summarized below:

- *Tom Sawyer*, Mark Twain
  1875   American 1,500,000 copies
- *Black Beauty*, Anna Sewell
  1877   British 1,000,000 copies

- *Ben Hur*, Lew Wallace
    1880   American 1,195,000 copies
- *Five Little Peppers and How They Grew*, Margaret Sidney
    1881   American 1,090,000 copies
- *Treasure Island*, Robert Lewis Stevenson
    1883   British 1,000,000 copies
- *Huckleberry Finn*, Mark Twain
    1884   American 1,000,000+ copies
- *Little Lord Fauntleroy*, Francis Hodgson Burnett
    1886   American* 503,000 copies
- *Looking Backward*, Edward Bellamy
    1888   American 500,000+ copies
- *Trilby*, George Du Maurier
    1894   British 1,000,000 copies
- *Beside the Bonnie Brier Bush*, Ian Maclaren
    1894   British 500,000+ copies
    * born British 1849, repatriated 1865
(Lehmann-Haupt, 1939, 160–161)

The disadvantages of this situation for foreign authors who were not compensated for their work are relatively clear. Less obvious is the problem for American authors, who were forced to place the product of their labor in ". . . direct competition with stolen wares. The reader must pay a dollar and a half for a novel by an American, while he can buy 'Middlemarch' or 'Daniel Deronda'— incomparable offsprings of genius—for twenty cents" ("The Blessings of Piracy," 1882, p. 944). Even indirect competition was a problem because of the expectations of unrealistically low prices, and the lack of appreciation for good quality printing and materials (Holt, 1888, p. 32–33).

Authors and publishers wrote of the lack of literary representation of American thoughts, values and society. In 1891, one publisher complained that there had been no American encyclopedia since before the 1880 census, and that even at that time the only revisions had been squeezed into already existing plates by taking something else out. Foreign encyclopedias were often inaccurate in their facts about and portrayals of America. He went on to cite Mark Twain's statement that 70 percent of library circulation was novels, and 90 percent of those were foreign, and this unduly influenced American readers with European ideas, standards and customs. To make matters worse, the injustices of those cultures were often avoided or covered up. Since residents could see for themselves the difficulties of American society, the comparison would inevitably make the reader overly critical of America (Holt, 1891, p. 444–445).

The total reading public was growing, and the variety of material available to them was becoming larger. Magazines, especially family magazines, might be the beginning of the reading habit, but these could lead to a taste for short stories, novels and other books. Political poets, local color and dialect authors also helped to satisfy a wide variety of tastes. Despite the lower cost of foreign work, American authors were becoming more popular. In 1820, an estimated 30 percent of the books published in the United States were by American authors. By 1840 this figure had increased to 50 percent, and by the 1860s, 80 percent. All of these figures, however, include school and text books, which presumably were increasing both in number and in proportion to the whole as school attendance increased (Lehmann-Haupt, 1939, p. 160).

Americans Pirated Abroad

It would be false to give the impression that piracy was only practiced by Americans against the British. Especially during the economically depressed years early in the nineteenth century, the desire for low-priced books was as strong in Britain as in America, and George Routledge, Henry George Bohn, H.G. Clarke and William Smith were the most prolific, but not the only, publishers willing to provide British readers with pirated American work. Like the Americans, British pirates offered their products in series, with three of the most popular being the "Railway Library," the "Popular Series" and the frankly-named "Cheap Series." Again, fiction was more in demand than non-fiction. Foreign authors, especially Americans, were pirated more frequently than British natives, but some British work was copied, particularly from journals (Barnes, 1974, p. 154).

An 1879 article described recent piracy of works from the United States by publishers in Canada (which had been separated from Britain in 1867). When the books were mailed back into this country for sale at very low prices, the protests from U.S. pirates weakened what little credibility had ever been held by their claims to motives of generosity toward the poor ("Copyright and Morality," 1879, p. 530).

The Berne Convention

In 1884, representatives of 14 countries, including the United States, met at Berne, Switzerland, to begin development of an international copyright agreement. By 1885, 20 nations were participating, but when the agreement was formalized in 1886, only 10—Belgium, France, Germany, Great Britain, Haiti, Italy, Liberia, Spain, Switzerland and Tunisia—signed. The basis of the Berne agreement is "national treatment," the assumption that foreign authors will be accorded the same rights with regard to publication as are citizens. Two specific provisions are key: first, the author's "Moral Rights" of paternity (use of his or her name in connection with the work) and integrity (control of adaptation and alteration), and, second, the prohibition of "formalities" such as notice, registration and deposit (Abelman and Berkowitz, 1977, p. 626–627; 633–634).

The incidents of piracy against American authors, their lack of protection on the international market, and the refusal of the United States to participate in the Berne agreement helped to show the truth of a statement by Charles Dickens in a speech in support of international copyright: "There must be an international copyright arrangement. It becomes the character of a great country, firstly because it is justice; secondly, because without it you never can have, and keep, a literature of your own" ("American Book-Piracy," p. 670).

THE RESPONSE: A STRONGER COPYRIGHT LAW

> It has been urged that an extended copyright would damage the public interest—that it would enhance the price of books. . . . Accordingly, I wrote to my butcher, baker, and other tradesmen, informing them that it was necessary, for the sake of *cheap literature* and the interest of the public, that they should furnish me with their commodities at a very trifling percentage above cost price. It will be sufficient to quote the answer of the butcher: "Sir: Respectin your note. Cheap literater be blowed. Butchers must live as well as other pepel—and if so be you or the readin publick wants to have meat at prime cost, you must buy your own beastesses, and kill yourselves."
>
> —Tom Hood (Copyright and Copywrong)
> ("American Book-Piracy," p. 670)

International Copyright Efforts in the United States

Agitation toward American participation in international copyright regulation began early in the nineteenth century; it was certainly underway by 1837, when Henry Clay approached Congress on the issue. In 1840, even before the opening of Wiley and Putnam's London office and its first royalty agreement with a foreign author, George Palmer Putnam published a pamphlet on the issue, *An Argument in Behalf of International Copyright*. Three years later, he gathered the signatures of 97 publishers, printers and binders on a petition to Congress protesting the lack of laws as "alike injurious to the business of publishing and to the best interests of the people." In 1853, five publishers lobbied Secretary of State Edward Everett with a proposal suggesting three conditions to be met for protection in the United States: (1) works by foreign authors must be registered here before publication abroad; (2) they must be issued here within 30 days of publication abroad; and (3) they must be manufactured in the United States. The same year, Everett negotiated an agreement with England under which authors copyrighted in each country would also be protected in the other, but the agreement was tabled by Congress. A visit by Charles Dickens to the United States in 1868, during which he spoke extensively about the copyright problem, prompted the formation of the "International Copyright Association." That year the Association presented to Congress a statement, "Copyright Association for the Protection and Advancement of Literature and Art," with 153 signatures, including 101 authors and 19 publishers. The Association would continue to present new or revised bills nearly every year until their goal was accomplished. In 1883 the "American Copyright League," a group of authors, was formed, and four years later the "American Publishers Copyright League" (Lehmann-Haupt, 1939, p. 162; Madison, 1966, p. 57; Putnam, 1891, p. 66–68).

In addition to the lobbying efforts, public opinion was shaped by the efforts, written and spoken, of journalists, authors, publishers, preachers, and others too numerous to count. Many of the prominent journals of the day featured frequent articles on the copyright question, with two of the most active being *The Nation* and *The Critic*. In England, *The Author* was one of the most outspoken.

As might be surmised from the many years of work involved in passage of the first law, opinion was far from united on this issue. In 1868, the same year as Dickens' visit, Harper and Brothers stated in a letter to the Committee for the Library of Congress: "any measure of international copyright was objectionable because it would add to the price of books, and thus interfere with the education of the people." (Ten years later, Harper had changed its position.) The Philadelphia publishers issued a joint statement in 1872 that: "Thought, when given to the world, is, as light, free to all." They went on to say that copyright was a domestic matter—and authors who wanted protection in the American market should become American citizens (Lehmann-Haupt, 1939, p. 163–164; Putnam, 1891, p. 70).

Two alternatives for international copyright legislation, known as the Hawley and Chace bills, were presented in Congress, and hearings were held by the Senate Committee on Patents on May 21, 1886. Testimony or letters were presented in favor of the bills by many well-known figures, including Librarian of Congress Ainsworth R. Spofford; authors Samuel Clemens and James Russell Lowell; publishers Henry Holt, George Ticknor Curtis, Dana Estes, R.R. Bowker, George Haven Putnam, George Munro and the Harpers. While concentrating on the issue of justice, the testimony also suggested that the bills could at least provide an important first step in international protection; would encourage improvement of the quality of writing and publication; and might actually lower prices by reducing the waste and disorder of the present system. Speaking against the bills were publishers Gardiner G. Hubbard, Henry C. Lea, Roger Sherman, and John W. Lovell, along with James Welsh of the Typographical Union. The opposing testimony focused on the desire for cheap reading matter, especially for the poor, the well-being of the typesetters, and an appeal to free enterprise (U.S. Congressional Hearings, May 21, 1886, passim).

The defeat of the bills, and the general lack of response by Congress, was not as much a result of hostility, or even indifference, to the treatment of authors and publishers as might be assumed. With the events leading up to, during, and following the War Between the States, Congress had many other things to occupy its attention. In addition, there existed an aversion to international agreements which was much broader than the copyright question (Lehmann-Haupt, 1939, p. 163; Gosse, 1890, p. 57). Divisions within the Congress on this issue were becoming visible, for an 1890 article in *The Fortnightly Review*, could single out Mr. Hopkins and Mr. Payson, both of Illinois, as the strongest opponents of the recently defeated international copyright proposal (Gosse, 1890, p. 57).

The turning point in the campaign probably came in 1890, when Judge Shipman, of the United States District Court, issued a decision in the case of Black, Scribners and Walker *versus* H.G. Allen and Co. Messrs. Black, of Edinburgh, were the publishers of the *Encyclopedia Britannica*, which sold in England for the equivalent of $9.00 per volume. Scribners held an agreement for publication in America, where it sold for $5.00 per volume. Allen had pirated the work through a photographic process, and was selling it for $1.50 per volume. The encyclopedia contained many articles and maps by American citizens, including General Francis A. Walker. The Americans either held their own copyright or had assigned it to Black. The copyright material had, of course, been reproduced along with the material ineligible for American copyright; this was the basis for the complaint. Allen's position was that if Americans chose to publish their work in volumes ineligible as a whole for copyright, they had thereby invalidated their claim to protection, and he went as far as to suggest that the entire matter was intentional entrapment. Judge Shipman decided in favor of the plaintiffs ("A Blow at the Pirates," p. 6).

The Chace Act

The Chace International Copyright Bill, or Chace-Breckenridge Bill, which included a provision that books must be typeset and printed in the United States, was presented to Congress, and hearings were held before the House Committee on the Judiciary on February 8, 1890. C. N. Bovee, Jr., representing Ignatius Kohler, publisher of German-origin books in English and German, recognized the complaints of American and foreign authors, but emphasized the need for inexpensive books for the reading public and the cost of the second typesetting and printing. William H. Arnoux, his "partner," reminded the Congress that neither the Bible nor the primer, "corner-stones" of the republic, were copyrighted. J.L. Kennedy, of the International Typographical Union, spoke in support of the bill's potential benefit to readers and, by extension, to society, as well as its benefit for the typesetters and printers. George Haven Putnam represented the American Copyright League in support of passage of this measure (U.S. House Committee on the Judiciary, February 8, 1890, passim).

In 1891 the Chace Act became America's first regulation on international copyright. The protection it offered was limited, however, by a provision that the person desiring copyright "shall, on or before the day of publication in this or any foreign country, deliver . . . or mail . . . to the Librarian of Congress, . . . two copies . . . printed from type set within the limits of the United States." Since

British law required publication in Britain, along with registration *after* publication, and various previous provisions of American law were still in effect, publishers had to adhere to a tightly scheduled order of procedures, most with lapses of only days in between. A relatively small delay in production or trans-Atlantic shipment could end the possibility of protection in one or both countries (Nowell-Smith, 1968, p. 65; Solberg, 1952, p. 56). The Act applied only to citizens of "proclaimed" nations, those recognized by Congressional proclamation as offering reciprocal treatment to citizens of the United States (Benko, 1987, p. 2). Its provisions were very similar to a bill which had passed the House in 1852, but had been defeated in the Senate. One historian comments: "Perhaps the final irony of all was that British authors, publishers, and politicians had to accept in 1891 what they resisted in 1854" (Barnes, 1974. p. 262). On a similar note, one legal scholar mentions the irony that the manufacturing requirement was designed for the protection of printers, rather than authors, in contrast to the Statute of Anne, which was designed to protect the authors from the printers (Patry, 1986, p. 313).

Movements Toward Revision

In an open letter addressed to the President of the American Copyright League, but sent to Congress, the French Association Litteraire et Artistique Internationale applauded passage of the Act, but urged removal of the provision for remanufacturing books in the United States, especially books in foreign languages, and of the same day registration clause. It suggested that American interests could be protected by forbidding entry of books written in or translated into English while still admitting foreign language books. The market for the latter was such a small part of the whole that few such works would be available in the United States if they had to be remanufactured. It also mentioned that most European countries granted copyright for the life of the author plus 50 years ("A French View of American Copyright," p. 136).

The British journal, *The Author*, expressed doubts about the value of the new law in view of its restrictions. They wondered if Americans would still want British works if they had to pay the higher prices necessary to cover the labor involved in a second typesetting. They stated that some British authors were choosing not to copyright under the new law, finding the old trade courtesy preferable ("Copyright in America," p. 167–168). A later article in the same journal mentioned a complaint from author John Strange Winter that his story "The Imp" (copyright 1887 in England) had been reprinted in the New York *Sunday News* under a different title. Winter's letter, inquiring about the News' authority for reprint and requesting remuneration, had yielded no response ("International Copyright," pp. 6–7).

In 1899, G. P. Putnam's Sons were sued by Rudyard Kipling for binding and selling purchased sheets of copyright material in the same volume with non-

copyright material, in a binding similar to the British authorized edition. Putnam's won the case, but in a similar case in 1903, damages were awarded
(Bowker, 1912, pp. 263–264).

As might be expected, however, not all of the violation, or questionable
observation, of the law was on one side. In 1900, Congress requested that the
Commissioner of Labor "investigate the effect upon labor, production, and
wages of the International Copyright Act." Their 99 page report included complaints from members of the International Typographical Union that many viola-
tions of the typesetting rule existed, most through the use of stereotype plates
("The International Copyright Act," p. 83–85).

In December 1906, the House and Senate committees on Patents held joint
hearings on bills to amend and consolidate the various copyright acts then in
force. By this time, legislation had come to include provisions for dramatizations
and translations as well as a variety of artistic media, along with procedural
matters such as deposit of copies with the Library of Congress and notice in the
book. The testimony represented several groups, including publishers George
Haven Putnam, Richard R. Bowker, W.A. Livingstone, Charles Porterfield,
William M. McKinney, Alfred Lucking and David C. Harrington; authors
Thomas Nelson Page, Samuel L. Clemens and the Rev. Edward Everett Hale;
librarians Arthur E. Bostwick (New York Public, representing the American
Library Association), Bernard C. Steiner (Enoch Pratt, Baltimore), H.C. Well-
man (Springfield, Massachusetts Public), and William P. Cutter (Forbes Library,
Northampton, Massachusetts), and C.P. Montgomery of the Customs Division of
the Treasury Department. The American Copyright League was represented
by Bowker, and the American Copyright Association by Robert Underwood
Johnson; several other associations related to publishing were also represented
(U.S. Congress, 1906, passim).

Copyright Acts of 1909 and 1976

The Copyright Code of 1909 added tighter restrictions to the Act of 1891 by a
provision that books must be bound, as well as typeset and printed, in the United
States (Lehmann-Haupt, 1939, p. 164). Conversely, it loosened restrictions by
extending to the President the power to proclaim that a nation offered reciprocal
treatment, (Benko, 1987, p. 2) and by removing the manufacturing requirement
for books not in the English language (Nowell-Smith, 1968, p. 65–66).

Between the years of 1922 and 1940, there were repeated attempts to revise
the provisions of American copyright law in order to remove the passages contradictory to the Berne Convention, thus paving the way for participation. The
necessary changes included: (1) making copyright automatic upon creation (removal of the "formalities" of notice, registration and deposit); (2) extending the
term of copyright to the author's lifetime plus some years (usually 50); and (3)
recognizing the concept of "moral rights" (Magavero, 1978, pp. 151–158).

In 1976, the copyright code was revised to move toward conformity with Berne. Revisions included: (1) extension of the term of copyright to the life of the author plus 50 years for works published after January 1, 1978, with provisions for joint, anonymous or pseudononymous authorship, works for hire and presumption of the author's death when date is unknown; (2) continuation of the requirement of copyright notice in books, but with provisions for errors and omissions; (3) clarification of the separate but related functions of deposit and registration, with encouragement (but not requirement) of registration; and phasing out of the manufacturing clause as of July 1, 1982. The Act (P.L.94–553) became effective January 1, 1978 (U.S. Library of Congress, 1977, introduction and p. 2:3, 10:1–5, 11:1–10, 12:1–2), but the manufacturing clause was extended to July 1, 1986 (Nasri, 1987, p. 122). Although these revisions did not remove all of the obstacles to joining Berne, the "authors and their representatives stressed that the adoption of a life-plus–50 term was by far their most important goal in copyright law revision," (Latman, Gorman and Ginsberg, 1985, p. 195) and this was accomplished.

It was also clear that American recognition of the need for participation in international agreements had increased, as evidenced by membership in the United Nations' Universal Copyright Convention from its founding in 1952 (Benko, 1987, p. 6).

Just as American law was being revised, so too was the Berne Convention: Berlin, 1908; Rome, 1928; Brussels, 1948; Stockholm, 1967 and Paris, 1971. The last two were concerned primarily with the need to be more inclusive of, and to make accommodations for, developing nations (Abelman and Berkowitz, 1977, p. 627, 630).

In 1959, referring to the Universal Copyright Convention, S.H. Steinberg stated: "The international regulation of copyright has put an end to the century-old twin-scandal of privileged and pirated editions—the former enriching publisher and author at the expense of the public, the latter ruining the respectable publisher and author with small benefit to the public" (Steinberg, 1959, p. 211).

Unfortunately, events would prove his words unduly optimistic.

THE RECURRENCE: PIRACY IN THE THIRD WORLD

Even as it applies to information in traditional delivery vehicles, such as this book, the idea of property rights in knowledge is tattered and torn. This was brought home to me when a young Chinese scholar, the nephew of an old friend, wrote to me from Hong Kong to say that he had translated an earlier book of mine (*The Future Executive*) and had arranged to market it in the People's Republic of China through a university press. I thought at first that my correspondent wanted to buy the Chinese rights to this copyrighted work, or at least was seeking my permission to use *my* words in *his* book. Not at all; my friend's nephew never raised those questions. Instead he asked me to write a

new introduction for the Chinese edition of my book. Intrigued by the prospect
of sharing my thoughts on management with a billion Chinese, I sat down the
very next weekend and wrote an introduction to this politely pirated edition of a
copyright work.

—Harlan Cleveland (1985, p. 74)

The Pirating of American Authors

Piracy of works by American authors has never completely disappeared. Matt
Roberts' bibliography includes numerous articles on piracy of American books in
China, Holland, Chile, Japan, the Philippines, South Africa, Latin America,
Mexico, Formosa/Taiwan, Iran and Cuba which appeared between 1904 and
1966 (1971, p. 310–314; passim).

An article in *Publishers Weekly* of March 11, 1988 cites a statement by U.S.
Trade Representative Clayton Yeutter that "the United States was losing from
$43 billion to $61 billion a year 'because of inadequate protection'." His figures
are extrapolated from a government survey of American publishers. While such
large numbers seem highly questionable, the smaller, more specific figures on
which they are based are also worthy of concern. Estimates vary depending on
the criteria used for judgement, but about 40 nations worldwide are believed to
have inadequate laws for protection of foreign works, or inadequate enforcement
of existing laws. The "top ten" offenders, with an estimated total of $427 mil-
lion, were: Taiwan and Singapore, $107 million each; Korea and the Philippines,
$70 million each; Malaysia, $20 million; Nigeria, $11 million; Egypt, $10 million; Brazil, $8 million; Thailand, $7 million; and Indonesia, $6 million (Fields,
March 11, 1988, p. 19). It is no surprise that textbooks and works in the sciences
are the items most in demand from the United States and European markets,
legally or illegally (Graham, 1988, p. 22; Taylor, April 1, 1988, p. 20–21).

Problems of Control and Access

Two problems are key to control of intellectual property in the world today.
The first is the end of control over "dissemination and distribution of . . . protected works" brought about by new technology, including "electronic storage,
distribution and retrieval of 'the printed word'. . . . The right to 'copy'—the
historic root of our copyright tradition—is slowly being displaced in importance
for some materials by the right to display." The other is "the widespread attitude
that the desire for 'access' should override proprietary interests" (Wagner, April
1, 1988, p. 19–20).

Philip Altbach points out that at least three factors have combined in a trend
toward possible improvement of the current situation. First, increasing willingness on the part of major publishers to consider and accommodate the particular

problems of Third-world nations has helped to provide goals and expectations more realistic and attainable in the economically and culturally pluralistic world of the late twentieth century. Second, fear of legal reprisals and trade sanctions from the United States and major Western European governments provides an incentive for tighter restrictions and enforcement within developing nations. Last, compliance of the Soviet Union with the Universal Copyright Convention in the last few years has improved perceptions in the Third world of both the concept and the effectiveness of that agreement (Altbach, 1987, p. 44).

It seems possible that there is another factor at work in the Third world. Altbach, in that same article, states:

In a way, copyright can be seen as a historically inevitable development as nations become more mature in their knowledge industries. The U.S. was one of the world's major pirates in the 19th century (with beneficial effects on its publishing and printing industries, but with great harm to its intellectual life at the time) and only joined the copyright system when America perceived it as advantageous. Pressure from Britain and other countries played a role, since copyright was lauded as a part of civilization. But the main motivation was self interest (Altbach, 1987, p. 44).

Relations with the Third World

The key point is that efforts on the part of industrialized nations to encourage education, scholarship, and publication *within* developing nations will eventually provide more lasting change than any system of punishments or rewards. This is because the developing nations will come to see protection of their own citizens through reciprocal copyright agreements and enforcement as necessary to their own intellectual progress. Altbach mentions the U.S.S.R.'s increasing compliance with the U.C.C. We could speculate that this recent change has been due to an acceleration of intellectual progress and a recognition of the need for self-protection in the recent environment of increased openness both internally and with the West.

Two problems were named by Wagner as contributing to the present situation: the end of control over protected material resulting from electronic technology, and the assumption of a right of access by people in need of information. These are in some ways reminiscent of two nineteenth century problems: the new technology, photographic reproduction, which led to the 1890 *Encyclopedia Britannica* case, and the attitudes satirized by Tom Hood's suggestion that his butcher should provide him with meat at reduced price in the interests of cheap literature for the public. Most scholars already know the weaknesses of the latter line of thought, but we might stop to consider the first.

What set the *Encyclopedia Britannica* case apart from those which preceded it was the logical result of that new technology—the fact that photographic reproduction included the work of American authors along with that by foreign. Once that was recognized, it quickly became clear that there was no effective way to protect the rights of the few other than to protect the rights of all, and action soon followed.

The Next Step: Trade Courtesy?

Until a similar situation arises in the Third world, it may be that the best practices will resemble the old trade courtesy—modest payments and reasonable concern for accuracy in return for the most recent originals and general coopera- tion. Cleveland demonstrates this in his recognition that he cannot prevent the translation and publication of his work, but that it is to his own benefit to cooperate and be allowed the opportunity for additional comments.

Sally Adamson Taylor, *Publishers Weekly* correspondent in the Far East, men- tions in her discussion of recent developments in Asia that Thailand, one of the major copyright offenders, belongs only to the Berne Convention. Since the United States has participated in the U.C.C., but had never joined the Berne Convention, the government of Thailand maintained "that the Americans are demanding copyright protection that they don't deserve—and that they should join the Berne like everyone else" (Taylor, April 1, 1988, p. 20).

The U.S. Complies with Berne

Even as her article was being published, movement was underway to do that. On May 10, 1988, the House passed, with no dissenting votes, HR.4262. This bill was designed with a "minimalist approach," making as few changes as possible to bring U.S. practice into compliance with Berne procedures. Among the necessary changes was recognition of two "Moral Rights," independent of economic rights: "paternity" (claim of authorship) and "integrity" (blockage of any distortion, mutilation, or alteration of a work which would prejudice the author's honor or reputation). It is mandatory for participation in the Berne convention that both of these apply, even if the author has given up all other copyright. A compromise in the registration requirement was developed after concern was expressed by Ralph Oman, Register for Copyright and Assistant Librarian for Copyright Services at the Library of Congress, that elimination of the requirement would undermine legal protection because those copies are now used in lawsuits as evidence of the existence and content of the work. The new law requires registration for works published in the United States, but not for works copyrighted in other countries ("Berne Adherence Bill," p. 126; Fields, May 27, 1988, p. 10). On October 8, the Senate voted 90–0 to pass S.1301, a slightly different version. The differences were worked out, and on October 15 the revised version passed the House (Cohadas, 1988 p. 2805; "United States to Join Berne Convention," p. 2980). Treaty Document 99–27, authorizing U.S.

entry into the Berne Convention, passed the Senate on October 20 ("Copyright: Berne," p. 9).

President Reagan signed both bills October 31, describing U.S. entry into Berne as a "major step in improving the protection abroad of America's most important export industries: motion pictures, television programming, computer programs, sound recordings, music, and books. . . ." The treaty became effective March 1, 1989, three months after the "instrument of accession" was deposited with the Director General of the World Intellectual Property Organization in Geneva ("The United States Joins the Berne Copyright Convention," p. 457–458). Egypt and Thailand, two of the nations numbered among the "top ten" pirates are members of the Berne Convention. Twenty-three other nations are in Berne, but not the Universal Copyright Convention: Benin, Brazil, Burkino Faso, Central African Republic, Chad, Congo, Cyprus, Gabon, Ivory Coast, Libya, Madagascar, Mali, Mauritania, Niger, Romania, Rwanda, South Africa, Surinam, Togo, Turkey, Uraguay, Zaire and Zimbabwe (U.S. Library of Congress. 1988, p. 2–8).

There are other signs that copyright relations with the Third World are improving. The General Agreement on Tariffs and Trade (GATT) talks have included discussion of piracy and copyright. The International Publishers Association Congress focused on the scarcity of books for over two-thirds of the world's population, and included discussion of the problem from the Third World's view as well as that of the more developed nations (Menkes, p. 20–26; Wagner, July 22, 1988, p. 22). In October, Taiwan found the Tan Ching Book Company guilty of illegally reprinting the *Encyclopedia Britannica* mainland Chinese edition for sale in Taiwan. The books were confiscated and the company president and the chairman were fined and sentenced to a year in prison. Another publisher has been authorized publication rights in Taiwan (Taylor, July 22, 1988, p. 14; "Taiwan Upholds 'Britannica'. . . " p. 22).

Public Lending Right: The Next Domestic Question?

The Public Lending Right may prove to be the next issue with international copyright implications. This concept, which has been put into practice in most of the nations of Europe, as well as Britain, Canada, Australia and New Zealand, provides payment by the government to authors as compensation for the use of their books in libraries. There are two basic models: the "Danish," calculated on the books owned by public libraries, and the "Swedish," calculated on an annual sampling of loans by public libraries. In most nations where this is in practice, payments are limited to authors who are citizens; a few allow payments to non-citizen residents, even fewer to any author who writes in the native language. Since the Berne Convention requires "national treatment" (that foreign authors be accorded the same rights with regard to publication as citizens), this is contradictory. So far, the conflict has been avoided by treating the payments as a government subsidy to the arts, rather than a copyright matter, but this seems tenuous, at best. There is no Public Lending Right bill in Congress now, but the issue is likely to resurface in the future (Stave, pp. 577–579; for treatment in individual nations, see various articles throughout this issue).

CONCLUSION: THOUGHTS FOR THE FUTURE

The expression "What goes around, comes around." certainly seems an apt summary of American involvement in book piracy and international copyright.

It would be naive to assume that now that the United States has joined the Berne Convention, all problems with piracy and copyright will disappear. Some of the issues which will continue to haunt authors and publishers can be foreseen; others will become clear only with time.

The most obvious ongoing problem will be relations with nations who do not participate in either of the two major copyright conventions. It was mentioned that two of the "top ten" pirating nations, Egypt and Thailand, are members of the Berne Convention; it seems reasonable to look for prompt—although not immediate—improvement in relations with those two countries. The eight remaining nations are responsible for $410 of the estimated $427 million, or over 95 percent. This hardly seems an encouraging statistic. However, it is important to remember that one of the basic premises of a Convention such as Berne is that an offense against one is an offense against all. Hence, if piracy does not show a distinct and rapid decrease, pressure from all the Berne nations, not just from the United States, will continue to grow. Since all of the pirating nations are poor and heavily dependent on foreign aid, none can afford to defy world opinion for long, especially when other poor nations are in compliance. Three signs already mentioned, an increasing willingness on the part of U.S. and European publishers and governments to design less rigid provisions for publishers, educators and governments in developing nations; an increasing tendency in developing nations to enact and enforce copyright legislation; and changes in attitudes and practices in the U.S.S.R. combine to indicate very encouraging trends.

The relationship between humans and the technology we have created remains an ongoing problem, and one which far exceeds the scope of this paper. In resolving this problem, however, it will be necessary to remember that the core of the problem lies with humans, not machines; the machines only make it possible for humans to act out age-old urges in new ways, for good or ill. If that is the case, solutions will also lie with people—probably with people using machines in various ways—but still with the people.

REFERENCES

Abelman, Lawrence E. and Linda L. Berkowitz. "International Copyright Law." *New York Law School Law Review* 22 (1977): 619–651.

Altbach, Philip G. "Toward a World Copyright Era." *Publishers Weekly* 232 (December 11, 1987): 44.

"American Book-Piracy." *Chamber's Journal of Popular Literature, Science and Arts* 62 (October 17, 1885): 669–671.

"American Copyright." *The Author* 2 (June 1, 1891): 232.

"American Copyright Act, The." *The Author* 2 (June 1, 1891): 5–11.

"American Society of Authors, The." *The Author* 2 (June 1, 1891): 388.

Barnes, James J. *Authors, Publishers and Politicians: The Quest for an Anglo-American Copyright Agreement, 1815–1854.* Columbus: Ohio State University Press, 1974.

Benko, Robert P. *Protecting Intellectual Property Rights: Issues and Controversies.* Washington, D.C.: American Enterprise Institute for Public Policy Research, 1987.

Benton, Wilbourn E., ed. *1787: Drafting the U. S. Constitution.* College Station: Texas A & M University Press, 1986.

"Berne Adherence Bills hit Snag Over Registration Requirement." *Publishers Weekly* 233 (May 13, 1988): 126.

"Blessings of Piracy, The." *Century Magazine* 23 (November 1881-April 1882): 942–945.

"Blow at the Pirates, A." *The Nation* 51 (July 3, 1890): 6–7.

Bonham-Carter, Victor. *Authors by Profession.* Vol. 1, *From the Introduction of Printing until the Copyright Act of 1911.* London: Society of Authors, 1978.

Bowker, Richard Rogers. *Copyright—Its History and Its Law: Being a Summary of the Principles and Practice of Copyright with Special Reference to the American Code of 1909 and the British Act of 1911.* Boston: Houghton Mifflin, 1912.

Boyesen, Hjalmar Hjorth. "Defense of the Eighth Commandment." *The Cosmopolitan* 4 (September 1887-February 1888): 485–489.

Carter, Robert A., "'Booming' the Book Throughout the Years." *Publishers Weekly* 233 (March 11, 1988): 74–76.

Chamier, D. "The Ethics of Copyright." *The Westminster Review* 135 (July to December 1890): 124–133.

Chan, James. "Today's New Opportunities." *Publishers Weekly* 233 (April 1, 1988): 23.

"Changes Expected When Berne Implemented." *Library of Congress Information Bulletin* 47 (November 14, 1988): 458–459.

Clemens, S. L. (Mark Twain). "Concerning Copyright: An Open Letter to the Register of Copyright." *North American Review* 180 (January 1905): 1–8.

Cleveland, Harlan. *The Knowledge Executive: Leadership in an Information Society.* New York: E.P. Dutton, 1985.

Cohadas, Nadine. "United States to Join Berne Convention: Congress to Clear Copyright-Protection Bill." *Congressional Quarterly Weekly Report* 46 (October 8, 1988): 2805.

Commerce Clearing House Editorial Staff. *Copyright Revision Act of 1976: P.L. 94–553, as signed by the President, October 19, 1976.* Chicago: Commerce Clearing House, Inc., 1976.

"Copyright and Morality." *Popular Science Monthly* 14 (November 1878- April 1879): 530–533.

"Copyright: Berne." *ALA Washington Newsletter* 40 (November 17, 1988): 8–9.

"Copyright in America." *The Author* 2 (June 1, 1891): 167–168.

Copyright Society of the U.S.A., compiler and editor. *Studies on Copyright.* Arthur Fisher Memorial Edition. South Hackensack, New Jersey: Fred B. Rothman and Co., 1963.

"English Copyright for American Authors." *The Nation* 46 (February 8, 1888): 110–111.

Feldman, Gayle. "The Second Beijing Book Fair." *Publishers Weekly* 234 (October 21, 1988): 19–22.

Fields, Howard. "House Votes Unanimously to Join Berne Convention." *Publishers Weekly* 233 (May 27, 1988): 10.

———. "Publishers Applaud New Trade Bill That Frees Some Books." *Publishers Weekly* 234 (September 9, 1988): 66.

———. "Senate Expected to Pass Berne Bill in September." *Publishers Weekly* 234 (September 9, 1988): 68.

———. "Senate Ratifies Berne Convention Treaty." *Publishers Weekly* 234 (November 4, 1988): 10.

———. "Trade Bill Veto Seen as Minor Setback in War Against Piracy." *Publishers Weekly* 234 (June 24, 1988): 16.

———. "Trade Commission Estimates $427 Million Lost to Pirates in 10 Nations Alone." *Publishers Weekly* 233 (March 11, 1988): 19.

"French View of American Copyright, A." *The Dial* 15 (September 16, 1893): 136–137.

Gosse, Edmund. "The Protection of American Literature." *The Fortnightly Review* 54 (July 1, 1890): 56–65.

Graham, Gordon. "Ten Years of Open Door." *Publishers Weekly* 233 (April 1, 1988): 22.

Hepburn, James. *The Author's Empty Purse and the Rise of the Literary Agent.* London: Oxford University Press, 1968.

Holt, Henry. "Our International Copyright Law." *The Forum* 11 (March 1891): 438–445.

———. "The Recoil of Piracy." *The Forum* 5 (March 1888): 27–46.

Hyatt, Dennis. "Legal Aspects of Public Lending Right." *Library Trends* 29 (Spring 1981): 583–595.

"International Copyright." *The Author* 3 (June 1, 1892): 6–7.

"International Copyright Act, The." *The Nation* 72 (January 31, 1901): 83–85.

Jones, Arthur. "Practical and Economic Considerations." *Library Trends* 29 (Spring 1981): 597–612.

Koch, Ole. "Situation in Countries of Continental Europe." *Library Trends* 29 (Spring 1981): 641–660.

Ladas, Stephen P. *The International Protection of Literary and Artistic Property.* Vol. 1, *International Copyright and Inter-American Copyright.* Harvard Studies in International Law Series, ed. Manley O. Hudson. New York: MacMillan, 1938.

Latman, Alan, Robert Gorman and Jane C. Ginsberg. *Copyright for the Eighties: Cases and Materials.* Second edition. Charlottesville, Virginia: The Michie Company, 1985.

Lehmann-Haupt, Hellmut. *The Book in America: A History of the Making, the Selling, and the Collecting of Books in the United States.* New York: R.R. Bowker, 1939.

Lottman, Herbert R. "Court Upholds Price-Fixing For Books in European Community." *Publishers Weekly* 234 (August 12, 1988): 321.

McClurg, Alexander C. "Justice to Authors." *The Dial: A Monthly Journal of Current Literature* 7 (May 1886): 5–9.

Madison, Charles A. *Book Publishing in America.* New York: McGraw-Hill, 1966.

Magavero, Gerard. "The History and Background of American Copyright Law; an Overview." *International Journal of Law Libraries* 6 (1978): 151–158.

Marke, Julius J. "United States Copyright Revision and Its Legislative History." *Law Library Journal* 70 (May 1977): 121–152.

Menkes, Vivienne. "A Publishing Summit: The IPA in London." *Publishers Weekly* 234 (July 22, 1988): 20–26.

Morrison, Perry D. "Situation in Canada and United States." *Library Trends* 29 (Spring 1981): 707–712.

Nasri, William Z. "Copyright." in *ALA World Encyclopedia of Library and Information Services 1985*, pp. 223–230. Chicago: American Library Association, 1986.

Nasri, William Z. "Copyright." *ALA Yearbook of Library and Information Services: A Review of Library Events 1986*, pp. 122–123. Chicago: American Library Association, 1987.

Nowell-Smith, Simon. *International Copyright Laws and the Publisher in the Reign of Queen Victoria*. Oxford: Clarendon Press, 1968.

Patry, William F. *Latman's The Copyright Law*, Sixth edition. Washington, D.C.: The Bureau of National Affairs, Inc., 1986.

"'Piratical Publishers', or a Piratical Government." *Popular Science Monthly* 22 (November 1882-April 1883): 702–704.

Pollock, Frederick. "Anglo-American Copyright." *The Contemporary Review* 59 (January-June 1891): 602–608.

"Public Laws." *Congressional Quarterly Weekly Report* 46 (December 10, 1988): 3495–3499.

Putnam, George Haven. "Fifty Years of Books: A Sketch of Book Publishing in the United States in the Half-Century Succeeding 1860." *The Nation* 101 (July 8, 1915): 62–66.

⸺. *The Question of Copyright: A Summary of the Copyright Laws at Present in Force in the Chief Countries of the World*. New York: G.P. Putman's Sons, 1891.

Rasmussen, Henning. "Situation in New Zealand and Australia." *Library Trends* 29 (Spring 1981): 697–705.

Roberts, Matt. *Copyright: A Selected Bibliography of Periodical Literature Relating to Literary Property in the United States*. Metuchen, N.J.: Scarecrow Press, 1971.

Scott, Leonard. "Piratical Publishers." *Popular Science Monthly* 22 (November 1882-April 1883): 656–659.

Shaw, Ralph R. *Literary Property in the United States*. Metuchen, N.J.: Scarecrow Press, 1950.

Solberg, Thorvald, compiler. *Copyright Enactments, 1783–1900: Library of Congress Copyright Office Bulletin No. 3*. Washington, D.C.: Government Printing Office, 1900.

Stave, Thomas. "A History of the Idea." *Library Trends* 29 (Spring 1981): 569–582.

Steinberg, S. H. *Five Hundred Years of Printing*. New York: Criterion Books, 1959.

Stern, Madeleine B. *Books and Book People in 19th Century America*. New York: R. R. Bowker, 1978.

⸺. *Publishers for Mass Entertainment in Nineteenth Century America*. Boston: G. K. Hall and Company, 1980.

"Taiwan Upholds 'Britannica'; Pirates Fined and Imprisoned." *Publishers Weekly* 234 (October 14, 1988): 22.

Taylor, Sally. "China Expands Copyright Protection to 'Compatriots' in Taiwan." *Publishers Weekly* 234 (July 22, 1988): 14.

⸺. "Copyright Protection in Asia." *Publishers Weekly* 233 (April 1, 1988): 20–21.

Tryon, W. S. "Book Distribution in Mid-Nineteenth Century America, Illustrated by the Publishing Records of Ticknor and Fields, Boston." *Papers of the Bibliographical Society of America* 41 (First Quarter 1947): 210–230.

⸺. *Parnassus Corner: A Life of James T. Fields, Publisher to the Victorians*. Boston: Houghton Mifflin, 1963.

U.S. Congress. House. Committee on the Judiciary. *Testimony Before the House Committee on the Judiciary on International Copyright*. 51st Congress, 1st Session, 8 February, 1890.

U.S. Congress. Joint Committee on Patents. *Copyright Hearing: Arguments Before the Committee on Patents of the Senate and house of Representatives, Conjointly, on the Bills S.63330. and H.R.19853. to amend and consolidate the Acts Respecting Copyright*. 59th Congress, 2nd Session, 7–11 December, 1906.

U.S. Congress. Senate Committee on Patents. *International Copyright*. 49th Congress, 1st Session, 21 and 29 January; 12 February; 11 March, 1886.

U.S. Congress. Senate Committee on Foreign Relations. *Berne Convention: Report (to accompany Treaty Doc. 99–27)*. (Senate Executive Report 100–17). 100th Congress, 2nd Session. 14 July, 1988.

U.S. International Trade Commission. *Study of the Economic Effects of Terminating the Manufactur-*

ing Clause of the Copyright Law. Washington, D.C.: United States International Trade Commission, 1983.

U.S. Library of Congress. Copyright Office. *General Guide to the Copyright Act of 1976 (September 1977).* Washington, D.C.: U.S. Library of Congress, Copyright Office, 1977.

U.S. Library of Congress. Copyright Office. *International Copyright Relations of the United States.* Washington, D.C.: Government Printing Office, 1988.

"United States Joins the Berne Copyright Convention, The." *Library of Congress Information Bulletin* 47 (November 14, 1988): 457–458.

"United States to Join Berne Convention." *Congressional Quarterly Weekly Report* 46 (October 15, 1988): 2980.

Wagner, Susan. "Copyright Issues at the Congress." *Publisher's Weekly* 234 (July 22, 1988): 22.

———. "In Search of a Publisher's Right." *Publishers Weekly* 233 (April 1, 1988): 19–25.

Wittenberg, Philip. *The Protection and Marketing of Literary Property.* New York: Julian Messner, Inc., 1937.

INVESTIGATION OF THE MOTIVATIONAL NEEDS OF CORPORATE LIBRARIANS:
A FRAMEWORK

Sohair Wastawy-Elbaz

INTRODUCTION

The main emphasis of this study was to identify the motivational needs of corporate librarians and test those needs against the hierarchy of needs set by the management and motivation theories.

The literature of information science revealed some questions regarding the personality characteristics of information professionals such as data processing personnel and system analysts. However, the personality characteristics and motivational needs of corporate librarians—as part of the information professionals—were not studied either in the information science or librarianship literature. Due to this lack of precise knowledge regarding the motivational needs of corporate librarians, it was considered an area which could be studied in depth.

Advances in Library Administration and Organization,
Volume 9, pages 105–139.
Copyright © 1991 by JAI Press, Inc.
All rights of reproduction in any form reserved.
ISBN: 1-55938-066-7

The theoretical foundation of this study involved five major management theories. These theories are: Herzberg's two factor theory, Maslow's needs hierarchy, Likert's System 1–4, Blake and Mouton's managerial grid and McGregor's theory Y and X. These theories provided a framework for defining and understanding the motivational needs.

The study focused on testing the levels of motivational needs and the effect of different variables on those needs. The main objectives of this study was to identify the motivational needs of corporate librarians and determine the strength of those needs and the effects of gender, age, education, organizational level and income variables on those needs. Also, the study sought to determine how the motivational needs of corporate librarians relate to the hierarchy of needs set by the management theorists.

Corporate libraries in the State of Massachusetts constituted the population for this study. The study presents in its conclusion a baseline description of the motivational needs of corporate librarians as well as the relationships between the motivational needs and the above mentioned variables.

THEORETICAL FOUNDATION OF THIS RESEARCH

In libraries, as in any organizational setting, managing and motivating people requires an understanding of their needs, their personality characteristics and a knowledge of what motivates them to produce to their capacity. When discussing the human needs and how these needs relate to motivation, it is necessary to bear in mind the theoretical dimensions leading to our present state of knowledge.

Basic to this understanding is the definition of motivation. Psychologists and theorists of motivation have identified motivation as a cause of behavior or a factor that helps the understanding of behavior.

After the turn of the century, we witnessed the formulation of more than 15 theories of motivation such as McDougall's Theory, Tolman's theory, Young, Allport, Lewin, Murray, Hall, Hebb and many others. Most of these theories are physiological oriented theories or learning theories of motivation. Few theories such as Murray, McClelland and Maslow made personalities their chief representatives.

The touchstone of all reflection about the hierarchy of human needs is Abraham Maslow's theory. It shows strong traces of psychoanalysis and has been the most well known to the managerial and educational psychologists, and the most used one. The need hierarchy proposed by Maslow includes the (1) physiological need, (2) safety need, (3) belongingness need, (4) esteem need, and (5) self-actualization need. These needs have a special order of precedence or domination. Once the first need is fairly well satisfied, the next level of need assumes priority (Maslow, 1970).

Maslow classifies his hierarchy as a two-level hierarchy. Needs 1 and 2 are considered lower-order needs, while 3–5 are called higher order needs. Lower needs are considered highly met for most people in the United States and other industrialized countries, but there is considerable evidence that many managers neglect the satisfaction of those lower-level needs thereby causing their subordinates to be distracted in their work by a lack of their fulfillment.

Another investigator, Frederick Herzberg, looked at the factors that motivate an individual within the organization. Herzberg's two-factor theory of motivation divides human needs into two categories. The first set of needs are called hygiene factors. The hygiene factors (almost equal to Maslow's lower needs) are associated with the job context or environment and seem to keep employees from becoming dissatisfied. These factors (organizational policy and administration interpersonal relationships with superiors, peers and subordinates, salary, job security) may cause dissatisfaction if they are absent from the work environment, but the presence of such factors will not motivate employees (Herzberg, 1969).

The hygiene factors are important and must be met in order to prevent job dissatisfaction. Herzberg explains that "hygiene factors fail to provide for positive satisfaction because they do not possess the characteristics necessary for giving an individual a sense of growth. To feel that one has grown depends on achievement in tasks that have meaning to the individual and since the hygiene factors do not relate to the task they are powerless to give such meaning to the individual" (Herzberg, 1969).

The motivational factors of Herzberg (the second set of needs) are associated with the job content. They include achievement, recognition, responsibility and advancement. The presence of these factors make individuals satisfied with their jobs and help to motivate them (Herzberg, 1969).

Although the theory has been criticized on a number of grounds and viewed by some critics as too universal, subsequent dual-factor studies have shown no clear direction of reinforcement or dismissal for Herzberg's theory (French, Metersky, Thaler, Trescler, 1973).

Motivational approaches reflect an underlying set of managerial assumptions or perceptions of the basic nature of people and their most likely response to multiple types of motivation. The best known classification of perception was furnished by Douglas McGregor in his theory X and Y. The theory X manager assumes or perceives the employee as fundamentally lazy, dislikes work, avoids responsibility and desires security as opposed to challenge. This manager believes that workers must be watched constantly, forced to work, threatened with punishment to achieve the organization goals and objectives.

Theory Y describes a different assumption based on the premise that man enjoys work and motivation comes from within, and that workers are responsible and prefer to be self-directed (McGregor, 1960). The conceptual framework of theory Y is represented by the motivation to achieve in Maslow's hierarchy as well as Herzberg's higher needs. Also, we find that the description of theory X corresponds with Herzberg's lower-needs where managers express a need to avoid pain or express higher needs for control. Although McGregor's assumptions are not in themselves leadership approaches or pursuits, they tend to exhibit a difference in motivational endeavor. Theory X managers tend to rely on disciplinary methods and penalties, where theory Y managers stress positive motivation and self-management.

The Managerial Grid Theory of Robert R. Blake and Jane S. Mouton falls into the same theoretical background, although it is viewed among management writers as an organizational tool to analyze interactions between significant variables of management.

The Managerial Grid shows managerial orientation in terms of two variables, concern for people and concern for production and cites five basic management styles. These are (1,9)-(9,1)-(1,1)-(5,5)-(9,5). The numbers indicate the strength of concern on a nine-point scale. The number 1 in each of these styles represents minimum concern. The number 5 is a middle of the road where both kinds of concerns are almost equal, and the number 9 represents maximum concern. If we take a deep look at the (1,9) management style where the management demonstrates a high concern for people and a low concern for tasks, we will find that this kind of manager falls in Maslow's hierarchy in the third stage of social needs of acceptance and belongingness is their ultimate motive. The (9,1) managers control and dominate the work environment for a greater production result and minimize concern for people which corresponds with McGregor's Theory X concept.

The third style of management is the (1,1) where the manager demonstrates minimum concern for both people and production. Unlike (1,1), contribution through commitment and caring characterizes the (5,5) management orientation where managers lean toward adequate performance and represent a combination of all concern for people and production and demonstrate a moderate need to achieve and self-esteem needs. The (9,9) theory of managing presumes an inherent connection between organization needs for production and people's needs for full rewarding experiences (Blake and Mouton, 1978).

It is clear that those characteristics of (9,9) manager correspond with Maslow's self-actualization and esteem needs, Herzberg's higher needs and McGregor's Theory Y.

Another popular theory is Rensis Likert's System IV. Likert's theory of supervision offers four management systems where organization management can range from System I "Exploitative-Authoritative" form that is characterized by the need for control and System II that is represented by the "Benevolent Authoritative" manager who also has a need for control but has little concern for people, to the "Consultative" and "Participative" form of management. In Likert's System III "Consultative," subordinates are often consulted before decisions are taken and usually motivated by desire for new experiences. In System IV management Likert emphasized the motivational forces that reinforce each other in a substantial and cumulative manner (Likert, 1967). By analyzing the motivational forces of each system of management we will see a great coherence between Likert's theory and all the above theories. For example, System IV, the participatory form of management, contains a combination of the achievement needs and concern for people of Maslow's theory, Herzberg's need for growth and McGregor's Theory Y as well as Blake and Mouton's (9,9) system.

Physiological needs, safety needs, belongingness needs, achievement, esteem needs and self actualization needs are the needs that are best known by motivation theorists. Research has shown that people of one profession have common primary motives with different strength on one need more than the other.

A knowledge of people's needs is a knowledge of their personality characteristics. Understanding what motivates corporate librarians and where the strength of their needs falls as it relates to the hierarchy of needs (as it is summarized in Figure 1) is the subject of this study.

STRUCTURE AND SCOPE OF THE RESEARCH

Study Problem and Significance

The research problem is best summarized as corporate librarians are probably motivated by various needs such as physiological needs; need for safety, protection and care; need for affection and belongingness; need for respect; and need for self-fulfillment. No research has investigated where the strength of corporate librarians' motivational needs lie and how these needs relate to the hierarchy of needs set by management and motivational theories (See Figure 1).

The significance of the study lies in its exploration into the personality characteristics of corporate librarians who are working in the profit making environment. It aims at an understanding of their motivational needs and the effect of education, age, sex, organizational level and income variables on those needs. These variables were used to analyze response to motivation measure and to characterize the sample by similarity or dissimilarity.

Because corporate librarians generally function outside formal library hierarchies, report to non-librarians and evaluated in a business-oriented, profit motivated mode, an understanding of motivational needs is very important. The results of this study should help library managers as well as corporate managers to have a clear understanding of their job environment and their employees needs; in turn, they may seek to redesign any job that lacks the necessary motivational dimension in order to promote employee satisfaction and productivity.

Objectives

The objectives of this study are:
1. To identify the need strength of corporate librarians on the hierarchy set by the motivation and management theories depicted in Figure 1.

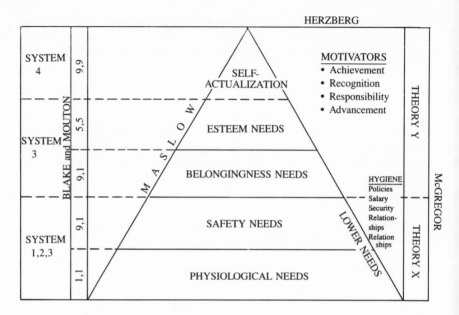

Figure 1. The Hierarchy of Needs as Depicted in the Motivation and Management Theories

2.   Compare the study variables (age, sex, education, organizational levels and income) with the motivational level of corporate librarians. Specifically, this objective will include an examination of the following:
    a. Older librarians (over 37 years old) vs. younger
       librarians (under 37 years old, based on the mean age of respondents).
    b. Females vs. males.
    c. Higher educational degrees (Ph.D. or DA) vs. basic library degrees (MLS, MS).
    d. Higher incomes ($30,000 and over) vs. lower incomes (under $30,000) based on U.S. Dept. of Labor Statistics of the median income of Massachusetts Librarians.

Hypotheses

The study is designed to test the following hypotheses:
1.   Corporate librarians have a high need for personal growth and development. They tend to score high in motivation for achievement, self actualization and concern for people and low in need for control and deterministic.
2.   There is no statistical difference (at 0.05 level of significance) between the level of motivation of:
    a. Male and female corporate librarians.

b. Manager and non-manager corporate librarians.
c. Higher and lower income corporate librarians.
d. Holders of higher degrees and holders of basic degrees corporate librarians.
e. Older and younger corporate librarians.

Operational Definitions

For the purpose of this study, the following terms are defined in the context of the study as such:

Achievement

The act of accomplishing or attaining something, a noteworthy and successful action or distinguished feat.

Behavior

A product of the combination of drives, needs, expectations and external demands and the capacities of people to deal with these forces (Levinson, 1968).

Corporation

(for profit) "A body formed by laws as a legal entity vested with powers and ability to contract, own, control, convey property and discharge business within the boundaries of the power granted" (Rosenberg, 1978).

Corporate Library

An administrative unit of an organization, owned, established and supported by a governing board legally constituted as a corporate body in the for-profit sector. Generally organized and dedicated to meet the information needs of the corporate members or staff in pursuing the goals of the organization and to satisfy a portion of their business area requirements that depends on information environment. The scope of the collection and service is limited to the subject interests of the host or parent organization. Normally collects, organizes, stores, retrieves, creates and disseminates documents and information and sometimes develops special interest packages and services for the members. Fundamentally, it is a place to have questions answered by subject specialist librarians.

Data Processing

The systematic performance of an operation or a sequence of operations upon data by one or more computer processing units to achieve a desired end result (ALA Glossary, 1983).

Growth

The process of development and advancement, and growing toward actualization of a person's potentialities and toward peak of experience (Maslow, 1970).

Information Center

An independent organization or an administrative unit of an organization which normally collects, organizes, stores, retrieves, creates and disseminates documents and information and performs such services as literature searches, compilations of bibliographies, building databases, offer reference and SDI services and training (also used as synonym for special libraries) (ALA Glossary, 1983).

Information Manager

A person who administers or manages information or an information system (ALA Glossary, 1983).

Information System

A complete system designed for the generation, collection, organization, storage, retrieval and dissemination of information within an institution, organization or other defined area of society (ALA Glossary, 1983).

Management

The act of coordinating the elements or factors of production toward the achievement of the purpose of an organization. It is the accomplishment of objectives through the use of human labor, material and machines (French and Saward, 1975).

Motivation

Processes or factors that cause people to act or behave in certain ways. To motivate is to ensure that people carry out effectively and willingly the tasks assigned to them by providing them with reasons for behaving in certain ways.

Productivity

"is a concept that expresses the relationship between the quantity of goods and services produced (output) and the quantity of labor, capital, land energy and other resources that produced it (input)" (U.S. Department of Labor, 1983).

Professional Staff or Personnel

Those staff members holding professional positions which require professional training and skill in the theoretical or scientific aspects of work in information centers as distinct from its mechanical or clerical aspects. The normal education requirements is a master's degree in library or information science or in another field (ALA Glossary, 1983).

Recognition

The formal acknowledgement of the management, organization or society to someone's efforts.

Satisfaction

The full gratification and fulfillment of desire, need or want.

Self Actualization

To realize fully one's potential, to become everything one is capable of becoming.

Self Esteem

Self confidence and satisfaction.

LITERATURE REVIEW

Effectively managing human resources has been and still is a pressing problem to all managers. But for corporate library managers, the personality and behavior of corporate librarians has been inadequately researched in the literature of library and information science, management and psychology. No empirical studies concerning corporate librarians' motivational needs was found. The reported empirical studies have focused on personnel issues related to the management of information system personnel. Part of these studies focused on individuals, others concentrated on groups and the organization. The populations addressed were Data Processing (DP) personnel, programmers, analysts and managers of information systems, with similar technical and educational backgrounds to librarian and information specialists. Daniel Couger and Robert Zawacki suggested that Information Systems (IS) professionals and managers tend to be characterized by high growth need strength and low social need in comparison with other groups of professionals. The high growth need refers to the degree to which individuals have a high need for personal advancement and development. The social need strength is the degree to which individuals wish to interact with others both on and off the job (Couger and Zawacki, 1978, 1979, 1980). C. K. Woodruff examined the possibility that IS personnel may have different personality profiles than other professionals in other fields. He utilized the Personality Research Form as a tool for twenty personality need scales. His sample included systems analysts, programmer analysts, programmers and operations personnel. The results showed that information processing employees tend to score high on need for achievement, cognitive structure, endurance, and harm avoidance (Woodruff, 1980). Elias Awad compared the preferences of programmers versus systems analysts for twenty occupational reinforcers using the Minnesota Questionnaire. His results showed that systems analysts gave higher ratings to nine reinforcers: ability, utilization, authority compensation, creativity, recognition responsibility, social status, supervision, human relations and variety (Awad, 1977).

In their study, Couger and Zawacki compared information system employees' perception of their jobs with the job perception of other professionals. They found that the lack of motivation is not restricted to IS employees only, but also true of their supervisors as well. By using the Job Diagnostic Survey (JDS), five important characteristics were found to be the lead to what is called internal motivation. These are: skill variety, task identity, task significance, task autonomy and feedback. When these conditions exist a person tends to feel good about him/herself. This, in turn, motivates the person to try to continue to do well. Internal motivations have more profound impact on these professionals more than the external ones such as incentive pay or compliments from the boss (Couger and Zawacki, 1980).

French, Metersky, Thaler and Trescler attempted to test Herzberg's theory of motivation using two different methods of data collection. Their sample contained systems analysts and systems engineers. Herzberg's two factor theory claims that basic motivational demands can be split into two categories labeled "hygienes" or "dissatisfiers" and "motivations" or "satisfiers." In the hygiene category, Herzberg identified some factors that are associated with the job context or environment and serve to keep employees from becoming dissatisfied. Herzberg considered achievement, recognition, responsibility and advancement motivators. The study of French and others supported the importance of achievement, work itself and responsibility as motivators. Company policy and administration was a significant hygiene factor. Other factors, such as advancement, growth possibilities, and working conditions were mentioned but did not clearly emerge as either motivators or hygiene factors (French, et al., 1973).

Kenneth Plate and Elizabeth Stone studied the factors that affect librarians' job satisfaction based on Herzberg's theory. The findings corresponded to those of Herzberg and indicated that the factors involved in producing job satisfaction are different from the ones that lead to dissatisfaction and the motivators are concerned primarily with the job content and the reasons for dissatisfaction found to be related to the job environment (Plate and Stone, 1974).

Along the same lines, Jac Fitz-Enz studied the job factors that were considered important by 1500 IS professionals. He found that achievement, possibility for growth, work itself, recognition, advancement needs, etc. form the most important needs for the IS professionals, which is almost identical with Herzberg's theory (Fitz-Enz, 1978).

J. H. Bryant investigated the rankings of nine job factors among IS employees in a state government agency and a utility company. The overall rankings by the sample was doing a good job, pay, satisfaction of users, satisfaction of supervisors, job security, participation in decisions, recognition, benefits and position title. Bryant divided the sample into five occupational groups and compared the ranking across all pairs of groups. Results showed that government data processing personnel evaluated job factors generally the same as personnel in a utility company. Programmers, analysts and supervisors gave similar rankings to the job factors. Computer operators rankings differed significantly from those given by analysts and supervisors. These results show that IS employees may differ in their job factors ranking according to their occupational differences (Bryant, 1976).

A recent study by Couger of maintenance personnel revealed that maintenance work tends to be demotivating to some DP personnel and it is viewed by some as an inferior, non-creative activity. This demotivating factor is considered one of the reasons for the turnover phenomenon. Turnover is a major problem for so many organizations because of the cost of replacing, hiring and training. The turnover phenomenon has been the subject of studies and discussions. According to Couger "the aura and excitement of being in a new and fast changing industry is wearing off" (Couger, 1985).

Carl Guynes believes that employees do not change their jobs without a good reason. Professional personnel, unlike other laborers, tend to stay with their organizations and need more justification for making a change. For this reasons Guynes assumed that computer personnel do change jobs frequently because they are not satisfied with their work environment (Guynes, 1979).

Another aspect of the job satisfaction problem was studied by Nathan Smith and Laura Nielsen. They attempted to test the severity of the burnout problem among corporate librarians by administering the Maslach Burnout Inventory. Results showed that corporate librarians' average scores were significantly lower in four of the six categories compared to scores derived by Maslach for other professional groups. It was also found that the greatest cause of high burnout is the librarians' feelings of no personal accomplishment followed by the inadequate positive feedback and the lack of control over the library operations (Smith and Nielsen, 1984).

Jack Baroudi examined the antecedents of job satisfaction, commitment and turnover intentions of 229 information systems personnel in the industrial field. The variables studied included: boundary spanning, role conflict and role ambiguity. A model of these variables was built and tested using path analysis. The results showed that role ambiguity is the most dysfunctional variable for IS personnel, accounting for 10.3 percent, 20.2 percent and 22.2 percent of the variance in turnover intentions, commitment and job satisfaction (Baroudi, 1985).

David Goldstein and John Rockart examined work-related correlates of job satisfaction of 118 programmer/analysts at four companies. The results indicated that both leadership variables correlated at least as highly with job satisfaction as job characteristics and that the addition of role and leadership variables to job characteristics significantly increases the explained variance in job satisfaction (Goldstein and Rockart, 1984).

Kathryn Bartol found that job satisfaction was a significant predictor or turnover among IS personnel (1979).

Cognitive style, attitude toward users and contact with them were found to be unpredictive of job satisfaction of IS personnel (Zmud and Cain, 1980).

Woodruff studied the job satisfaction levels of IS professionals using the Minnesota Satisfaction Questionnaire to evaluate employee's satisfaction with their jobs. He compared the IS personnel level of satisfaction with samples of accountants and engineers. The research results showed that IS personnel level of satisfaction was lower than their counterparts (Woodruff, 1980).

Research by Bartol examined the relative importance of two individual factors versus two organizational factors (that is, personality and professional attitudes versus professional reward system and tenure) in prediction of job satisfaction and turnover among computer professionals. Results showed that the organizational variable and professional rewards are the strongest predictor of job satisfaction (Bartol, 1979).

As mentioned, turnover continues to be a serious problem to organizations as well as to individuals. Managers fear the potential harm that can be caused by disgruntled employees. This includes malicious damage to computer programs, damage to files, and the dissemination of false information.

T. C. Willoughby estimates that annual turnover in the IS field ranged between 15 percent and 20 percent during the 1960s, declined to 5 percent in the early 1970s, and began to rise again by the end of the decade (Willoughby, 1977).

A 1979 study carried out by Datamation set the rate of IS employee turnover at about 28 percent annually. R. A. McLaughlin points out that at this rate the equivalent of half a work unit turns over every two years. This is a serious matter in a profession where it frequently takes twelve to eighteen months before a new employee makes significant work contributions (McLaughlin, 1979).

A *Computer World* study reported that 26.6 percent of IS managers interviewed have problems at their installation as a result of turnover (Dooley, Laberis, and Paul, 1981). Madeline Weiss found that the low level of social support among IS employees creates strain and stress. Social support can reduce these symptoms of strain, and, in turn, job satisfaction (Weiss, 1983).

The research on information system personnel groups is relatively small. G. J. Myers tried to evaluate the effectiveness of a group over individuals working in testing and debugging programs. By comparing the experimental group and individuals, group showed marginal effectiveness over individuals in locating more errors, but took more time per error (Myers, 1978).

On the organizational level, the role of IS managers and their type of leadership was discussed. The changing role of the chief information officer (CIO) was the research subject of Robert Benjamin, Charles Dickinson and John Rockart. The results of their survey in 25 large organizations indicated that CIO responsibility is rapidly being distributed and that the senior IS executive is emphasizing staff responsibilities and is becoming proactive in business strategy issues. The role of managers in motivating IS employees was emphasized as an emerging role for managers (Benjamin, et al., 1985).

Motivational research with IS personnel as subjects has followed a rather narrow band of rating and ranking job factors. However, the research has been generally supportive of the notion that the nature of work, achievement and growth are important job factors for data processing personnel. There has been little research on current approaches which go beyond job factors in attempting to understand the process through which people become motivated to perform.

DESIGN AND METHODOLOGY

Research Method

Based on the aim of the study which is identifying what motivates corporate librarians the survey method of research was employed to fulfill the research purposes.

The methodology as Fred Kerlinger points out has the advantage of wide scope where a great deal of information can be obtained as well as accuracy when the sample is properly drawn (1973). Herbert Goldhor adds that the survey research pattern lends itself much more readily than does the experimental approach to the study of a large number of cases, of changes which are too personal or too large to be made deliberately or within a reasonable time, and of relationships about which we are still largely ignorant (Goldhor, 1969).

Using a self-administered questionnaire is advantageous considering the other survey methods. It has some advantages over the interview in obtaining honest answers for sensitive questions that might embarrass respondents, and it maintains people's privacy.

The case for using self-administered questionnaires has been summarized by S. Sudman and M. Bradburn " . . . if the topic is threatening, more complete reporting may be obtained from self-administered rather than the interviews—where a socially desirable answer is possible on attitudinal questions there is greater tendency to conform on personal interviews than on self-administered questionnaires" (Sudman and Bradburn, 1974).

Self-administered questionnaires can be used to survey large groups of people simultaneously. Also, self-administered procedures make it possible to lower costs below those incurred by expensive face-to-face interviews.

Finally, the self-administered questionnaire can be hand delivered when there is a limited geographical dispersion among potential respondents and when the elimination of interviewing time will allow large numbers to be contacted in a short period of time. However, the success of the procedure depends on the quality of the original contacts and persistence of follow-ups.

The Study Universe

The State of Massachusetts was chosen as the geographic area for the study. The population of this study is drawn from the *Directory of Special Libraries and Information Centers*, 1987. Under the geographical location of Massachusetts the directory contains a number of units that do not meet the definition of the corporate library in the for-profit sector used in this study. Thus, various categories of entries were excluded. These include all libraries located in all educational institutions either publically or privately supported and governmental agencies, all entries headed U.S., U.S. plus the name of an agency or department, all quasi-governmental agencies, all state agencies, all religious agency units, all municipally supported units as well as professional societies and associations. Entries that contained terms that might be applied in a profit-making context, although their meaning in general usage might indicate a not-for-profit organization, were checked against the descriptive part of the same directory as well as the *Directory of Special Libraries in Boston and Vicinity* and purged unless the parent organization appeared in a directory of profit-making organizations.

This process identified 167 corporate libraries and information centers centered and supported by profit-making, mission oriented entities and they exist to serve the needs of the parent organization. This pool of libraries range in size from large research libraries offering services on a branch basis to corporate location nation and worldwide to one professional single room units.

The diversity extends to subject coverage as well as size. Libraries range in subject areas from financial and taxonomy, law, management, telecommunications and satellites to the biological, pharmaceutical and environmental and chemical engineering.

Although the geographic area is limited to one state, the diversity of such a population had an obvious appeal. Inference drawn data gave promise of being generalizable beyond the geographic area.

Sampling Technique

The purpose of the sample was to obtain the names of the organizations whose participation in the study would be sought. By using a confidence level of .50 the number of libraries identified for the study was **n = 27**. The list of libraries was arranged alphabetically and a simple random sampling process was applied. A random digit table was generated on an IBM microcomputer using STATPack software. The first 27 numbers on the table were chosen and applied against the list of libraries and information centers extracted from the directory. In addition to the 27 numbers, 5 more numbers were chosen to be used as a backup to the sample in case one of the libraries refused to participate in the study.

The Instrument

The Meta Motivation Inventory (MMI) is a self-administered measure designed to measure 32 personality dimensions which have been found to be important to personal and managerial style. These are motivation for achievement, perfection, assertiveness, independence, achievement, meta-achievement deterministic, approval, conventional, dependent, avoidance, helplessness, need for control, persuasiveness, manipulation, reactive, authoritarian, exploitative, concern for people, cooperation, affiliation, humanistic, synergy, meta-humanistic, self-actualization, stress, repression, anger, judgmental, creativity and growth potential. The four major scales, Deterministic, Motivation to achieve, Need to control others and Concern for people are each made up of the 15 items of five of the subscales.

Each of the above profiles describes special personality characteristics and each one of them is tested by a set of self-descriptive statements.

The motivation for achievement is manifested in a style of thinking which is represented by an independent striving for accomplishment of self set goals. The perfection subcategory of the achievement profile tests the amount of perfection expressed in the concern for excellence respondents have. This was exhibited in different statements to test how people express their self esteem through quality performance such as Statement 46 or 26 "one of my primary traits is persistence when the odds are against me" and the concern for details that is expressed in Statement 6 "I make long lists of things I have to do."

The subcategory, assertiveness, is the measure of an individual's drive to secure what he/she wants out of life, the determination to succeed and to achieve one's goals in spite of the obstacles encountered. Statements such as (**7.** I assert myself with hard work to get what I want) and (**27.** I don't let obstacles prevent me from accomplishing my goals) exhibit this characteristic as well as Statement 47. Independence subdimension demonstrates the individual's need for experiencing independence and uniqueness and sense of self responsibility.

This was well expressed in the self-descriptive stalemates in this category such as (**8.** I establish my own realistic goals), (**28.** I tend to be unique and independent), and (**48.** I am free to be me). People who position themselves where the responsibility for success of failure rests on their shoulders and who enjoy challenging activities and adventures are the ones described in the achievement dimension.

The meta-achievement dimension goes beyond the achievement one to describe the meta-needs of the self-actualizing process. The meta-achievement motivated people are perceived as visionaries, dreamers and idealists. They work more for satisfaction than for survival. They are dedicated to achieving the best they and the organization can produce. This was tested by the self-descriptive statements (10, 30, 50).

The deterministic profile of the inventory tests different aspects of the personality. People who tend to have deterministic personality traits believe that they have little if any control or influence over their own destiny. They believe that pleasing others and securing their approval makes them more virtuous persons and adding in their own self-interest is selfish. The five sub-categories of the deterministic dimension are approval, conventional, dependence, avoidance, and helplessness.

People who share the approval style tend to actively seek approval by consistently being friendly (**1.** I want everyone to like me). Managers who embrace approval as a predominant style may be more concerned with looking good and winning the approval of superiors and subordinates than getting the job done. (**21.** I am concerned about what other people think about me), (**41.** I find it difficult to tell people no.)

The conventional part of this dimension test is the tendency of being conventional in life's orientation. Managers who adapt this style believe that an organization should be run by the book and people need considerable structure as mandated by the rules and regulations. (See self-descriptive statements 2, 22, 42).

The dependency approach is described in statements 3, 23, 43. The primary characteristic of this style is being eager to please others. The dependent people usually worry about whether they are meeting other's expectations and often are dependent on others for advice. They tend to be uncertain, experiencing self-doubts and subsequent lack of assertiveness. Dependent managers tend to let others decide and delegate responsibility and authority.

The subdimension avoidance is the personal style of the people who indulge in avoidance behavior. The primary characteristics of this style are procrastination, lack of planning, indecisiveness and abdication of responsibility. (See 4, 24, 44.)

The last category in this dimension is helplessness. It is tested through statements 5, 25, 45. People who demonstrate this behavior tend to complain, focus on the negative, and be goalless or at least be vague about what they want.

The third dimension of this inventory is need for control, a characteristic of individuals who rely upon the authority of their position and enjoy bossing others.

Persuasiveness, manipulation, reactive, authoritarian and exploitative characteristics are the profile dimension. Persuasiveness is described in statements 11, 31 and 51. The behavior of a persuasive manager exhibits a desire to be the best in the organization and always attempt to persuade others to do the job his or her way. They usually enjoy a good argument as long as they are winning. Manipulation is a form of indirect persuasion where a person tends to use others in the work environment to get ahead or satisfy their own needs. Statements 12, 32, 52 describe this kind of behavior.

The dimension reactive is a measure of how stubborn and skeptical some people can be. People who share this style tend to be critical and fault finding, which often promotes conflict. They usually resist change and are uncooperative in their work relationships. This style is best described in Statements 13, 33, and 53.

Authoritarian is the fourth subcategory tested on the need for control dimension. It is well described in statements 14, 34 and 54. Authoritarian people are often abrupt, intimidating and critical of others as a result of a rigid, dogmatic and judgmental thinking style. As a managerial style, they accept limited input from others, make unilateral decisions and demand loyalty from their subordinates. They inhibit achievement in others which, in turn, encourages dependency and determinism in the work force.

The fifth subcategory tests in this dimension is exploitative. The exploitative personality is a combination of the manipulative and authoritarian styles. In addition to that, they tend to climb the organizational ladder without regard for the means (See Statements 15, 35 and 55).

Concern for people is the fourth main category of the Meta-Motivation inventory. It is tested through 15 self-descriptive statements that form five subcategories. These are cooperation, affiliation, humanistic, synergy and meta-humanistic.

The cooperation dimension is simply a measure of how much a person has a tendency to cooperate in joint ventures with others. This is described in Statements 16, 36 and 56.

Affiliation is the core of social relationships. It is important for the effective manager in order to build a healthy social atmosphere in the organization. This dimension is tested through Statements 17, 37, and 57.

The humanistic and meta-humanistic are tested in questions 18, 38, 58, and 20, 40, 60 respectively. Humanistic people perceive others as basically good. They are sensitive to the needs of other people and take them into account in their plans. The humanistic manager expresses confidence in subordinates' abilities and they delegate responsibility with authority to get the job done. They create a non-threatening, open-door work environment that promotes excellent communication and feedback.

Meta-humanistic is a higher level of the humanistic dimension. It is a behavior evolved with the maturation of the self-actualizing process. Synergy is the cost subcategory in the concern for people dimension. It is tested by Statements 19, 39, and 59. Synergistic managers are very effective team leaders. They like to consult with peers, subordinates and superiors in pursuit of excellence. They encourage leadership to shift from person to person in their meetings and demonstrate little need to control the session. Synergistic people tend to be intuitive and enjoy the realm of creative ideas. They usually seem free to pursue their thoughts to the end of their imagination.

The self-actualization dimension is tested by sixteen statements that constitute a compilation of all the four main dimensions of the inventory. Self-actualization is a process of significant personal growth. Self-actualizing people have a unique perspective on life. They tend to be non-defensive-defensive, feel that they have nothing to prove to others or themselves. They enjoy a secure sense of self-esteem. Balance seems to be a key factor in their personality makeup. They are equally dedicated to tasks, people and themselves.

The MMI is a useful device to provide feedback to people regarding their characteristic management and thinking style. The dimensions each scale and index assess are derived from Maslow, Herzberg, McGregor, Likert, and Blake and Mouton theories.

The Validity and Reliability of MMI
Validity

Responses from 5,000 managers who have taken MMI confirmed the original norms for all scales except the reactive scale, which measured 0.6 of a point higher than the original norm. Face validity is claimed on the merits of the clinical experience of the author, which is supported by the fact that 87 percent of the sample in the original norm study indicated that they felt the results were an accurate description of their personalities. (Walker, 1985).

The author reports that the MMI does share 12 dimensions with another well established self report inventory, and that correlations between the shared items average over .50. The Achievement Motivation dimension of MMI is significantly related to income. The Stress scale and several of the subdimensions indicated a very high correlation with responses about short and long term medical symptoms which are listed on the back of the inventory. Further, the MMI discriminates between management levels, between female managers and female non-managers, and between top and bottom sales people (Walker, 1985).

Reliability

The Meta-Motivation Inventory was subjected to a test-retest reliability study in 1980. Thirty-three educators were administered the MMI without benefit of scoring or feedback on results. Six weeks later they took the inventory again and their results were compared to the first test.

The correlations between the scores on both tests ranged from .84 to .87 with an average of .86 for the six dimensions of the inventory. These findings compare very favorably with reliability studies of other major personality inventories including the Minnesota Motivation Personality Inventory (Walker, 1985).

To test the reliability of the instrument on this environment two randomly chosen libraries were contacted and librarians agreed to fill out the questionnaire for the second time. After 21 days of receiving their first questionnaire the second questionnaire was mailed to them.

The correlations between the scores on the first and second tests for the major five dimensions were used in the study are reported as follows:

> Self-actualization **.93**
> Need for control **.97**
> Deterministic **.89**
> Motivation to achieve **.95**
> Concern for people **.97**

The average correlation for the five dimensions is **.94** which is a significant factor of reliability.

Data Collection Procedures

In April 1987, a telephone call to the director of each corporate library in the sample was made to solicit the approval of conducting the survey in their library. Library managers were asked about the number of professional librarians they have in their libraries in order to send the right number of questionnaires to the librarians.

Twenty-six library managers agreed to answer the questionnaire. Only one library manager did not approve of conducting the survey in his library. The twenty seventh library was selected randomly from the backup list, and its manager agreed to participate in the study. To avoid some of the usual problems with mail surveys, managers were given the choice of either hand-delivering the survey package or mailing it. Fourteen libraries (51.85 percent) preferred hand-delivery and thirteen libraries (48.14 percent) preferred the mail process.

Survey packages consisted of:

1. A cover letter from the researcher explaining the purpose of the survey and encouraging the librarians' cooperation and ensuring confidentiality of the response.
2. The survey instrument.
3. A handout showing the scores and profile interpretation.
4. A self-addressed, first class stamped envelope.

A code number was assigned to each library and was written on the back of the questionnaire for follow-up purposes.

The return rate in the first week was 56 percent. By the beginning of the second week the return rate reached 74 percent. Toward the end of the second week, telephone calls were made to each library that had not returned the questionnaire. The overall rate of return was twenty seven libraries, or 100 percent. Only one librarian failed to fully complete the questionnaire, therefore, that library was not included in the study.

The final sample consisted of 27 libraries. Of these, 27 library managers and 25 librarians responded for a total of 52. The returned questionnaires were coded and entered into a microcomputer for analysis using the statistical package SPSS. Hypotheses were tested using multiple regression and frequency distribution.

DATA ANALYSIS

Demographic Profile of Respondents

The population utilized in this study was corporate library managers and professional corporate librarians in the state of Massachusetts. Twenty seven libraries were seen as the needed study sample sufficient for statistical analysis and feasible in terms of resources.

The number of librarians in each library ranged from eight to one with a mean of 1.92.

Age

The median age of library managers on the one hand and the librarians on the other hand was close. The median age of library managers is 39 years with a mean of 40.5 years. The median age of librarians is 32 years with a mean of 34.8. The mean age of both groups is just above 37 years, the skew of the data indicating that a slightly larger number of library managers than of librarians is above the mean age.

These data indicated that the managers of librarians in business and industrial, for-profit environments are a "middle-aged" group. Over 52 percent of this group are over 37 years of age. Of the librarians group, 80 percent are under 37 years of age. The distribution of the sample in terms of age, however, shows considerable dissimilarity within this overall generalization. Table 1 presents the age of managers and librarians by frequency, percentage, and total numbers.

Sex

The six distribution patterns of librarians and library managers was not surprising. Women outnumber men in librarianship by a rate of approximately 5:1.

Table 1.   Age of Respondents by Frequency, Percentage
and Total Numbers

Age Span	Library Managers		Professional Librarians	
	Frequency	*Percentage*	*Frequency*	*Percentage*
Under 32	5	18.51	10	40
32–37	8	29.62	10	40
38–43	4	14.85	2	8
44–49	2	7.50	1	4
50–55	7	25.92	2	8
56–above	1	3.70	0	0
Total	27	100.00	25	100

Managerial Levels

The titles of the libraries and information center managers correspond with the name of the facility. Six units of the sample were identified as information centers (22 percent); therefore, their manager titles emphasized the orientation of function of these units. The titles of those six managers ranged among information manager, technical information manager, information director, information specialist and technical information analyst. Those bearing the title librarians or a modification thereof, library manager, supervisor, director, or head librarian totaled 78 percent of the study population. The age of managers is presented in Table 1. The distribution of library managers by sex is presented in Table 3.

The reader must bear in mind that the small number of male respondents in the study sample affects the study results.

Educational Levels

Based on the definition of professional librarian used in this study, librarians and managers who only hold library and information science degrees (the first professional degree) were asked to complete the questionnaire. None of the 52 respondents had a doctoral degree or Ph.D. in library and information science or

Table 2.   Distribution of Respondents by Sex

	Number	Percentage
Female	43	82.70
Male	9	17.30
TOTAL	52	100.00

Table 3.   Distribution of Library
Managers by Sex

		Number	Percentage
Female		21	78.0
Male		6	22.0
	Total	27	100.0

any other field, as it was assumed. All 52 librarians and managers hold MLS degrees. For this reason the education variable will not be of any value in comparing the motivational needs of librarians who hold basic or higher library degrees.

Income

The median income of special librarians in the State of Massachusetts was reported by the U.S. Department of Labor to be $29,750. This number was rounded and taken to be the variable limit. Any income falling under $30,000 was considered to be low income and any income reported over $30,000 was considered a high income. Table 4 presents the sample distribution of income.

Generalization to the Population

The sample of corporate library managers and professional librarians upon which the foregoing analyses are based are statistically representative of the population from which they are drawn. Thus, the summary of the characteristics that follow are generalized such that the population, corporate library managers, is a "middle-aged" group; nearly half of the group is between 38 and 58 years of age.

Corporate librarians fell in the lower age group where 80 percent are under 37 years of age. Seventy-eight percent of library managers are female. All libraries and information center managers have formal education in librarianship.

Table 4.   Distribution of Respondents by Income

	$30,000 and under	%	Over $30,000	%	N
All respondents	23	44	29	56	56
Managers	3	11	24	89	27
Librarians	20	80	5	20	25

None of the population tested held a doctorate degree in librarianship. The vast majority of corporate librarians hold Masters of Library and Information Science degrees.

Most of the corporate library managers (89 percent) have a yearly income over $30,000. On the contrary, 80 percent of the librarians have a yearly income of less than $30,000.

Test of Hypotheses

The advice of the statistical consultant was employed throughout the analysis of the data. The data were manipulated using the SAS program. The principal tests of significance used was student's t-test.

The hypotheses were formulated for investigation in this study. In this section, the hypotheses are restated and a discussion of findings pertinent to each is included.

Corporate librarians have a high need for personal growth and development; they tend to score high in motivation for achievement, concern for people and self-actualization, and they score low in need for control and deterministic characteristics.

Scores from the 25th to the 75th percentile represent the low to high average range with the 50th percentile the mid-point. The motivation for achievement characteristic was tested by statement numbers 6, 7, 8, 9, 26, 27, 28, 29, 46, 47 and 48 (See Appendix 1).

This characteristic or style is manifested in people who have concern for excellence in the performance of tasks. They focus on results and require continuous feedback on performance effectiveness more than recognition or achievement. They enjoy moderate risk taking and challenge. They demonstrate a considerable amount of assertiveness and independence and pursue their self-set goals in a creative, innovative style. High scores in this part of the inventory mean that these people need their work to satisfy their deepest needs.

The mean score of all participants (52 librarians and their managers) in this category is 56, which is higher than the mid-point (50).

In the subcategories of the motivation to achieve, the mean scores are as follows:

Perfection	**10.2**
Assertiveness	**12.0**
Independence	**11.7**
Achievement	**11.7**
Meta-achievement	**11.0**

The concern for people characteristic was tested through statements 16, 17, 18, 19, 20, 36, 37, 28, 39, 40, 56, 57, 59 and 60. People who shared this characteristic receive a great deal of satisfaction from interacting with other people. In a service oriented profession such as librarianship, a supportive, open, humanistic and synergistic environment is necessary.

By testing this hypothesis corporate librarians ranked high. The mean score for the concern for people category is 56.42, and on the subcategories the mean scores are:

Cooperation	**10.71**
Affiliation	**12.65**
Humanistic	**12.55**
Synergy	**11.33**
Meta-humanistic	**9.9**

Manifesting this style of behavior means that corporate librarians are motivated by a concern for others and enjoy working synergistically with people and experience deep, genuine feelings for humanity.

In the self-actualization characteristic, the mean score of the study participant is fairly high -60.21. Self-actualization is a process of significant personal growth commensurate with a deeper level of understanding of self and others. Self-actualizing people are devoted to their tasks, career or work outside of themselves. They experience a sense of mission and a significant purpose to be accomplished in life. They are dedicated to tasks, people and themselves. The mean score in this category is 60.21 on a scale of 25–85. There is no subcategory for this characteristic. Scores are divided from the four main categories of the inventory.

The need for control characteristic was tested by questions 11, 12, 13, 14, 15, 31, 32, 33, 34, 35, 51, 52, 53, 54, and 55. The mean score was a low as 36.46 as it was hypothesized. Need for control is a characteristic of individuals who feel a strong need for control in their lives. They generally are persuasive and enjoy having influence over other people. They are usually concerned with status, prestige, and material possessions to create the impression of a charismatic life style.

As it was assumed, corporate librarians have low need for control and tend not to rely upon the authority of their positions. In the need for control subcategories the study participants' mean scores are:

Persuasiveness	**8.84**
Manipulation	**7.34**
Reactive	**7.20**
Authoritarian	**7.26**
Exploitative	**5.76**

The last part of the first hypothesis is the characteristic deterministic, where people who share this style are considered conservative and prefer the status quo to rapid changes in their lives. As it was hypothesized, corporate librarians' mean scores in this part of the inventory was as low as 42. The mean scores of the subcategories are:

Approval	**10.78**
Conventional	**9.09**
Dependence	**8.59**
Avoidance	**8.55**
Helplessness	**5.30**

The scores on the subcategories range from one to fifteen. The closer to fifteen the mean score, the less favorable the characteristic of the respondents to that particular scale item, as opposed to achievement and concern for people characteristics. On the basis of these results, the first hypothesis was accepted. Figure 2 presents the results of the first hypothesis.

The second hypothesis states that there is no statistical difference between the overall level of motivation of:

a. male and female,
b. managers and non-managers,
c. higher and lower income,
d. holders of higher degrees and holders of basic degrees, and
e. older and younger corporate librarians.

As shown in Table 5, there was not a significant relationship between the motivational levels of corporate librarians and the variables stated above. The reader must bear in mind that the low significance could be due to the small sample size.

Since all of the study participants have Masters of Library Science degrees, no correlation was made between the motivational levels of corporate librarians and their educational levels. As a result of the correlations made and presented in Table 5, the relationships in the second hypothesis were also satisfied:

A. Sex—the null hypothesis was **accepted**.
B. The Organizational Level—the null hypothesis was **accepted**.
C. Income—the null hypothesis was **accepted**.
D. Level of Education—the null hypothesis was not **tested**.
E. Age—the null hypothesis was **accepted**.

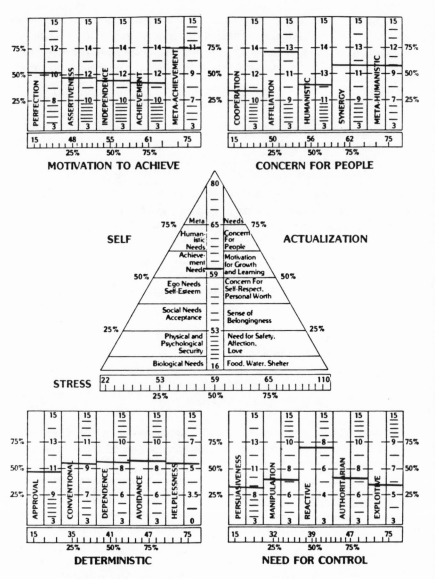

Reprinted by permission from John A. Walker, *Meta Motivation Inventory,* Meta Visions: Plymouth, Michigan, 1979. p. 53.

Figure 2.

130

Table 5. Means, Standard Deviations and t-tests
on Overall Level of Motivation

Group	n	Mean	S.D.	t	Significance
Males	9	255.4	25.5	1.07	n.s.
Females	43	247.6	18.9		
Managers	27	249.4	23.2	0.23	n.s.
Non-Managers	25	248.1	16.6		
High Income	29	251.6	22.6	1.02	n.s.
Low Income	23	245.9	16.7		
Under 37 (age)	31	251.8	18.6	1.21	n.s.
Over 37 (age)	21	245.0	22.3		

SUMMARY, FINDINGS, CONCLUSIONS AND RECOMMENDATIONS

Summary

The main objective of this study was to identify the motivational needs of corporate librarians and to test those needs against the hierarchy of needs depicted in various management and motivational theories. The related library and information science literature have revealed some questions regarding the personality characteristics of some groups in the information science profession such as, data processing personnel, programmers, and systems analysts. However, the corporate librarians were not included in any of the reviewed studies.

The theoretical foundations of this study involved five major management theories. These theories are Herzberg's Two-Factor Theory, Maslow's Needs Hierarchy, Likert's System 1–4 Theory, Blake and Mouton's Managerial Grid, and McGregor's Theory X and Theory Y. These five theories provided a framework for defining and understanding the hierarchy of needs.

All of the five theories agreed that human needs somehow follow an order (hierarchy) starting at the level of basic needs to the self-actualization need. However, every level of those needs does not have to be satisfied 100 percent before the next level of the hierarchy emerges. Maslow alludes to this fact by stating "a more realistic description of the hierarchy would be in terms of decreasing percentages of satisfaction as we go up the hierarchy of prepotency" (Maslow, 1970).

The study focused on testing these levels of motivational needs and the effect of different variables on those needs. Figure 3 shows the scores of the respondents in accordance with the management theories.

Management Systems Profile

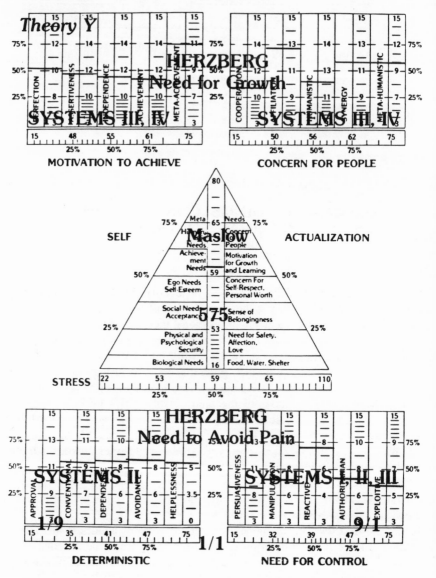

Reprinted by permission from John A. Walker, *Meta Motivation Inventory,* Meta Visions: Plymouth, Michigan, 1979. p. 47.

Figure 3.

132

Statement of the Problem

The purpose, then, of this study was to identify the motivational needs of corporate librarians and determine the strength of those needs and the effect of a group of variables on them. Also, this study sought to determine how the motivational needs of corporate libraries relate to the hierarchy of needs set by the management theories.

The instrument, along with a cover letter and a handout for background information on the profiles and the interpretation of the scores, was addressed to the respondents. Respondents were requested to react to each item on MMI by citing a number that indicates their self-description, such as: (1) almost never like me; (2) seldom like me; (3) sometimes like me; (4) often like me; (5) almost always like me.

Corporate libraries in the State of Massachusetts constituted the population for this study. A random selection of 27 libraries met the minimal criteria for a sample, for there were 27 responses from 27 corporate library managers and 25 librarians.

Collection of the Data

The first mailing and hand-delivering of the instrument brought a return of approximately 75 percent. A follow-up telephone call was made to those who had not responded. The instrument was coded so that the researcher could identify the corporate names who responded. The overall return was 100 percent.

Treatment of the Data

A demographic profile was constructed which included background information for all respondents. Differences between scores of managers and non-managers, male and female, high income and low income, old and young corporate librarians, were analyzed by using paired t-tests. All data were summarized to acquire means, standard deviations, correlations, frequency and percentage.

FINDINGS AND CONCLUSIONS

This section will present the findings and conclusions from the analysis of data resulting from this study. A *finding* is specific information derived from the data-gathering procedures. A *conclusion* is a judgmental statement supported by the data. The findings of this research present a baseline description of the motivational needs of corporate librarians.

The conclusions will be divided into several categories. There will be conclusions dealing with: (1) the demographic data, (2) the motivational needs of corporate librarians, (3) the relationships between the motivational levels and several variables such as age, sex, income and organizational levels of the respondents.

Demographic Data

Analysis of the demographic data brought these findings:

1. All corporate library managers had master's degrees in library and information science.
2. The average age of library managers was over 40.
3. The average age of librarians was 37.
4. Fifty-two percent of library managers were over 37 years of age.
5. ighty percent of librarians were under 37 years age.
6. Seventy-eight percent of library managers were female; twenty-two percent were male.
7. Forty-four percent of all respondents had income under $30,000 a year, and fifty-six percent had income over $30,000 a year.

A conclusion is that corporate library managers and librarians in Massachusetts are predominantly female and the managerial positions in the field of corporate librarianship is not a "male" occupation since 78 percent of the randomly selected libraries in this study were managed by females.

A second conclusion is that corporations are becoming aware that advanced degrees (MLS) are needed for any library manager because 100 percent of the library managers had master's degrees in library and information science.

A finding is that the motivational needs of corporate librarians fit the theoretical frameword set by the management theories depicted in Figure 1.

Assuming that the physiological needs of most individuals in industrialized countries are met, there were no questions concerning these needs. Corporate librarians ranked low in the second stage of the hierarchy (mean 49.7), higher on the third level of needs (56.4) and scored almost the same on the fourth level (56.3) and higher on the fifth level of self-actualization (60.2). Figure 3 illustrates these levels within the theoretical framework.

The conclusion about this find is that corporate librarians are motivated by achievement, concern for people and self-fulfillment. These are the primary needs of corporate librarians.

Although workers are motivated by different needs at different times, and those needs follow the hierarchy from lower order to higher order needs, managers should evaluate where their workers are on the depicted hierarchy of needs and adjust rewards accordingly. In order to build a healthy work environment, motivators must be perceived by the subordinates as a motivator. If librarians are striving to achieve and to be self-fulfilled, a challenging and reachable task should be assigned to help them, taking into consideration that a satisfied need is not a motivator, and lower needs must be satisfied before the higher level needs become motivators.

The data showed that age is not a factor in placing a priority on needs. Young librarians have a priority on higher needs as much as older librarians.

Age, income, sex and organizational levels may not have any significant effect on motivational needs of corporate librarians.

Corporate librarians have the highest need for self-fulfillment and growth and a low need for control.

The low scores in the need for control dimension showed low managerial abilities. A modest amount of persuasiveness is of value, the deficiency on this dimension could be increased through training and education.

Library managers should assess their employee motivational needs and re-structure some jobs to improve their motivating potential if necessary. In the dynamic business and industry field, reassessment of employee motivational needs and perceptions should be made no less than every two years. With a 25 percent turnover in the field of information, new employee populations come to work every four years. Periodic use of a diagnostic instrument keeps manage-ment informed of the degree of match between each job's motivating potential and the incumbent's need for growth.

The library and information industry has placed a great emphasis on keeping pace with the new technologies. To enable the information professionals to keep pace with the technological improvements, equal concern needs to be placed on the motivational environment. Improving the working environment is an en-hancement to productivity and employee satisfaction; it puts into play a number of mutually beneficial forces.

RECOMMENDATIONS FOR FURTHER RESEARCH

The findings of this study identify a number of areas that can profit from further research. One of the major areas relating to motivation is job satisfaction, which has been the subject of professional concern for a number of years. Although job satisfaction was not the subject of this research, the present study has delineated certain parameters of the motivational needs of corporate librarians in its descrip-tion of the study participants scores.

Future research into the subject of the motivational needs of the business and industrial libraries is needed to further define the levels of motivation in a substantive way.

The present study identified a few variables; more variables should be em-ployed in future studies. The data available did not permit any interpretation of the relationship between the educational levels and the levels of motivation.

The study identified a group within the sample of business and industrial librarians whose titles were different than the rest of the group studied. Also, the name of the facility was different or mixed, such as library or information center. The group exhibiting these characteristics in the for-profit environment should form the population sampled in a future study.

The motivational needs should be explored in greater depth and detail in view of the findings of this study that indicated that these motivational needs were not associated with the management technique in the work situation.

In recommending future research in the area of motivation, the researcher is conscious of the fact that motivation research in librarianship had not reached the point where general statements could be made. More complex variables need to be developed to address the complex relationship between the librarians needs and their work places. More sophisticated techniques to refine responses need to be developed. The population to be sampled needs to be larger or nationwide. In many respects motivation research, a developing field in librarianship, is challenging. More research is needed to develop this ground work and to establish a theoretical base for the motivational needs of corporate librarians and information professionals.

Finally, the research presented here is the first study of the motivational needs of corporate librarians based on actual data that addressed their needs. The major contribution of the study is the demonstration of strength of corporate librarians needs.

Like any baseline, exploratory study, the research presented here has raised more questions than it has answered. The identification of the motivational needs was in itself an objective of this research in addition to providing a foundation from which to assess the job dimensions in corporate libraries to contain all the necessary motivational forces. The research will have value insofar as it contributes to the knowledge of motivation in librarianship.

The present study, by broadening the context in which the motivational needs of corporate librarians are addressed, has implications for the discussion of library management and the corporate productivity and, in turn, profitability. If the study contributes to the achievement of an enriched understanding of the motivational needs of corporate librarians, it will have achieved its purpose.

APPENDIX 1

Meta Motivation Inventory

1. I want everyone to like me.
2. I am uncomfortable with changes.
3. I feel that pleasing others is more important than pleasing myself.
4. I face the same problems weekly.
5. Sometimes I just can't cope.
6. I make long lists of things I have to do.
7. I assert myself with hard work to get what I want.

8. I establish my own realistic goals in life.
9. I enjoy challenges that require full use of my ability.
10. I work for satisfaction more than survival.
11. I am a very persuasive person.
12. I am good at getting others to do what I want.
13. I don't like to be told what to do under any circumstances.
14. I believe in running things myself and making people do the right job.
15. I feel a need to tell people what to do for their own best self-interest.
16. People describe me as cooperative and easy to get along with.
17. I feel warm interpersonal relationships are more important than things.
18. Helping others grow and develop makes me feel good and is worth the effort.
19. Other people stimulate creative ideas in me.
20. I treat everyone the same whether they are six or sixty.
21. I am concerned about what other people think of me.
22. I like to do things by the book.
23. Something always keeps me from achieving my goals.
24. I wish I were more certain about things in my life.
25. I am afraid I won't get what I want in life.
26. One of my primary traits is persistence when the odds are against me.
27. I don't let obstacles prevent me from accomplishing my goals.
28. I tend to be unique and independent.
29. I get bored with routine tasks and reach out for new adventures.
30. I sense there is a significant mission I must complete in my lifetime.
31. I enjoy having influence over others.
32. I take advantage of every opportunity with people to meet my needs.
33. People in authority often don't know what they're doing and impede my growth.
34. I have little confidence in most people and think they need direction.
35. I don't care if people like me, as long as they respect me and do what I want.
36. I am considered tactful and diplomatic.
37. I like to be around children—they're fun.
38. People often come to me for advice and assistance.
39. I find that differing with others often produces better ideas.
40. I need to help others to help myself.
41. I find it difficult to tell people no.
42. I believe in a "proper" upbringing of children.
43. I often ask people for advice.
44. I tend to procrastinate a lot.
45. Fear tends to overwhelm me.
46. Sometimes I feel driven to be successful.
47. I am dedicated and ambitious.

48. I am free to be me.
49. I often take calculated risks in life.
50. I live my dreams.
51. I believe winning makes you a winner.
52. Sometimes I think it's fun to cheat if no one gets hurt.
53. I don't trust many people.
54. I believe it is necessary to be tough and aggressive.
55. I think using people is often justified.
56. At times I compromise to get along with others.
57. I enjoy meeting and interacting with new people.
58. I believe people are basically good.
59. I produce better results working with others than
    working alone.
60. I often see pain in strangers' faces and feel a compulsion to help.

Reprinted by Permission from John A. Walker, *Meta Motivation Inventory*, Meta Visions: Plymouth, Michigan, 1979.

REFERENCES

The ALA Glossary of Library and Information Science. Chicago: American Library Association, 1983.

Awad, Elias M. "Job Satisfaction as a Predictor of Tenure." *Computer Personnel* 7 (Autumn 1977): 7–10.

Baroudi, Jack C. "The Impact of Role Variables on IS Personal Work Attitudes and Intentions." *MIS Quarterly* 9 (December 1985): 341–356.

Bartol, Kathryn M. "Individual Versus Organizational Predictors of Job Satisfaction and Turnover Among Professionals." *Journal of Vocational Behavior* 15 (August 1979): 55–67.

Bartol, Kathryn M. *Turnover Among DP Personnel: A Causal Analysis*, University of Maryland Working Paper, College Park, Maryland, 1981.

Benjamin, Robert; Dickinson, Charles Jr., and Rockart, John F. "The Changing Role of the Corporate Information Officer." *MIS Quarterly* 9 (September 1985): 177–188.

Blake, Robert and Mouton, Jane. *The New Managerial Grid*. Houston: Gulf Publishing Company, 1978.

Bryant, J. H. "Survey of Values and Sources of Dissatisfaction." *Data Management* 14 (February 1976): 34–37.

Couger, J. Daniel and Zawacki, Robert A. "What Motivates DP Professionals?" *Datamation* 24 (September 1978): 116–123.

Couger, J. Daniel and Zawacki, Robert A. "Compensation Preferences of DP Professionals." *Datamation* 24 (November 1978): 96–102.

Couger, J. Daniel and Zawacki, Robert A. "Something's Very Wrong With DP Operations Jobs." *Datamation* 25 (March 1979): 149–158.

Couger, J. Daniel; Zawacki, Robert A. and Opperman, Edward. "Motivation Level MIS Managers Versus Those of Their Employees." *MIS Quarterly* 3 (September 1979): 49–56.

Couger, J. Daniel and Zawacki, Robert A. Motivating and Managing Computer Personnel. New York: Wiley Publishing, 1980.

Couger, J. Daniel. "Motivating Maintenance Personnel." *Computer World* 19 (August 12, 1985): 5–14.

Directory of Special Libraries and Information Centers. 9th ed. Edited by Brigitte T. Darnay. Detroit, Michigan: Gale Research Company, 1987.

Dooley, Ann; Laberis, Biss and Paul, Lois. "Staff Turnover, No Problem: Surveyed Managers Report." *Computer World* 15 (February 23, 1981): 1–4.

Fitz-Enz, Jac. "Who is the DP Professionals?" *Datamation* 24 (September 1978): 125–128.

French, Derek and Saward, Heather. *Dictionary of Management.* New York: International Publication Services, 1975. p. 247.

French, E. B.; Metersky, M. L.; Thaler, D. S. and Trescler, S. T. "Herzberg's Two Factor Theory: Consistence Versus Method Dependency." *Personnel Psychology* 26 (Autumn 1973): 369–375.

Goldhor, Herbert. *An Introduction to Scientific Research in Librarianship.* Urbana, IL: University of Illinois, 1969.

Goldstein, David K. and Rockart, John F. "An Examination of Work Related Correlates of Job Satisfaction in Programmer Analysts." *MIS Quarterly* 8 (June 1984): 103–115.

Guynes, Carl Stephen. "The Care and Management of EDP Specialists." *Personnel Journal* 58 (October 1979): 703–706.

Herzberg, F. *Work and The Nature of Man.* Cleveland, Ohio: World Publishing, 1966.

Kerlinger, Fred N. *Foundations of Behavioral Research.* New Jersey: Holt, Rinehart and Winston, 1973.

Levinson, Harry. *The Exceptional Executive.* Cambridge: Harvard University Press, 1968.

Likert, Rensis. *New Patterns of Management.* New York: McGraw-Hill, 1961.

Maslow, Abraham H. *Motivation and Personality.* 2nd Edition. New York: Harper & Row Publishers, 1970.

McGregor, Douglas. *The Human Side of Enterprise.* New York: McGraw-Hill, 1960.

McLaughlin, R.A. "The Old Bugaboo Turnover." *Automation* 25 (October 1979): 97–101.

Myers, G. J. "A Controlled Experiment in Program Testing and Code Walkthrough Inspection." *Communication of the ACM* 21 (September 1978): 760–768.

Plate, Kenneth H. and Stone, Elizabeth W. "Factors Affecting Librarians' Job Satisfactor: A Report of Two Studies." *Library Quarterly* 44 (April 1974): 97–110.

Rosenberg, Jerry. *Dictionary of Business Management.* New York: John Wiley and Sons, 1978, p. 107.

Smith, Nathan M. and Nielsen, Laura F. "Burnout: A Survey of Corporate Librarians." *Special Libraries* 75 (July 1984): 221–227.

Sudman, S. and Bradburn, M. *Response Effect in Surveys: A Review and Synthesis.* Chicago: Aldine Publishing, 1974, p. 66.

U. S. Department of Labor. *Occupational Outlook Handbook.* Washington, DC: Government Printing Office, 1986.

U. S. Department of Labor. Bureau of Labor Statistics. *Productivity and the Economy: A Chartbook.* Washington, DC: Government Printing Office, June 1983.

U. S. Department of the Treasury, Internal Revenue Service. *Cumulative List of Organizations Described in Section 170 of the Internal Revenue Code of 1954.* Washington, DC: Government Printing Office, 1983.

Walker, J. A. "The Motivation Inventory: Administration, Validation and Reliability." Plymouth, Michigan: Meta Visions, [1985].

Weiss, Madeline. "Effect of Work Stress and Social Support of Information Systems Managers." *MIS Quarterly* 7 (March 1983): 29–43.

Willoughby, T. C. "Computing Personnel Turnover." *Computer Personnel* 7 (Autumn 1977): 11–13.

Woodruff, C. K. "Data Processing People Are They Satisfied/Dissatisfied with Their Jobs?" *Information and Management* 3 (December 1980): 219–225.

Zmud, R. W. and Cain, D. D. "Conceptual Framework and System Analyst Job-Fit. *Computer Personnel* 8 (December 1980): 3–6.

LIBRARIES, TECHNOLOGY, AND ACCESS:

THE STATEWIDE AUTOMATION PLANNING PROCESS IN NEW YORK

Frederick E. Smith and George E. J. Messmer

Library resources sharing in New York State formally began 35 years ago with the organization of libraries into systems. There are now three types of systems which cover the entire State and include all types of libraries. The systems provide the means by which library resources are made available to all residents in the State. These systems, and the New York State Library, have a long-standing commitment to the use of technology to improve services, increase efficiency, and constrain cost increases.

The origins of the first statewide plan for library automation are found in the New York State Governor's Conference on Libraries held in 1978. As one of the many outgrowths of the Governor's Conference, a Committee on Statewide Library Development was appointed by the Commissioner of Education in 1980. The Committee was charged with preparing recommendations for State policy

Advances in Library Administration and Organization,
Volume 9, pages 141–164.
Copyright © 1991 by JAI Press, Inc.
All rights of reproduction in any form reserved.
ISBN: 1-55938-066-7

regarding services, financial support, use of technology, and governance in the light of library needs and resources during the next decade. In 1981, the Committee submitted its report entitled *Meeting Information Needs of the 80's: Report of the Commissioner's Committee on Statewide Library Development*. This report, commonly known as the Commissioner's Committee Report, grouped its recommendations into seven categories, one of which was automation. The first recommendation in the automation category was: "The State Library should develop and implement a statewide plan for library automation in consultation with the library community." This was the foundation for a process which eventually resulted in a statewide automation plan for the libraries of New York.

The next step of that process also took place in 1981, actually at the same time that the Commissioner's Committee Report was being developed and issued. In anticipation of the recommendation that a statewide automation plan be developed, the State Library prepared and circulated within the library community a draft *Library Automation Plan for New York State*. After discussions with the field, an outside consultant was engaged to work with a State Library staff committee to revise and expand upon this draft plan. Based upon this work, the State Library issued a new draft plan titled *A Library Automation Plan for New York State: 1984*. To obtain responses to this draft, the State Library's Division of Library Development held a statewide hearing later that year and also requested written input both to support statements made at the hearing and to give those who were not able to testify at the hearing the opportunity to express their points of view.

There were three primary results generated by the 1984 draft plan and responses to it. First, the basic premise of the plan—that statewide library automation be developed according to a three-part program—was accepted. Second, it became clear that the best approach to developing a final plan would be to appoint a statewide automation committee from among the librarians of the State. Third, this plan provided the basis for the 1984 legislation which created the funding for the statewide automation program.

Based upon the 1984 draft plan, the Board of Regents of the State Education Department adopted in 1986 the following three-part program for automation: (1) Continued development of the statewide database; (2) A distributed network of linked systems encompassing all of the bibliographic records in the State converted into machine-readable form; and (3) A strong and formal automation consulting capability within the State Library. Later that year, the Director of the State Library's Division of Library Development appointed a 16-member Statewide Automation Committee broadly representative of automation concerns in all types and sizes of libraries. The Committee was asked to develop a plan for accomplishing the Regents automation program.

STATEWIDE AUTOMATION COMMITTEE

The Statewide Automation Committee met seven times over the course of a year. Working within the three-part program just described, questions were developed at the outset by Library Development staff as a starting point for addressing issues involved with the database, linking, and consulting and training. After initial discussion of these questions by the entire Committee, three subcommittees were appointed to examine these questions in more detail, to develop a set of recommendations for each of these three areas, and to report back to the full committee.

Many issues were discussed first by the subcommittees and then by the entire committee. Some were typical of other statewide library issues and were, therefore, not unique to automation. These included the ongoing questions about funding for upstate versus downstate, the relative merits of funding for different types of libraries, and state level versus regional or system level authority. The automation issues discussed most extensively by the Statewide Automation Committee and the decisions made about these issues are as follows:

1. Should the goal of database development be the conversion of 100 percent of the records in the State? The Committee decided that comprehensive conversion of all library records in the State should not be established as a goal in the Statewide Automation Plan, but no other percentage was agreed upon as the goal which should be met for records to be converted. Instead, it was decided that it would be better to leave this as a question to be answered sometime in the future with the determining factor being the percentage of records that need to be converted for the libraries of the State to reach a level of satisfaction in terms of meeting their resource sharing needs. When that satisfaction level is achieved, the percentage of the database to be converted will have been determined.

2. Should the emphasis of funding shift from conversion to access projects? Similar to its decision about #1, the Committee decided that this issue could not be resolved in the report but only over the passage of time.

3. Should the database be distributed on multiple computers or centralized on one or just a few computers? The recommendation made in the 1984 draft plan that the statewide database be decentralized rather than monolithic was affirmed by the Committee.

4. Are unique records or holdings more important to the database? It was decided that unique records and holdings serve different purposes that are of equal value. Therefore, both are needed.

5. Must materials for which records are converted be accessible to library users or should records be converted because knowledge that materials exist and about where they are located is important even if there is little or no access to them? After considerable debate, the Committee emphatically decided that mate-

rials represented in databases by records converted with State funding must be accessible to library users.

6.   Should there be performance standards for lending libraries responding to interlibrary loan requests if the records for the requested materials have been converted using State funding? The decision was that there should be suggested performance standards for this purpose.

7.   Should State funding be provided for the maintenance of the database? The Committee agreed that the cost of database maintenance must be the responsibility of local funding.

8.   Should there be challenge grants provided in order to make the records of uncataloged collections available in machine readable form? It was decided that such grants should not be provided because there are too many other priorities for funding.

9.   Should the Committee adopt the recommendation included in the 1984 plan that there be a central index to facilitate access to library records stored on computers located throughout the State or should it recommend that linkages be established among these computers? The Committee decided in favor of linkages since there were major questions as to how a central index would be implemented and since future technology is moving in the direction of linkages.

After resolving these and other issues, a draft plan listing 17 recommendations was prepared and distributed to libraries and library systems throughout the State. Three hearings were held to enable librarians and other interested parties to respond to the draft. The primary issues raised in the hearings and the way in which the Committee dealt with them are as follows:

1.   Several responses to the draft plan took issue with a statement that said that State monies could not be expected to fund all library automation and that local funding would also be needed for this purpose. Why should this be the case when dramatically higher levels of funding are provided for the public schools than for libraries even though both fall under the jurisdiction of the State Education Department? Although the Committee thought that the realities of State funding required that the essence of the original statement remain in the plan, it did place increased funding for libraries as the first of eight priorities.

2.   In the recommendation dealing with access to materials, what was meant by "qualified users"? Might this terminology exclude anyone from using materials represented in a database by records converted with State funding? The Committee responded to this issue by deleting the reference to "qualified users" from the report.

3.   Also in the access recommendation, particularly the part discussing suggested performance standards for lending libraries, questions were raised about the statement, "Performance standards are suggested as inclusionary, not exclusionary, with the state supporting efforts by libraries to meet them." What did this

mean and should it remain in the report? The Committee decided to leave this statement in the report because it thought it was important to convey the message that libraries would not be excluded from receiving future funding if they could not meet the suggested performance standards due to inadequate resources, although it was recognized that it would be difficult to provide State funding to enable libraries to meet the standards.

4. Wasn't the lack of mention of CD-ROM technology in the draft plan a serious omission? The Committee agreed and included a recommendation about the importance of CD-ROM in the final plan (Compact Disk-Read Only Memory).

5. Should the report recommend providing State monies for linkages between and among computer systems since a high percentage of the materials needed by libraries could be obtained without this expensive technology? The Committee decided that the linkage recommendations must remain in the report because they are important to realizing the ultimate goal of access to all library records in the State by any library user.

6. Shouldn't more public funding be put toward mechanisms that would increase the circulation of materials from individual libraries than toward the sharing of resources among libraries? Since the objective of the plan was automation on a statewide basis, the Committee decided that the thrust must continue to be resource sharing.

7. There was criticism that the plan was too philosophical and not sufficiently detailed. The Committee agreed and responded with the determination that this document should be the strategic part of the Statewide Automation Plan and that a second Statewide Automation Committee and three task forces should be appointed to develop an operational plan. The goal of the operational part of the Statewide Automation Plan would be to determine how the strategic recommendations should be implemented.

LIBRARIES AND TECHNOLOGY

Based upon extensive work and after reviewing substantial input from the field, the Statewide Automation Committee issued a plan in May, 1987, under the title of *Libraries and Technology: A Strategic Plan for the Use of Advanced Technologies for Library Resource Sharing in New York State*. The 20 strategic recommendations included in *Libraries and Technology* are organized into four broad categories: General, Database, Linking, and Consulting and Training. The recommendations as they are stated in the document are as follows:

General Recommendations

1. In order to ensure that the strategic goals of this plan are met, an operational plan with estimated costs of implementation shall be developed

by a Committee with Library Development Division staff, appropriate consultant help and the participation of other relevant state-level agencies.

This planning document can provide immediate guidance for ongoing regional and local automation efforts while an operational plan is being developed at the state level. The Phase II Committee will include some members of this Statewide Automation Committee, which now has concluded its work, and others who will convert philosophic and strategic goals into specific operational steps.

2. The Library Development Division, a Library Telecommunications Task Force and other library leaders must participate in the development of a state-financed or state-assisted telecommunications network, assuming a leadership role, so the State's libraries can effectively participate in and take full advantage of such development.

State-financed, state-assisted telecommunications programs are vital to accomplish this plan. There are numerous players, many of whom do not yet recognize library interests in these developments. It is essential that the library community be involved in forums in which telecommunications policies and plans are being developed—resulting in a higher profile for library interests. A Library Telecommunications Task Force will undertake the important ongoing work in the area of telecommunications that is vital to the linking recommendations.

3. The Library Development Division should convene a committee biennially to review administration and technological progress on the statewide automation plan and recommend updating and revision.

The Committee emphasizes that the dynamic and rapid pace of current technological change quickly renders planning documents obsolete. At the same time, the administrative infrastructure required to accomplish key recommendations usually matures more slowly. A mandated review every two years recognizes the dichotomy and therefore the need to monitor commitment and fine tune priories in any statewide plan for automation for libraries.

Database Recommendations

A machine-readable database encompassing bibliographic, holdings, and related information on the contents of more than 7,700 libraries is a massive undertaking. The concept raises fundamental questions of definition, scope, priorities, use and cost. For the continued development of the database, the Committee makes five basic recommendations.

4. For purposes of library automation planning, the statewide database is defined as the aggregate of machine-readable records describing and locating materials in all physical data storage media and formats in New York institutions and support files. While issues of records ownership may affect database integration and linkage, the State goal is to facilitate global and inclusive access to the totality of such records.

The term "statewide database" constitutes a basic building block of the state-wide automation plan. The database comprises:

a. bibliographic information describing collections in institutions in the state, including all physical data storage media (e.g., videotape), and formats, including CONSER (serials);
b. holdings statements providing location data for discrete titles;
c. ancillary data essential for database maintenance and use, such as name authority files or name and address directories;
d. community and data referral information files created by libraries or library agencies.

The database is closely related to commercially produced secondary sources such as abstracting, indexing, and numeric databases to which referral access is purchased by libraries. These databases, when searched, generate requests for materials found in the statewide database for direct on-site access or interlibrary loan.

Every unique record in the statewide database is supported by at least one holding record. The database exists within the context of the international database as follows: library system; region of the state; New York State; contiguous states; United States; international.

5. Leadership in statewide database investment decisions should be provided by the Library Development Division, even though the program is in large part regionally administered. The Library Development Division and the regions should be guided by the priorities recommended in this automation plan.

The major role the regions play in determining priorities that reflect different regional needs is endorsed. It is an effective means of keeping all libraries, large and small, public, academic, special and school, interested and actively participating in the State's automation program. The Library Development Division's leadership role, the priorities recommended in this plan, and increased use of appraisal procedures at the regional level can mediate competing interests and ensure the feasibility of accomplishing the goals within the available funds.

6. Continued statewide database development efforts should give high priority to ensuring the inclusion of a reasonable balance of unique items, scarce items, ubiquitous items and high demand items within the statewide database.

Unique, scarce, and ubiquitous items are defined in terms of distribution, location, and search expectations: a unique item would be represented by one record in the state in all sources, and fewer than two holdings; a scarce item, less than three records in different sources and fewer than ten holdings; ubiquitous items, more than two records in different sources and more than ten holdings in the state. High demand items may be unique, scarce, or ubiquitous.

7. The criteria which define reasonable balance include the likelihood of

use of materials represented in the database both locally and for interlibrary loan, the value to the State's program of economic development, the contribution to research and scholarship in all disciplines, and the numbers of users in all types of libraries served by the database.

While development efforts incorporate the four components of bibliographic records, holdings statements, ancillary data, and information and referral files, funding decisions about the database will be governed by the usefulness of the database, with priority given to user needs. That is, reasonable balance is an attribute that should pertain to the material listed in the database.

Appraisal criteria and procedures which should be used by the region and the State to assess the likelihood of potential use of statewide resources will be developed by a Criteria Task Force to be used as a part of fund application assessment and in planning.

8.   Institutions that use public funds for database development must ensure ongoing commitment from local funds for entry of current materials, ensure continuing maintenance and security of the database, and provide access to the materials listed in the database within defined performance standards.

The State's financial assistance for development of the database is intended to facilitate resource sharing and public access to information. Acceptance of public funds by an institution therefore carries a responsibility for maintaining and securing the database and for providing access both to the database and to the materials listed in the database.

Performance standards are suggested as an integral program component of database development investment decisions. The suggested standard or guideline is for a respondent agency to be required to transmit a response to each request within two working days of receipt of the request, with the "standard" met 95 percent of the time for 95 percent of responses. "Transmit" may include a paper response as well as electronic transmission. Performance standards are suggested as inclusionary, not exclusionary, with the state supporting efforts by libraries to meet them.

Access to listed materials, either direct or through some form of resource sharing, is also important. Meeting the legislative and program objectives of the program requires that the public will have access to such converted materials in accord with reasonable conditions established by owning institutions and approved by Library Development Division and/or regional surrogates for such access.

Linking Recommendations

The linking of computer systems to communicate and exchange information with other computer systems and system components is basic to this plan. Linking mechanisms, standards and issues are under discussion at local, state and national levels. The "Linked Systems Project" of the Library of Congress, the Research Libraries Group, OCLC, and Western Library Network (WLN), and funded by the Council on Library Resources, should prove helpful to New York State. Linking will be made possible through national efforts and collaboration with vendors. The ultimate resolution will be in large part driven by forces outside New York State.

To capitalize on national developments in achieving this plan, the State Library, with the assistance of a state-level committee and technical advisors, should work closely with other state and national efforts and commercial vendors to ensure that communications standards and library applications software provide (1) the widest possible database access to the State's citizenry, (2) compatibility and transportability of the output from library applications software, and (3) electronic linkage with related public and commercial resources that would enhance the breadth of automated resources available. The Committee makes five basic recommendations for linking.

9.   The Library Development Division should constitute a Linkage Standards Task Force including representation of libraries in the State and technical advisers to recommend standards and specifications for enabling computer systems and system components to communicate and exchange information.

Complex problems, costs and objectives are involved in the linking of computer systems. The Library Development Division should use the best advisory resources available to achieve the goal of accessing multiple databases from a single station through computer-to-computer linkage designed to bridge differences among data sources, computer systems presently in use, and application differences among those systems. A means should be developed for assessing the cost/effectiveness of particular linkage mechanisms. The work of the Task Force would include identifying, with wide input from librarians in the State, various classes of linkages to be established and the criteria for judging those linkages. A family of recommended linkages would be devised which vendors and utilities could be encouraged to develop and support.

10.   These standards should conform to the International Standards Organization/Open Systems Interconnection (ISO/OSI) reference model and should be adopted by New York State.

More specifically, the specifications should be consistent with the protocols of the Linked System Project Standard Network Interconnection (LSP/SNI) as specified in "SNI Protocol Specifications," available from the Library of Congress. The SNI protocols are based on the ISO/OSI protocols.

The standards being developed in conformance with the seven layers of the ISO/OSI model are the protocols needed for communication among bibliographic utilities, regional systems, local systems and system components. Protocols for the lower three layers of the OSI model have been widely accepted for several years. Protocols for layers 4 and 5 of the OSI model have become standardized and are being increasingly accepted. Protocols for some library applications based on the upper layers are expected to become international standards within a year. The nature of the OSI networking architecture permits implementation and migration to the developing international standard. Interim standards can be adopted and replaced when necessary as national and international work proceeds on the ISO/OSI model. Thus, by adopting the ISO/OSI reference model, libraries in the State can make progress toward interconnecting systems and system components while national efforts proceed.

Local systems will need to be augmented with facilities conforming to the standards in order to effect communication with various systems.

11.   The Library Development Division should pursue and support programs to link systems and system components consistent with national efforts such as the Linked System Project (LSP).

National efforts through the Linked Systems Project (LSP), the Library of Congress, the national utilities and cooperating vendors will result in the facilities needed to permit the exchange of bibliographic data. With a commitment to conform to international standards for system interconnections, State efforts will articulate well with national efforts. The prototype system now being tested at New York University is being used to link NYU's local computerized system with the Research Library Information Network (RLIN). To carry out this recommendation, the Library Development Division should require that the standards developed as a result of recommendations 9 and 10 be observed in State-funded projects at the earliest feasible date.

12.   The Library Development Division should have the capacity to test specific systems offered by vendors and verify that they meet these New York State standards.

The Library Development Division must be able to review and test whether a vendor's proposed linkage mechanism meets the standards adopted for libraries in New York State. New York State should make use of the Library of Congress's Standard Network Interconnection (SNI) test facility and other qualified facilities to the extent feasible. Vendors should be expected to demonstrate their compliance to national and State standards by using this test.

13.   Plans for a statewide network must recognize the continuing importance of offline databases and the probability that some human intermediation will be needed to access these records.

The overwhelming majority of linkages will be online computer to computer linkages. When appropriate, traditional manual facilities may be employed. Centers with bibliographies and indexes of materials not conveniently maintained in machine-readable form may be accessed by human assistance responding to queries via telephone or electronic mail.

Consulting and Training Recommendations

Libraries and library systems involved in automation face complex information needs. The Committee examined various roles of libraries, library systems, library schools and related organizations in meeting these information needs through consulting and training. The Committee makes six recommendations for consulting and training.

14. The Library Development Division should develop an interactive online database of providers of library automation training and consultant services.

An information gathering and referral service is needed to help libraries find help at the most appropriate level. An interactive database should list the consultative and training resources of all systems, the Library Development Division itself, vendors, bibliographic utilities and outside independent consultants. Listing would not constitute endorsement.

15. The Library Development Division should seek and dispense technical information about vendors which do and do not meet international and national standards for bibliographic records, telecommunications standards, and linking capabilities.

Securing and dispensing technical information is most efficiently done at the state level to minimize duplicative efforts at the regional level. This will allow libraries and library systems to make intelligent, appropriate and cost-effective choices for their automation needs.

16. All library systems, using intersystem cooperation and resources, should identify needs, sponsor training, introduce new technologies and provide automation information.

Because the circumstances and resources of the automation program differ from region to region, particular responsibilities of public library systems, reference and research library resources systems, and school library systems in consulting and training will vary. The regions offer opportunities for intersystem cooperation to meet training needs through automation conferences and workshops, demonstrations, automation information centers, and participation in a statewide bulletin board.

17. Library schools within the State should be provided with access to automation systems developed by the Library Development Division for the statewide database.

Graduate library schools within the State can be encouraged to inform students about the State's programs for automation, resource sharing and database quality control. Library schools should be utilized as demonstration and training sites for new automation systems for accessing the statewide database.

18. Advanced technology internships should be supported by the State Library.

Internships can make effective use of library sites in the State. Beyond their value as opportunities for continuing professional education, advanced technology internships in libraries can provide short-term infusions of specialty skills.

19. The Library Development Division, using the resources of the Edu-

cation Department and other external resources, should develop library automation training and support programs using, for example, video, teleconferences and internships.

The potentially high cost of developing training curricula and support materials requires the utilization of specialized state-level training resources already in place, such as the Center for Learning Technologies. This level of development enhances the capacity for replication across the State.

20.   The possibility of statewide cooperation and negotiation to obtain deep volume discounts on software and hardware should be explored by the Library Development Division and information on discounts should be disseminated to library systems.

State agreements are used effectively by libraries for purchases of office supplies, audiovisual equipment, and other non-library-specific acquisitions. System-level and regional-level negotiated discounts sometimes exceed industry-wide levels. The possibility of extending and improving on regional-level discounts should be explored.

PHASE II STATEWIDE AUTOMATION COMMITTEE AND TASK FORCES

Since *Libraries and Technology* is a strategic plan, further work was required to move it to the operational level. The plan, therefore, recommended the establishment of a Phase II Statewide Automation Committee and three Task Forces— Database Criteria, Telecommunications, and Linkage Standards—as the means to do this. These four groups were appointed by the Director of Library Development in June 1987. The work of the Phase II Committee and Task Forces required two years, nearly 50 people, and 28 meetings before the operational plan was completed. For each group, the charge, the most significant issues reviewed, and the decisions made in response to these issues are discussed below:

Phase II Committee

Charge

The Phase II Committee was responsible for developing an overall plan for implementing the 20 recommendations included in *Libraries and Technology*. The Committee's specific responsibilities fell into two categories: (a) Working directly with the recommendations not assigned to the task forces; and (b) Incorporating into the operational plan the proposals made by the task forces about the recommendations assigned to them.

Issues/Decisions

1.   What would be the best way for the Committee to present the implementation plan? The Committee initially attempted to be as specific as possible by

outlining the steps, establishing a timetable, and estimating the costs required to implement the strategic recommendations. But after making little progress with this approach, it shifted gears and took the less specific approach of grouping recommendations into four categories based upon whether they require new legislation, existing State and/or Federal funding, changes or amendments to regulations or guidelines, or endorsement.

2.   An organizational question that the Committee had to answer was: What is the relationship between the Phase II Committee and Task Forces? Specifically, does the Committee have the responsibility to review, accept, or reject recommendations made by the Task Forces? This was not an easy question to answer, but it was finally agreed that all four groups were equal and that the Phase II Committee had the responsibility to decide how to effectively integrate the recommendations of the Task Forces into the final plan but not to pass judgment on those recommendations.

3.   As the report began to come together, the Committee felt that, although the work of all four groups was invaluable, the report was shaping up to be a "bloodless" document e.g., recommendations that there be more committees, studies, etc. It was out of this perception that the "Electronic Doorway" concept was born. It was agreed that this concept would breath life into the report and that it would be the linchpin for the rest of the report.

4.   The adoption of the "Electronic Doorway" concept helped in two other ways. It first responded to an issue that was not resolved by the original State-wide Automation Committee. By adopting this concept, the Phase II Committee took the position that a gradual shift should be made away from placing heavy emphasis on conversion, as had been done up to that time, and toward providing more funding for access activities. The Committee agreed, however, that this shift should be evolutionary rather than abrupt. And this concept then took this decision one step farther by stating that not only should greater emphasis be placed on access activities but that access should also be available to end users. This point was included in the plan in order to respond directly to the Regents program for automation.

5.   Had circumstances changed so as to cast a new light on any of the 20 recommendations from the *Libraries and Technology* strategic plan? After carefully reviewing each recommendation, the Committee decided that Recommendations 14 and 15 should not be pursued. These were the recommendations that the Division of Library Development should develop a database of automation consultants and that it should dispense information about the adherence to standards by vendors.

Database Criteria Task Force

Charge

The Database Criteria Task Force was responsible for considering those issues involved with the development of the statewide database, particularly as they pertain to applications for funding for conversion of records to machine-readable form. Toward this end, the Task Force was asked to develop appraisal criteria and procedures which should be used by the regions and the State to assess the likelihood of potential statewide use of resources as proposed in Recommendations 6 and 7 of *Libraries and Technology*. It was also responsible for Recommendation 8.

Issues/Decisions

1.   Although Recommendation 6 speaks about unique items, the Task Force came to realize that the definition of a unique record should be subdivided into two parts: Unique in the Database and Unique in New York. The reason behind this decision was that it is only for records that are Unique in the Database that the extra effort is required to convert the records into machine-readable form. Therefore, it is only for these records that a higher level of funding per record is justified. Records that are Unique in New York only require attaching a holding symbol to a record that has already been entered into the database and, thus, do not deserve a higher level of funding.

2.   The Task Force originally thought that three levels of funding would be provided depending upon whether records are ubiquitous, scarce, or unique. That is, libraries would receive a basic amount per record for ubiquitous records; they would receive a higher level of funding for scarce records; and the highest level of funding would be awarded for unique records. Since the first level of funding above the basic level would be for scarce records, it was decided, based upon a statistical study done for the Task Force, that a sample size of 269 records would be needed to adequately sample scarce records. At the same time, this sample size would automatically be large enough to sample unique records as well. When it was determined that the only category of records really deserving of a higher level of funding are those that are Unique in the Database, the Task Force agreed, based upon the same study, that the sample size could be reduced to 136 records. (As a related matter, the Task Force also decided that a library could declare a candidate collection to be ubiquitous and thereby be exempt from the sampling requirement if it is willing to forego the opportunity for a higher level of funding and settle for the minimal amount per record).

3.   The Task Force decided that the concept of a library database should be separated into sampling and recipient databases. The Task Force agreed that there are only four databases against which a library may sample to determine what percentage of records in a candidate collection are Unique in the Database. The four sampling databases are OCLC, RLIN, UTLAS, and MILCS—a regional utility based at the New York Public Library. The selection of the sampling databases was based upon two factors: (a) A sampling database must be a national or major regional bibliographic utility; and (b) A searching library must be able to view all records of all libraries participating in the utility in one search.

Although the number of sampling databases is limited, the Task Force also agreed that records may be entered into a wide range of recipient databases both online and offline. This decision was in concert with Recommendation 4 in *Libraries and Technology* which states that the statewide database is distributed on multiple computers systems.

4.   Although Recommendation 6 states that a library must check all databases existing in the State in order to determine whether records are unique, scarce, or ubiquitous, the Task Force determined that this recommendation was really looking toward the time when all databases would be connected through linkages. The decision was, therefore, made that until that time a library must sample against only one of the four sampling databases.

5.   There was considerable debate as to whether funding should continue to be provided to libraries which input records into offline databases since these records may not be accessible for resource sharing purposes. The debate revolved primarily around the cost of imputing into online versus offline databases compared with the availability of funding to input into one or the other. It was finally agreed that this would be earmarked as an issue that would need to be considered by the first Biennial Review Committee, and that funding should continue to be provided for imputing records into to both online and offline databases in the meantime.

Telecommunications Task Force

Charge

The Telecommunications Task Force was asked to address the need for cost-effective electronic transmission of interlibrary loan requests to remote databases. This Task Force, appointed as an outgrowth of Recommendation 2 in *Libraries and Technology,* was also asked to identify and evaluate the feasibility of using existing and planned telecommunications facilities within the State for all library networking purposes.

Issues/Decisions

1.   Should the library community develop its own network or should it utilize the capacity of an already existing network(s)? The Task Force quickly decided that the library community should not develop its own network and that the only reasonable choice would be to use the services of another network(s).

2.   Of the three statewide educational networks (TNT, SUNYNET, and NYSERNET), should the Task Force promote one as being best for libraries to work with or would the libraries of the State be better served by working with all three networks? The Task Force agreed that it is unlikely that all of the libraries in the State would be served by one network and that all three networks (and maybe

others yet to be developed) would probably play a role in library resource sharing.

3.   Assuming that multiple networks will serve libraries in the future, how easy will it be to establish connections among these networks? The Task Force found that there is considerable similarity among the existing or planned backbone structures of the three statewide educational networks which means that gateways can be easily established among them.

4.   It is possible that EmpireNet, the network being planned by the State Office of General Services to link State agencies, might be a factor in the mix of network solutions for libraries? The Task Force agreed that even if EmpireNet does not play a direct role in providing library services, it may play an indirect role since any or all three of the statewide educational networks might rent circuits from EmpireNet.

5.   Since communications costs present a greater problem over the "last mile" than across a network, should State funding and the emphasis of this Task Force be concentrated on the former rather than the latter? It was agreed that at this stage the primary concern should be to make network capacity available to libraries at an affordable price and that "last mile" costs should be addressed at a later stage.

Linkage Standards Task Force

Charge

The Linkage Standards Task Force, which was assigned the responsibility of carrying out Recommendations 10 and 11, was asked to examine the issues involved once a user has effectively reached a remote database through a telecommunications network and wants to access and manipulate the records in that database. This task force was specifically asked to: (a) Recommend standards and options necessary to ensure the exchange of information between and among computer systems; (b) Develop models representing typical linking configurations to establish future compliance criteria; (c) Recommend a series of pilot projects demonstrating the feasibility of adherence to adopted standards; and (d) Develop strategies to allow the State Library to participate in and benefit from national efforts such as the Linked Systems Project.

Issues/Decisions

1.   Would it make sense to have CD-ROM serve as a short-term strategy to improve statewide access to bibliographic records while awaiting the availability of effective linkages which would be the long-term strategy? More specifically, should funding be initially channeled into a statewide CD-ROM database since this is a well developed technology, and have this be the stepping stone to

providing funding for linkage activities once the linkage standards are complete and products based upon these standards are developed? The Task Force agreed that this strategy would not be advisable for two reasons. First, the completion of the linkage standards and the availability of affordable products that adhere to the standards are not as far away as some might imagine. Second, the development of a CD-ROM database is a halfway measure in that it only provides access to bibliographic records, whereas some type of electronic communication must also be available if resource sharing is to take place.

2.   Would a statewide conference about linkage standards be useful or would it be more productive to hire a contractor to work with librarians on a small group or even a one-to-one basis to determine linking needs? The Task Force decided that both approaches would be useful: a statewide conference should come first and have as its objective education about linkage standards in general terms; this conference should be followed by regional programs and workshops; and, tied in with or subsequent to the programs/workshops, a contractor should begin to work with small groups and individuals to help them carefully define what they want linkages to accomplish for them.

3.   Should the educational efforts and the contractor promote a direction in which linkage development should take place (e.g., interlibrary loan) or should the work done by the contractor be completed before deciding upon and promoting a direction? After substantial discussion, it was decided that it would be premature to promote a direction because an incorrect decision(s) could be made and time and resources wasted if a direction is promoted without having sufficient input beforehand.

4.   Should pressure be put on vendors (primarily in terms of guidelines as to how libraries and library systems may use State funding) to develop products that adhere to linkage standards? After initial enthusiasm for this approach, the Task Force decided that it would be preferable to begin with motivation of vendors toward this end, and that leverage and pressure should only be applied once the standards have been completed if still necessary by that time.

5.   Should New York State follow the lead of the Federal Government and mandate GOSIP (the U.S. Government Open Systems Interconnection Profile) beginning in 1990 or some later year? It was decided that the GOSIP mandate should be carefully monitored at the Federal level and that it should be applied in New York State but at a time to be determined in the future.

TECHNOLOGY AND ACCESS

In August, 1989, a plan incorporating the work of all four groups was issued by the Phase II Committee under the title of *Technology and Access: The Electronic Doorway Library. Technology and Access* includes 18 recommendations which outline steps to implement the recommendations in *Libraries and Technology.* As stated earlier, the recommendations are organized into four categories based upon whether they require new legislation, existing funding, changes to guidelines or regulations, or simply endorsement (and two of the recommendations from *Libraries and Technology* have been reconsidered). Foremost among the recommendations included in *Technology and Access* is Recommendation (A2) which states that legislation be proposed to make it possible for any library in the State regardless of size, type, or location to become an Electronic Doorway. The recommendations as stated in *Technology and Access* are as follows:

A. Implementation steps requiring new funding levels acquired through new legislative initiatives

A1.   The Regents 1989 legislative proposal for libraries includes increased funds for: the Regional Bibliographic Data Bases and Interlibrary Resources Program, system automation, acquisition of microcomputers, technology internships, and the linking of library systems to telecommunications networks such as Technology Network Ties (TNT). This legislation supports a basic growth level for library automation and should be enacted at the earliest possible date.

A2.   In 1990 the Regents should propose legislation to bring about a program that makes it possible for any library in the State, regardless of size, type, or location to become an *Electronic Doorway*. The Electronic Doorway Library would provide users needed information electronically from any part of the State through use of automation and resource sharing programs which are currently operating and being developed. In this legislation the Regents should propose to underwrite the costs of enabling any library which meets basic standards for its type of library and participates in State-supported systems and automation programs to meet the guidelines of a carefully designed prototype as an Electronic Doorway site and to be formally designated as such by the Regents. Designation would denote that the library has a board or administration, director, and staff fully committed to using technology to provide quality library service, is connected by one or more computer systems to electronic databases for resource sharing purposes, and expects to work with its library system in making full use of future technologies.

Electronic Doorway Libraries might be among the first to offer users the opportunity to access the local library catalog by microcomputer from home or work place. Through the Electronic Doorway Library, a user could also access the catalogs of other libraries for bibliographic references or tap into various information data banks to obtain articles or materials.

The concept of the Electronic Doorway Library as the threshold to the State's library and information resource sharing system will require education and training, public information, and consultation. In some cases, a library may need to acquire equipment, software or telecommunications capacity. A unifying symbol could be developed to help the public identify libraries that met the Regents standards as Electronic Doorway Libraries. The 1990 legislative proposal should provide funds for such purposes.

If this initiative is accompanied by continued and expanded State support of resource sharing systems, it has the potential to implement both the philosophy and the actuality of *Libraries and Technology* recommendation #4 to provide global and inclusive access to records of all of the State's information resources. Some libraries in the State may already qualify as Electronic Doorway Libraries. The goal is to help all libraries qualify. An appropriation of $1.3 million annually over the next few years should enable the State to develop Electronic Doorway Libraries systematically.

A3.   The Regents 1989 legislative proposal for libraries includes $50,000 for internships to implement *Libraries and Technology* recommendation #18 for advanced technology internships. In addition, continuing education, consultation and training, and advanced library technology internships should form the focus of new, separate library legislation in 1990, developed specifically to finance *Libraries and Technology* recommendations concerning: use of library schools as demonstration and training sites for automation initiatives (*L&T* #17); advanced technology internships (*L&T* #18); and training packages utilizing videos and teleconferences (*L&T* #19). In this new, separate legislation the Regents should propose a broadly comprehensive initiative with separately-enacted funding to benefit both students and experienced practitioners. Students and practitioners should be able to apply from the field as well as from professional schools to work in appropriate sites throughout the State for periods varying from one month to an academic year.

A4.   The Regents 1990 legislative proposal for libraries should include at least one additional automation consultant position in the Library Development Division.

B. Implementation steps to be carried out by the Library Development Division, other agencies, and the library community in programs and pilot projects funded primarily by present pools of State and LSCA Title III funds.

B1.   By the end of 1990, the Library Development Division should appoint the first Biennial Review Committee to carry out *Libraries and Technology* recommendation #3. The committee should include 11–15 members (representative of the field by type of library and system, selected from rural and urban areas, with broad geographic representation, and technical expertise). To facilitate effective appointments, the Library Development Division should seek nominations from the field by October 1990. The Committee will issue a report by December 1991.

B2.   To take continued leadership in telecommunications (*Libraries and Technology* #2), the Library Development Division must continue to build both formal and informal working relationships between and among the existing educational networks and the library networks in New York State. By the end of 1990, the Library Development Division should appoint a telecommunications task force or advisory group comprised of leading players in telecommunications in the State (such as the Office of General Services, EMPIRE NET; New York State Education and Research Network, Inc., NYSERNet; State University of New York, SUNYNET; State Education Department Technology Network Ties, TNT; and others). A task force or group involving (or representing) leading players is essential in the absence of an interagency task force convened by the Governor or another State agency. Such a telecommunications task force or advisory group would provide a regular focus on libraries as needs are identified and cooperation is explored.

B3.   The Linkage Standards Task Force has pointed out the need for a continuing advisory group on linkage standards "to review and recommend policy" and to recommend when the U.S. Government OSI Profile (GOSIP) should be mandated in New York State. The Library Development Division should appoint such a group by the end of 1990.

The work of the Linkage Standards and Telecommunications advisory groups would need to be coordinated. The two groups would be involved with activities that are both different enough and large enough to warrant their being separate. However, there should be effective interplay between the two groups and they should hold an initial joint meeting to clarify and establish their respective responsibilities. The two committees should meet jointly, as appropriate, either on a periodic basis or as needed, even after the initial meeting.

B4.   The Library Development Division should seek and use field and State government expertise (and contract funds) to secure and provide the consultant help needed to develop a strategic plan to determine the most effective telecommunications solutions to the needs of libraries on a statewide basis.

B5.   The Library Development Division should commit to a multi-year educational undertaking consisting of a well organized and high-quality statewide conference to initiate the linkage standards education effort in the State, and follow-up programs and workshops in each of the nine regions.

Education of the New York State library community about linkage standards is critical to accomplishment of the *Libraries and Technology* strategic plan. The Library Development Division and library systems should work together to develop and maintain a knowledge base among library leaders and other individuals involved with library automation about linkage standards and their importance to libraries. Education about linkage standards should impress upon librarians the need to work together to motivate vendors to comply with standards.

The State-level conference should be mounted sometime late in 1990, with plans for regional follow-up developed as part of State-level conference planning. Video tapes and teleconferences should be considered to ensure quality and conserve resources. LSCA Title III, funds from the legislative initiative, and joint use of State and system funds could support this education effort.

B6. The Library Development Division, systems, and others concerned should develop a statewide plan for linkage standards compatibility between and among libraries, systems, and regions. In doing so, the Library Development Division should engage a contractor to: determine needs; develop functional requirements, specifications, and models; and determine application protocols for linking computer systems.

B7. The Library Development Division should encourage systems to conduct (in cooperation with the Library Development Division) one or more phased pilot projects for the purpose of investigating improved telecommunications options and establishing linkages among library computer systems. Phase one should test alternatives to local and intra-LATA communications (within the area served by one or more local telephone companies) for the purpose of achieving more cost-effective transmission of bibliographic data. Phase two should use the contractor's recommendations to test the linking of disparate library computer systems. The phased pilot project(s) should be carried out within the next three years, using an appropriate combination of LSCA, regional database, and other existing resources.

B8. In its regular review of regional and system planning documents and project applications, the Library Development Division should be alert to opportunities to encourage and assist in the negotiation of deep volume discounts for mass purchases of software or hardware (*Libraries and Technology* #20).

C. Implementation steps requiring changes or amendments to current Library Development Division regulations or guidelines.

C1. The Library Development Division should incorporate the database criteria assessment definitions and instrument developed and field tested by the Criteria Task Force, as appropriate, into guidelines, regulations, and formulas for allocation of funds for database development. Formulas should continue to provide a higher level of per record funding for the conversion of records that are unique to the database.

Systems and other planners should reflect in regional planning documents and regional priorities the *Libraries and Technology* recommendations calling for balanced development of the statewide database among unique, scarce, ubiquitous, and high demand items (*L&T* #6); balanced development of the database taking into account likelihood of use of materials, value to the State's program of economic development, contribution to research and scholarship, and numbers of users in all types of libraries (*L&T* #7); and ongoing commitment from local funds for entry of current materials, continuing maintenance and security of the database, and access to materials listed in the database within defined performance standards (*L&T* #8).

C2. To implement the *Libraries and Technology* recommendation requiring all library systems to identify needs and sponsor training (*L&T* #16), the Library Development Division should: (1) adopt LSCA policy guidelines that require each system applying for funds for a technology-related project to document needs, show intersystem consultation and cooperation, and provide for appropriate training; and (2) see that its LSCA policy guidelines are parallel to the regulations, guidelines, instructions, and forms used in the Regional Bibliographic Data Bases Program.

D. Implementation steps involving non-financial issues of endorsement, etc.

D1. The Library Development Division, the New York Library Association, and the library community should support American Library Association efforts that seek to establish special favorable telecommunications tariffs for libraries and other educational institutions.

D2. State Education Department staff should incorporate International Standards Organization/Open Systems Interconnection (ISO/OSI) standards into plans for the redesign of the State Library's Collection Management System (CMS) to the New York State Information Network (NYSIN).

D3. The State Librarian should work with the Chief Officers of State Library Agencies (COSLA) "to urge State Librarians to form counterpart task forces in other states to promote the linkage standards and to inform constituencies of the importance of linking computer systems in this manner." As recommended by the Linkage Standards Task Force, this effort should also be continued with the Chief Officers of State Libraries in the Northeast (COSLINE), particularly through the COSLINE Networking Group.

D4. The Library Development Division should monitor the progress of the U.S. Government OSI Profile (GOSIP). The United States government has indicated that it will mandate GOSIP at the Federal level in 1990 with lenient waiver procedures. The Federal experience should be helpful in determining when it may be possible to mandate GOSIP in New York.

E. Reconsidered *L&T* Recommendations

After extensive discussion of the current need, value, timeliness, and cost effectiveness of *Libraries and Technology* recommendations #14 and #15, we recommend the following changes of direction.

E1. For referral sources of providers of library automation and consultation services we recommend, instead of an interactive online database suggested in *L&T* recommendation #14, an informal network of practitioners, with Regional Automation Committees and system automation staff serving as first lines of automation expertise.

E2. The complexity and deliberate pace of development of national linkage standards now compel postponement and reconsideration of the *L&T* recommendation #15 for the Library Development Division to dispense vendor information. The library community needs a more widespread understanding and commitment to linkage standards to motivate vendors to make progress with these standards.

CONCLUSION

The completion of *Technology and Access* marks the end of a three-year statewide automation planning process beginning in May 1986 and ending in May 1989. The 20 strategic recommendations included in *Libraries and Technology* and the 18 operational recommendations in *Technology and Access* together comprise the Statewide Automation Plan. These 38 recommendations provide the blueprint needed to make the best use of existing and future funding, and they also provide the foundation and benchmark for the reexamination of these recommendations in the years ahead by successive Biennial Review Committees.

The implementation of these recommendations will be administered and funded through the Regional Bibliographic Data Bases and Interlibrary Resources Sharing (RBDBIRS) Program, a statewide program administered through the State Library's Division of Library Development which funds automation activities for resource sharing purposes. Established in 1984, this program provided State funding for library automation purposes for the first time. It is primarily through this program that Library Development has provided some $17 million over five and a half years to support automation programs at the State, regional, and local levels.

The process of integrating the recommendations from the Statewide Automation Plan into the RBDBIRS Program has already begun. The most significant example is the use of the Database Criteria Assessment Instrument, as proposed in Recommendation C1 of *Technology and Access,* which must be submitted by any library that applies for funding to convert records into machine-readable form. To justify their requests for funding, libraries are asked to respond to questions which address Recommendations 6–8 in *Libraries and Technology.* The Assessment Instrument requires that Recommendation 6 be addressed with a sampling process if a library wishes to obtain funding above the minimal amount per record; Recommendation 7 be dealt with by the use of a scaling system supplemented by written statements; and Recommendation 8 be met with a written statement. After prolonged development and two field tests, this instrument is being used on an operational basis in the RBDBIRS Program.

Five-Year Plans to cover the period 1990–1994, which is the second five years of the RBDBIRS Program, have just been submitted to the Division of Library Development by the State's nine library regions and 23 public library systems. Most or all of the recommendations in *Technology and Access* will be implemented during the life span of these Five-Year Plans. Any that are not will be integrated into the RBDBIRS Program in subsequent years.

As stated at the beginning of this paper, the Statewide Automation Plan is rooted in the 1978 New York State Governor's Conference on Libraries. More than a decade later, work is underway on the Governor's Conference on Library and Information Services scheduled for Fall 1990. It is significant that the State-wide Automation Plan, which originated with the 1978 Conference, is available as an important resource document for the 1990 Conference. Although the agenda for the 1990 Conference has not yet been developed, it is clear that this will be a timely and useful document since planning is far enough along to know that delegates will be discussing topics to which automation is central.

The Statewide Automation Plan will have a major impact on the RBDBIRS Program in the years ahead, and it will influence other Library Development programs as well. But the document may also play a role in ways which cannot even be foreseen at this time. The Statewide Automation Plan will guide the development of library automation across New York State in many ways well into the future.

NOTE

A shorter version of this paper was published in *Library Hi-Tech* Consecutive issue 26 volume 7, no. 2 (1989):85–89.

REFERENCES

The University of the State of New York/The State Education Department/New York State Library. *A Library Automation Plan for New York State* (Draft). Albany, 1981.
The University of the State of New York/The State Education Department/New York State Library. *A Library Automation Plan for New York State: 1984* (Draft). Albany, 1984.
The University of the State of New York/The State Education Department/New York State Library. *Libraries and Technology: A Strategic Plan for the Use of Advanced Technologies for Library Resource Sharing in New York State.* Albany, 1987.
The University of the State of New York/The State Education Department/New York State Library. *Meeting Information Needs of the 80's: Report of the Commissioner's Committee on Statewide Library Development.* Albany, 1981.
The University of the State of New York/The State Education Department/New York State Library. *Technology and Access: The Electronic Doorway Library.* Albany, 1989.

THE NATIONAL SZECHENYI LIBRARY:

BUDAPEST-HUNGARY

Elizabeth Molnar Rajec

As an International Research Exchange grant scholar and a Fulbright-Hays recipient I visited libraries in Budapest, Hungary in 1983, 1985, and 1988. During my first visit I used the National Szechenyi Library still at its old headquarters in Pest. By my second visit the library had moved into its beautiful new home, in the impressive rebuilt castle, the former Royal Palace in Buda. This report intends to summarize my findings about the above mentioned libraries.

Every library has its own peculiar history, and so does the National Szechenyi Library. Although the library was founded in 1802 by Count Ferenc Szechenyi, collecting of books as a national treasure can be traced back to a flourishing medieval culture around the universities (Pecs, 1367; Obuda 1389; Pozsony 1467;—incidentally my place of birth), but most of all to the royal library of King Matthias (1458–1490), the Bibliotheca Corviniana, which was exceptionally rich in codices and incunabula. During the Turkish occupation, which lasted one and a half centuries, a lot of national treasures disappeared, and during

Advances in Library Administration and Organization,
Volume 9, pages 165–169.
Copyright © 1991 by JAI Press, Inc.
All rights of reproduction in any form reserved.
ISBN: 1-55938-066-7

the long reign of the Habsburg dynasty Hungarian national interests were not considered priorities. This explains the relatively late date of the establishment of a national library.

The Bibliotheca Szechenyiano, according to its charter, opened its door to the public for research, study, and self-improvement on Thanksgiving Day, the most important national holiday which commemorates the memory of St. Stephen, the first king of Hungary, August 20, 1803. The collection consisted of approximately 13,000 printed books, 2,000 manuscripts as well as several hundreds of maps and engravings. Already in 1804 the library requested the deposit of a single copy of all material published in Hungary. (The 1897 copyright law and its reinforced 1928 version made the copy deposit mandatory; by 1951 a two copy deposit was made obligatory!)

In 1808 the National Museum of Hungary was established into which the National Szechenyi Library was incorporated. By 1846 this impressive building in the classicist style was completed. Under these favorable circumstances the museum as well as the library were able to enlarge its accumulated treasures by generous private donations which included some of the lost codices, incunabula and other rare items. New purchases and unique acquisitions rapidly enlarged the holdings of the collection. Since the library shared the stately building with the museum it was also known as the Library of the National Museum.

By 1866 an efficient reading room accommodating 80 readers opened. Statistics of this period reveal that about 5,000 patrons used the library yearly and about 15,000 titles were consulted annually. In 1876 the Department of Manuscripts was established, and a year later the first journal of librarianship was launched with great emphasis on the history of book publishing and bibliographies. (By the way the journal *Magyar Könyvszemle* is still flourishing. A truly meritorious accomplishment!) In 1892 the Archives and in 1884 the Department of Periodicals were established.

By the centennial anniversary, the holdings of the library consisted of 350,000 books, 20,000 periodicals, and 3,000 maps, 1,100 incunabula, and 400 codices. Unfortunately, these prosperous years did not last long. The devastating events of World War I were soon followed by even greater hardship. Perhaps the only worthwhile fact to mention here is that the collapse of the Austro-Hungarian monarchy inversely helped in the acquisition of scattered valuable items of the national treasure. For example, 33 valuable medieval codices and 16 Corvina codices (which had been carried away to the Court Library of Vienna) were safely returned. Also, that during the years between the two world wars, the library was able to reclassify its collection. Its holdings were classed into the Universal Decimal Classification System.

A far-reaching reorganization plan included, among other things, the establishment of departments. All musical material was housed by 1928 in the Music Collection which includes the priceless manuscripts of Haydn, Liszt, Bartok, and Kodaly, to mention just a few. By 1935 the Collection of Small Prints and

Graphics became an independent division. The Theatre History Collection (which I consulted most frequently for my research on Ferenc Molnar on whose play the American musical *Carousel* was based) was set up by 1949; the Microfilm Collection in 1952; and the Centre of Library Science and Methodology was founded in 1952. Among other things, the Centre's scope of duties included modernization and development from a theoretical, as well as from a practical, point of view. Training of professional librarians, co-ordination of tasks, implementation of new policies, adherence to standards and up-keep with technological changes and numerous other aspects are administered by this division.

It took several years to restore the devastating impact of World War II. By 1949 the library was separated from the National Museum and was known hereafter as the National Library. It started the compilation of a yearly bibliography under the title *Bibliographica Hungarica. Catalogus systematicus librorum in Hungaria editorum.* Retrospectively accumulated volumes cover the period from 1945 to 1978 as well as the years 1921–1944. Since 1978 the MARC-II format is followed, which includes the ISBN and the ISSN numbers. Older publications are included in *Res litteratia Hungariae vetus operum impressorum (1473–1600)* published in 1971 and up-dated in 1983. In addition bibliographies compiled by professional librarians and scholars are also available. Henceforth, the tracing of published titles is possible without ado.

In 1956 a Library Act was introduced (re-enforced in 1976) which regulated in details all library functions. Its primary emphasis was the scope of future activities. Its directives covered, for instance, the Bookbinding and Restoration Laboratories, national bibliographic services, union catalogs, and interlibrary services on the local as well as the international level. Moreover, an international exchange of publications was launched. Since 1957 the *Yearbook of the National Szechenyi Library* annually summarizes pertinent information in professional articles. By 1971 the holdings of the library reached about 5 million titles, the patrons exceeded 62,000 and services were provided by 26 departments and units.

As a general rule, the National Szechenyi Library collects works published in Hungary, foreign titles related to Hungarica as well as translated titles which touch upon their interests. In addition the library acquires basic foreign materials, with a great emphasis on reference titles. It subscribes to nearly 2,500 periodicals published in Hungary and in other countries. In order to preserve the rapidly deteriorating newspaper and periodical collection about 3 million pages per year are microfilmed. About 20 million squares of negative films preserve the aging materials. Since 1976, colored film processing is also available; and from about 1980, the more efficient Pentakta processing method is used.

In spite of all the above mentioned improvements, by 1950s the library could no longer provide adequate space for its holdings or its services. It simply outgrew its boundaries. Even two supplementary buildings and additional storage space could not satisfy the library's and the users' ever-growing needs.

Already by 1959 a law was passed which recommended the rebuilding of a wing of the former Royal Palace (damaged heavily during World War II), which would be large enough to accommodate the library's collections. This plan took historical continuity into consideration, by commemorating the Bibliotheca Corviniana and its priceless treasures, but also reached out to the twenty-first century. Thus, the historical past became the link to the present as well as to the future.

On October 3, 1984, the move to the reconstructed "F" wing of the neo-baroque Royal Palace started. The festive opening ceremony took place on April 4th, 1985, on an important national holiday which commemorates the end of the Nazi years. In its new and splendid location, the library houses over 6 million titles; 700 staff members assist about 65,000 users annually.

The new library occupies a *brutto* space of 249,000 cubic meters based on 44,300 square meters base area. A very impressive marble covered entrance hall and spacious marble staircases lead to the main reading room as well as to the specialized departments. In spite of the castle's historical past (actually dating back to the Medieval Ages) and the palace's formal settings, which impose obviously, certain architectural limits, the renovation process implemented technological innovations whenever possible. For instance, the library can be approached from the downtown area of Buda via fast moving elevators piercing through the entire castle hill, thus sparing the patron a time consuming, winding bus ride. The old cogwheel railway was also modernized, which provides in addition to an express ride of a few minutes a breath-taking panoramic view of Pest when it lifts up from the picturesque riverbank of the only sometimes blue Danube.

The interior design of the library utilizes new technical devices, too. From compact moveable shelves requested titles are transported horizontally as well as vertically by a "Telelift," an electronically operated book-forwarding system especially designed for the library in West Germany. This system carries books over a 1,000 meter distance to 56 stations gathering material from a total of about 75,000 meter shelf space.

The elegant and spacious new reading room accommodates about 700 patrons and about 80,000 reference items can be consulted at the surrounding open shelves. Furthermore, the Szechenyi National Library utilizes TS terminals, is equipped with DARO and FACIT displays and printers in addition to IBM, Siemens, and Farranti computers. Thus, at the present location the treasures of the past as well as more up-dated reference tools can be consulted by the serious scholar or patron. Be the need for a beautifully illuminated codex or simply an entry verification in the *National Union Catalog of the Library of Congress*, the Szechenyi National Library can provide it.

The new library is a truly outstanding accomplishment; indeed, the laudable achievement of a small nation of about 10,000,000 people whose national treasures, including valuable library collections, suffered much dissevering over the span of its history, starting with the invasion of the Mongols, the Tatars, and the

Turks, only to be continued by a greedy and patriotically biased Habsburg rule, a savagely devastating Nazi dictator and the merciless purge of the Stalin years. This new library deserves a better fate and hopefully it will be spared from future disasters. It is elegant, spacious, and efficiently planned for further growth. On a national level planning for the future, especially considering the unpredictability of the rapidly growing information industry, is a tremendous task. From this even the new library cannot be spared. Perhaps its future accumulations will eventually have to be stored in a paperless library. Be this as it may, at present, the National Szechenyi Library is a precious stone illuminating not only the often culturally deprived wasteland of the past but also enlightening the present as well as the unknown future to come.

REFERENCES

The National Szechenyi Library. Edited by Magda Joboru. Budapest, 1972.
Az Orszagos Szechenyi Konyvtar. 3rd edition edited by Ilona Kovacs, 1985.

THE ROYAL SCIENTIFIC SOCIETY LIBRARY OF JORDAN

Nahla Natour

RSSL was established in 1970 as a special library to meet the needs of researchers in various fields. These fields include: Electronic, Mechanical, Civil Engineering and Building Research, Industrial Chemistry, Computing and Information Science, Economics and Management, Solar Energy, Physics and Mathematics.

As part of its services, RSSL includes microform services, and bibliographies of the 45,000 books and 1500 periodicals available. RSSL has made provision to furnish its users and local researchers with access to one of the world leaders in scientific and technical publications, namely NTIS.

NTIS: National Technical Information Services provides researchers with technical and scientific information in the form of reports. In addition to fields mentioned above, the information covers a wide range of topics such as: Agriculture and Food, Biomedical Technology and Human Factors Engineering, Health Planning and Health Services Research, Natural Resources and Earth Sciences, Transport and many other topics.

The RSSL is the focal point of the (NTIS).

Advances in Library Administration and Organization,
Volume 9, pages 171–181.
Copyright © 1991 by JAI Press, Inc.
All rights of reproduction in any form reserved.
ISBN: 1-55938-066-7

The library, which is considered the basic source of information for local search operations especially in fields of science and technology, contains a large number of books in different fields of knowledge, international and local reports, international and national standards, micro films, and maps in addition to new technologies such as optical disk storage media and laser printers. The library has holdings of about 70,000 titles in books, periodicals, and scientific documents. A computerized library system has been developed to fully automate the operations and contents of the library.

STIC coordinates with other organizations in Jordan to build their own data bases it analyzes their information needs, designs and implements the necessary information systems and conducts training courses for better utilization of information. These courses are directed to managers, administrators and technicians, including information scientists and librarians.

The Scientific and Technical Information Center (STIC) at the Royal Scientific Society (RSS) as a part of the National Information System (NIS), of Jordan, is now developing and expanding its services to cope with the information revolution which is currently spreading all over the world. STIC started to provide its services to decision makers, researchers, university students, individuals and companies since the date it was established. It provides scientific and technical information in the fields of energy, civil engineering, construction, industrial chemistry, mechanical, engineering, information technology, computer science, economics, electronics topology, natural and medical sciences and history, especially the history of art and Palestine. STIC also provides latest information in an efficient and rapid way through computers and on-line facilities. This enables direct access to international data services, consisting of many data bases and data banks covering various fields such as pure sciences, applied sciences, social sciences and others. Thus, access to the latest publications and research results in those areas, in addition to all past publications, is facilitated.

The information experts at the RSS can retrieve on-line information from these data banks/bases quickly and efficiently simply by specifying the type of information needed by the researcher. Information specialists at the center set up a search strategy, and communicate on-line with the required data banks through the use of computer facilities, thus retrieving the information needed within a few minutes. In general, the cost of on-line search ranges from JD 20 to 25 per search which only covers the cost of the telephone call and the cost of using the international data bases. This service started one year ago and the number of users is increasing continuously. The average number of on-line search operations for information at the center is approximately 30 operations a month.

The RSSL uses INTERNATIONAL data banks DIALOG, BRS, ORBIT.

ROYAL SCIENTIFIC SOCIETY LIBRARY

Books	45,000
• Arabic	15,000
• English	30,000
Periodicals	1500
• Arabic	350
• English	1100
• German	50
Standard and Specifications	18,000
Newspapers	16
Theses	350
Non-book Material	
• Video Cassettes	4
• Microfiche	1000
• Maps	450
• Films	200
• Tapes	200
• Slides	500
• Cassettes	200
• CD-ROM	2
• ON-LINE SEARCH	

NATIONAL INFORMATION SYSTEM IN JORDAN

Introduction

Information is one of the basic elements needed in the process of development. Preparing, providing and conveying the information to decision makers and researchers throughout Jordan has become an urgent necessity.

Therefore, Jordan has decided to set up the National Information System (NIS). The objective of NIS is to prepare, manage and coordinate economic, social, scientific and technical information and to offer information services to various levels of decision makers, researchers at beneficiary institutions with the aim of rendering support to the development plans in Jordan.

The Objectives of NIS

The aim for setting up the NIS is to prepare and provide information as an aid to the formulation of policies and to conduct economic, social studies and scientific research.

By linking the NIS with local and foreign information banks the beneficiary will be able to obtain the required information. The basic objectives of NIS are:

- To coordinate and regulate the process of acquiring economic, social, scientific and technical information.
- To study the needs of officials for various types of information, to reach agreement with beneficiaries on the form and content of the required data to the extent that they are available as potential sources of information, and to help prepare the required preliminary information and data in agreement with branch administrations.
- To set up and modernize bases of information.
- To provide information services to beneficiaries.
- To provide advanced scientific techniques enabling beneficiaries to easily define the sources of information needed as well as the method of obtaining the information.

NIS Structure

NIS is structured in such a way as to make it efficient in administrative matters and flexible enough to handle any type of requirement within its mandate. Hence the basic elements that form NIS are:

1. The Central Management Committee.
2. The Economic and Social Information Center at the Ministry of Planning.
3. The Scientific and Technical Information Center at the Royal Scientific Society.
4. Subcenters and Managements at various institutions.
5. A specialized communications network.

The Central Administration of the NIS consists of a council chaired by the Minister of Planning, and includes the following as members:

1. The President of the RSS.
2. The Secretary General of the Hashemite Royal Court.
3. The Secretary General of the Ministry of Planning.
4. The Director General of the General Statistics Dept.
5. The Director General of the Telecommunications Corporation.
6. Representative of the Prime Ministry.

7. The Director of the Economic and Social Information Center at the Ministry of Planning.
8. The Director of the Scientific and Technical Information Center at the Royal Scientific Society.

The Central Administration will be in charge of supervising and managing the NIS. The Economic and Social Information Center and the Scientific and Technical Information Center will discharge the functions of the technical secretariat, each in its own field of speciality.

Branch Administration of the NIS will be located at computer centers and information centers at government ministries and departments, universities, institutions and research units of both the public and private sectors. These could be utilized at the national level where information is coordinated and processed in cooperation with the Economic and Social Information Center or the Scientific and Technical Information Center according to the nature of the information required and the compatibility of the information with the specialization of each of the two centers.

Services

The NIS will be utilized for the service of various sectors, including managers, planners, and officials as well as researchers, professionals and others.

Among the services offered by the NIS is to coordinate information with branch administrations, to prepare and classify information in forms and within frameworks appropriate for processing and analysis according to the requirements of the beneficiaries through the NIS communication network and according to the constraints and confidentiality agreed upon with the Central Administration. The NIS will furthermore, build up data bases and offer consultations to researchers and beneficiaries with the aim of guiding them to the potential sources of information needed.

ROYAL SCIENTIFIC SOCIETY
FOREWORD

The Royal Scientific Society (RSS) is a research and development institution whose main function is to provide research, testing and evaluation services in scientific and technological fields, using highly qualified and well-trained manpower and utilizing the best advanced equipment in order to achieve the highest level of performance.

The basic mission of RSS is to promote scientific research and the scientific spirit, to take part in creating an effective climate which helps the process of qualitative construction, and to participate in meeting Jordan's needs and development requirements in an appropriate manner.

Table 1. Qualifications of RSS
employees as on December 31, 1988

Degree or Certificate	Number
Ph.D	41
M.A./M.Sc	60
Diploma	23
B.A/B.Sc	144
Assistant Engineer	05
Community College	72
General Secondary Certificate	54
Others	130

RSS plays its role within the context of a general policy drawn up for science and technology which reflects the aspirations of His Majesty King Al-Hussein, the leader of Jordan and the pioneer of its development process. It has been helped in its progress by the enthusiastic spirit and determination of His Royal Highness Crown Prince El-Hassan to whom thanks are due for his patronage of RSS and his continued support since RSS came into existence in 1970.

GENERAL INFORMATION

- The Royal Scientific Society was established in 1970 as a research and development institution to work in fields related to the development process in Jordan.
- RSS is a national institution enjoying financial and administrative independence.
- RSS has been made one of the scientific and technological centres of the Higher Council for Science and Technology, established in 1987 under the chairmanship of His Royal Highness Crown Prince El-Hassan, with the following eminent persons as members:

  - The Commander-in-Chief of the Jordanian Armed Forces.
  - The Minister of Planning.
  - The Minister of Industry and Commerce.
  - The Minister of Finance.
  - The Minister of Higher Education.
  - The Minister of Agriculture.
  - The President of the Royal Scientific Society.
  - The Chairman of Amman Chamber of Industry.
  - The Council Secretary General.

In addition, there are three other qualified and experienced persons by the chairman for four years.
- RSS is administered by a President, four Vice-Presidents and department directors.
- RSS started its activities at the offices of the Central Bank of Jordan. It then moved to a rented building in Amman before acquiring its present permanent site at Jubaih, near Amman, which it occupied in February 1972.
- The area of the permanent site is 342,000 square metres.
- The buildings and laboratories cover a floor area of 28,127 square metres.
- The budget of RSS is derived from self-generated revenues from technical services and consultations, research contracts, an annual grant from the Government of Jordan, grants and donations from local institutions, and technical assistance from a number of industrial countries as well as from international and regional organizations.
- RSS consists of the following departments and centres:
  - Mechanical Engineering Department.
  - Industrial Chemistry Department.
  - Electronic Services and Training Centre.
  - Economic Research Department.
  - Administrative Affairs Department.
  - Solar Energy Research Centre.
  - Building Research Centre.
  - Computer Department.
  - Budget, Follow-up and Audit Department.
  - Public Relations Department.

RSS cooperates with a number of research institutions, universities, organizations, councils, centres and establishments at the Arab, regional and international levels through agreements, memoranda of understanding and contract research and studies.

RSS is a member of several Arab, regional and international unions, federations, councils, associations, organizations and societies.

AIMS AND FUNCTIONS

Aims

The Royal Scientific Society aims at conducting scientific and technological research and development work related to the development process in Jordan with special attention to industrial research and services. It also aims at disseminating awareness in the scientific and technological fields and at providing specialized technical consultations and services to the public and private sectors.

It seeks to develop scientific and technological cooperation with similar institutions within the Arab world and internationally.

Functions

1. Carrying out studies and conducting applied scientific research related to industry in particular and to the various areas of development in general.
2. Conducting economic and technical feasibility and analytical studies with regard to development projects which fall within the Society's scope of interest.
3. Carrying out studies and research in the field of vocational and industrial education and producing books and publications in support of training and the industrialization process.
4. Conducting research on a contract basis with institutions within Jordan and abroad.
5. Carrying out joint research with scientific, production-oriented and service institutions at the national, Arab and international levels.
6. Conducting research and development work leading to the production of prototypes for possible application in industry.
7. Developing its laboratories, providing them with up-to-date equipment and orienting them towards serving the objectives of scientific and technological research and the needs of the public and private sectors.
8. Carrying out tests and experimental work on materials as well as on finished and intermediate goods and providing related technical consultations to the users.
9. Contributing to the solution of technical problems facing the various organizations, particularly industrial establishments.
10. Cooperating with agencies concerned with the establishment of national technical standards and specifications and providing technical services which would facilitate their application and ensure proper quality control of goods and materials.
11. Attracting qualified Jordanian and Arab personnel and providing them with favorable working conditions.
12. Upgrading human capabilities and technical skills through the provision of distinctive training opportunities.
13. Producing books and other publications in the areas of science and technology which contribute to the effective dissemination of scientific and technological concepts.
14. Preparing the servicing information systems in addition to processing, programming and implementing computer systems.
15. Contributing to the transfer and adaptation of technology and selecting appropriate technologies related to the Society's scope and field of expertise.

16. Cooperating in science and technology with local, Arab and other organizations for the purpose of exchanging information and expertise and conducting joint research.
17. Developing the instruments of scientific and technological management, the methods of setting up national science and technology policies and providing consultations in this regard at the national and Arab levels.
18. Contributing to the development of the Arab region through providing technical services and consultation and creating opportunities for highly specialized technical training.

FUTURE OUTLOOK

The Royal Scientific Society, as an effective research and development institution in the field of science and technology, feels that it has to keep up with the latest developments and innovations in that field. In accordance with this perception, it had, first, to rearrange its priorities, upgrade its scientific and technical capabilities and develop its specialized personnel in order to become better prepared for the new work areas it intends to enter. Within this context come, for example, the efforts it exerts to upgrade the function of scientific research it carries out, to give it more attention and maintain a more efficient balance between research and specialized technical services. Another example is the practical steps which have been taken to introduce the computer into the operations of the Society's departments and centres in order to make it the common language for handling these operations, especially in relation to scientific research. Necessary equipment has been acquired and suitable training has been conducted while studies and the required programmes have been prepared.

Prominent among the new specialized areas, which RSS is looking forward to entering, are biotechnology, computer-aided engineering design, informatics, computer manufacturing, fibre optics, applied systems analysis, highly specialized professional training, project formulation for industrial purposes, patents and investment in science and technology.

RSS has undertaken considerable measures towards achieving these aspirations. A patent office, an applied systems analysis unit, a unit for highly specialized professional training have been established at the Society in addition to a technology development fund that serves as an investment outlet for turning technological accomplishments into feasible investment projects that enable RSS to reinforce its effective role in the development of Jordan and the Arab region. Moreover, contacts have been conducted and agreements have been signed with the relevant bodies inside and outside Jordan. Efforts are being exerted to secure assistance and expertise through specialized foreign agencies for establishing a biotechnology research centre and a computer-aided engineering design centre. Measures are underway to establish a standards and specifications centre in cooperation with the Ministry of Industry and Trade, an environment research centre in cooperation with the Ministry of Municipal and Rural Affairs and the Environment and a radiation protection centre. Furthermore, RSS has secured a nearby plot of land for the establishment of a science park which will, in cooperation with the universities and industrial sector, convert the findings of scientific and technological research into industrial projects.

RSS believes that these aspirations and efforts exerted to achieve them will enhance its endeavour to become an advanced scientific and technological centre which serves the development purposes in the region, starting with Jordan, of course. In accordance with this endeavour, RSS has recently established, in cooperation with the concerned Yemeni parties in Sana's, a Jordanian-Yemeni technical centre for investment to act as an appropriate communication and cooperation channel through which the services required in the two sister countries can be fulfilled.

RSS also believes that to cover and get involved in the fields of investment, industrialization and services in cooperation with the private sector is an integral part of its work. Therefore, it has established the Technology Development Fund to be its investment arm that adopts promising ideas and converts them into feasible investment opportunities reassuring the linkage between investment and research and development.

All this shows that numerous steps have been taken to reinforce the leading role RSS plays in Jordan and the rest of the Arab world to maintain its dynamism and continuous efforts for the good of the community and its growth in Jordan.

RSS COOPERATION RELATIONS WITH ARAB AND INTERNATIONAL ORGANIZATIONS AND INSTITUTIONS

RSS is connected with a good number of Arab and international organizations and institutions through:

A. Agreements or Protocols of Cooperation, with the following institutions:
- Arab Industrial Development Organization/Iraq.
- Arab Organization for Standardization and Metreology/Jordan.
- Islamic Foundation for Science, Technology and Development, Organization of Islamic Conference/Jeddah.
- Scientific Research Council/Iraq.
- Kuwait Institute for Scientific Research/Kuwait.
- Academy of Scientific Research and Technology/Arab Republic of Egypt.
- King Abdul Aziz City for Science and Technology/Kingdom of Saudi Arabia.

- The Academy of Sciences of the USSR.
- Scientific and Technical Research Council of Turkey/Turkey.
- Renewable Energy Development Centre (Centre de Development des Energies Renouvelables)/Morocco.
- National Technical Information Service/USA.
- Council of Scientific and Industrial Research/India.
- Council of Scientific and Industrial Research/Pakistan.
- Friedrich Ebert Stiftung/West Germany.
- German Agency for Technical Cooperation (GTZ)/West Germany.
- Cambridge Applied Nutrition, Toxicology and Biosciences Group (CANTAB)/United Kingdom.
- The Polish Academy for Science/Poland.
- Scottish Agency for Development/U.K.
- Bahrain Centre for Research and Studies/Bahrain.
- International Development and Research Centre.
- United Nations Development Program (UNDP).
- Economic & Social Committee for West Asia.

B. Membership in the following organizations:
- Federation of Arab Scientific Research Councils/Iraq.
- Intergovernmental Bureau of Informatics (IBI)/Italy.
- World Association of Industrial and Technological Research Organization (WAITRO)/Denmark.
- International Council of Scientific Unions (ICSU)/France.
- International Foundation of Science (IFS)/Sweden.
- International Association for Housing Science/USA.
- The International Federation of Institutes for Advanced Studies (IFIAS)/Canada.
- International Measurement Confederation (IMEKO)/Hungary.

A COLLECTION FOR A BROKERAGE FIRM LIBRARY

Kris Sandefur, Lori Rader, Bernard Schlessinger,
and Rashelle Karp

The Latin term *investire* means "to clothe," or "to surround." Today, an investment is a commitment of something, usually money, in order to provide a financial return, and "to clothe or surround" the investor in security. Millions of Americans are taking crash courses in investment strategy. Stockbrokers are finding new competition for investment capital springing up daily in the form of innovative investment devices. The complexities of today's economy forces investors to become more and more specialized in their knowledge. But, before turning to the vast array of investment advisory reference tools available, it is interesting to trace briefly the history of the American economy.

The U.S economic rollercoaster had its beginnings with the establishment of the New York Stock Exchange in 1792. This quite literally started the largest capital market in the world. However, in 1837, depression struck and caused the failure of the state banking system. After a slow recovery, businesses, especially the railroads, began expanding—too quickly. Beginning in 1873 there was a

Advances in Library Administration and Organization,
Volume 9, pages 183–198.
Copyright © 1991 by JAI Press, Inc.
All rights of reproduction in any form reserved.
ISBN: 1-55938-066-7

6-year depression followed by major banking reforms. After another period of recovery a sharp recession hit in 1893, causing many railroads to fold. In 1900, the country adopted the gold standard, which would become a major force over the years.

World War I spurred the economy somewhat but on its heels came the Stock Market Crash of 1929, followed by the Great Depression. In 1941, upon the U.S. entry into World War II, a business boom started. The New Deal had opened the door for federal involvement in the economy, and President Johnson's Great Society, along with the war in Vietnam, planted the seeds for double-digit inflation. Productivity dropped sharply in the mid-1960s while at the same time it rose dramatically in countries like Spain. By 1981, public debt had reached one trillion dollars, and there was a drive to restrain government's role in the economy, which has continued to this date (1989).

Within the last fifteen years the country has experienced three recessions: 1973–75, 1980, and 1981–82. In 1980, the U.S. experienced spiraling, double-digit inflation. Silver and gold hit all-time highs of $50.35 and $875 an ounce respectively. Prices rose at an annual rate of 17 percent in the first quarter. Escalating prices ate away at corporate profits and discouraged thousands from investing much-needed capital for business growth and development. Inflation pushed credit out of the reach of many. Nineteen eighty-one became the year of the merger—larger companies merged or acquired other companies to diversify into more profitable areas and bring in money to offset wage increases, soaring energy costs and foreign competition. In 1981, consumer prices rose 10.3 percent.

During the first 3 months of 1982, prices rose only 1 percent and economists were predicting an annual inflation rate of 5 to 6 percent. By May, gold was down to $331 and silver to $6.66 per ounce. Real estate prices fell 1.3 percent. Interest rates remained high. Braniff International, the Nation's ninth largest airline, declared bankruptcy. Auto workers gave up recent wage gains to salvage jobs and companies.

The abrupt slowdown in inflation coupled with still-high inflation rates caused many financial advisors to suggest more traditional stocks and bonds. Treasury bills and corporate bonds, providing up to 14 percent on the investment, appeared sound with an inflation rate of 5 percent–6 percent. Even government bonds at 13 percent seemed a good investment.

Despite the availability of discount brokerage services at over 700 banks and thrift institutions, companies in the brokerage business experienced an incredibly successful year in 1983. Pretax returns on equity of as much as 100 percent were not unusual for some of the larger privately held firms, and brokers electing to go public were able to obtain selling prices of $3^1/2$–$5^1/2$ times their prepublic book values.

Currently, about 47 million Americans own stock valued at over one trillion dollars. Speculation that the economy is due for another recession increased through 1986 and 1987 with astronomical gains in the stock market. That was followed in October of 1987 with a rapid fall of the stock market and a period of instability extending into 1988. Financial advisors, investment analysts and the individual investor have the unenviable task of keeping up with, even predicting, all of the changes in the economy. On a typical day, 100–300 million shares of stock exchange hands at the New York Stock Exchange. Information sources for investors have to be the most up-to-date available. Month- or even week-old data are often irrelevant.

Few business fields have such a wide array of advisory and statistical reference tools available. But because of their high cost, especially the cost of the comprehensive looseleaf services, few individuals or small companies can afford even the modest collection available at most medium-sized public libraries. Instead, they rely on public library collections to supply what they cannot afford. The following list of materials represents what should be available as a collection at most medium- to larger-sized public libraries. It is arranged in the categories of statistical sources and services, directories, indexes and abstracts, handbooks and manuals, biographical sources, dictionaries and encyclopedias, bibliographies, periodicals, and government documents. The total cost of the sources (August 1988) is approximately $21,836.65, obtained using the lowest figure (i.e.—weekly) when multiple prices are given. The cumulative cost also includes various duplicate sources, such as *Moody's* and *Standard and Poor's* services, although it is recognized that most libraries will choose one or the other.

STATISTICAL SOURCES AND SERVICES

American Stock Exchange Fact Book. New York: American Stock Exchange. Annual $3.
 Quick and easy reference to stock market activity, listed companies, and price trends is provided in this inexpensive source.

Creditweek. New York: Standard and Poor's Corporation. Weekly. $1238.
 Written for fixed income investors, coverage is designed to notify subscribers of developments which may potentially affect bond prices and yields. Regular sections include "Credit Forum," providing discussions on market and economic conditions by nationally recognized economists.

Moody's Bond Record. New York: Moody's Investors Service, Inc. Monthly. $125.
 Statistical background and facts related to marketing position are given for over 48,200 issues and situations, with 9,100 treated in greater detail.

Moody's Bond Survey. New York: Moody's Investors Services, Inc. Weekly. $895.

Commentary, analysis, and opinions on the bond and money markets and on individual markets are presented, accompanied by ratings of bank and finance, commercial, corporate, industrial, municipal, and government bonds.

Moody's Dividend Record. New York: Moody's Investors Service, Inc. Twice weekly with annual cumulations and 3 tax supplements. $345.

Entries for 13,000 securities provide data on dividend changes, amounts, frequency of payment, and totals for prior year's payments and dates. Special features include a table of 15-year monthly dividend changes, stockholder's rights, and special stock exchange rulings.

Moody's Manuals. New York: Moody's Investors Service, Inc., 1955–. Annual with semi-weekly supplements. $2,081 special library rate.

Bank and Finance Manual includes over 10,000 national, state, and private banks, plus insurance companies, mutual funds and closed-end investment companies, real estate firms, etc.

Industrial Manual covers every industrial firm listed on the New York and American Stock Exchanges, plus some of the more important unlisted companies.

International Manual highlights financial and business information for over 5,000 international corporations incorporated outside the United States in 100 countries.

Municipal and Government Manual covers the U.S. federal and state governments plus state agencies and over 16,000 bond-issuing municipalities.

OTC Industrial Manual provides information on approximately 3,200 over-the-counter industrial corporations and enterprises.

Public Utilities Manual provides detailed facts and financial data on all U.S. public and some privately-owned utilities.

Transportation Manual offers important information on numerous transportation companies including air, rail and bus lines, barge and steamship lines, etc.

National Bond Summary. Jersey City, N.J.: National Quotation Bureau. monthly—$264. Semiannual hardbound editions—$150.

Daily bond offerings and wants are summarized for all inactive listed and over-the-counter issues.

National Quote Sheets. Jersey City, N.J.: National Quotation Bureau. Daily— $504.

Often referred to as "pink sheets" because of their color, the *Quote Sheets* provide listings of companies not found in some of the larger sources, due to size or infrequency of trading. Presented alphabetically, information on both foreign and domestic common and preferred stocks is included.

National Stock Summary. Jersey City, N.J.: National Quotation Bureau. Monthly—$300. Semiannual hardbound editions—$150.
Listings of all inactive and over-the-counter stock offerings are presented, including name changes, mergers, stock splits with dates, and last known quotations of prices from named trading organizations.

New York Stock Exchange Fact Book. New York: New York Stock Exchange. Annual. $5.
Intended as a convenient reference tool for the investing public, and government and financial press, the *Fact Book* offers statistics on market activity, listed companies, stock price trends, securities market credit, and shareholders.

Standard and Poor's Analysts Handbook. New York: Standard and Poor's Corporation. Annual. $550.
Composite per share data for the companies and industries included in the S & P 400 Industrial Stocks Index, plus 15 transportation, financial and utility groups are summarized, with statistics and percentages covering 13 components including sales, operating profits, depreciation, earnings, and dividends.

Standard and Poor's Bond Guide. New York: Standard and Poor's Corporation, 1938–. Monthly. $145.
Statistical data on the performances of over 6,500 domestic and foreign corporate bond issues are provided in tabular format along with S & P Quality Ratings for each issue.

Standard and Poor's Statistical Service. New York: Standard and Poor's Corporation. $450.
Statistics from both government and private sources are provided in looseleaf format. Although specific source publications are not cited, agencies providing data are included.

Standard and Poor's Dividend Record. New York: Standard and Poor's Corporation. Daily—$550. Weekly—$235. Quarterly—$97.
More than 10,000 listed and unlisted issues are covered in an alphabetical listing by corporation of preferred and common stock dividends. Complete yearly dividend payments, with tax information, are summarized in an annual issue.

Standard and Poor's Monthly Stock Guide. New York: Standard and Poor's Corporation. Monthly. $84.

Comprehensive statistical data on over 5,300 common and preferred stocks, plus approximately 400 mutual fund issues traded on numerous North American exchanges, are given, with ratings based on ability to pay dividends and sinking fund obligations.

Standard and Poor's Stock Reports. New York: Standard and Poor's Corporation. 3 sets, NYSE—$797; AMEX—$615; OTC—$615. Quarterly with new reports several times a week.

This source reports on 3,750 companies, covering all those listed on NYSE, AMEX, and nearly 1,200 active and widely held companies traded OTC and on regional exchanges. Each company profile is supported by statistical data and includes charts showing 6–7 years of monthly stock price ranges and trading volumes.

Value Line Investment Survey. New York: A. Bernhard and Company, 1936–. Looseleaf with weekly additions. $495.

Evaluations of stocks and industries through stock charts and tables are included in 3 parts. Part 1 provides a summary and index to stock information with rankings for timeliness and safety. Part 2 contains forecasts and commentary covering current economic data and stock market activity. Part 3 includes industry analyses, and highlights selected companies with predictions of future trends.

Wall Street Letter. New York: Institutional Investor Systems, Inc., 1969–. Weekly with revised semiannual index. $775.

The *Letter* highlights developments at brokerage firms, institution trading desks, and on the regulatory scene.

Wiesenberger Investment Companies Service. New York: Wiesenberger Financial Services, 1941–. Annual with supplements. $345.

Basic information on mutual funds and investment companies is presented, covering 10-year histories of approximately 5,000 investment companies, including over 900 mutual funds, arranged alphabetically.

DIRECTORIES

Blue Book of Pension Funds. Mountain Lakes, N.J.: Dun's Marketing Services. Latest edition 1985, 6 volumes. $595 per set; $215 per volume.

Plan sponsors maintaining at least one retirement plan with assets in excess of $1 million are included in 6 regional volumes: New England, Mid-

Atlantic, Southeast-South Central States, Midwestern, Rocky Mountain-Southwest, and Far West.

Capital Changes Reports. Chicago: Commerce Clearing House. Weekly. $635.
Historical company information is covered. Details regarding name changes, security offerings, stock splits, bankruptcy proceedings, and dividend repayments are given alphabetically by corporate name.

Directory of Business and Financial Services. Mary M. Grant and Riva Berleant Schiller, ed. New York: Special Libraries Association, 1984. $35.
Business, economic, and financial services that are published periodically or with regular supplements are described.

Directory of Municipal Bond Dealers of the United States. New York: Bond Buyer, Inc. Semiannual. $70.
Listings of municipal bond dealers of the United States, financial consultants, and municipal bond attorneys are provided. An alphabetical listing of dealers and advertisers is included.

Dun and Bradstreet's Million Dollar Directory. New York: Dun and Bradstreet, 1964–. Annual. 5 vol. $1195.
Approximately 160,000 companies with an indicated net worth of over $500,000 are included, with information on officers and directors, products or services, SIC number, approximate sales, and number of employees.

Money Market Directory. Charlottesville, VA: Money Market Directories, Inc. Annual. $535.
Comprehensive descriptions of the entire tax-exempt institutional market are presented. Part I is tax-exempt funds, Part II is investment services, Part III is master trustee banks and their clients, Part IV is research departments by industry groups, and Part V is tax-exempt funds ranked by assets.

Mutual Fund Directory. New York: Investment Dealer's Digest. Semiannual. $90.
Background information, current statistics and a 10-year statistical record are presented for each of the 400 mutual funds included.

Polk's World Bank Directory. Nashville: R. L. Polk and Company, 1895–. Semiannual. $168.75 per issue.
Entries for over 15,000 banks and branches worldwide are given, including data on the Federal Reserve System and other U.S. and state government banking agencies.

Security Dealers of North America.   New York: Standard and Poor's Corporation. Semiannual. $320.
> Geographic access to over 14,000 U. S. and Canadian brokers and investment banking firms is provided, with up-to-date listings completely revised twice a year

Standard and Poor's Register of Corporations, Directors, and Executives.   New York: Standard and Poor's Corporation, 1928–. Annual. 3 vol. $425.
> Volume 1 is an alphabetical listing of over 36,000 U. S. and Canadian companies, with information on officers, products, SIC number, sales ranges, and number of employees. Volume 2 is a biographical listing of executives and directors. Volume 3 contains indexes by corporate family, SIC number, and location.

INDEXES AND ABSTRACTS

American Statistics Index: A Comprehensive Guide and Index to the Statistical Publications of the U.S. Government.   Bethesda, Maryland: Congressional Information Service, Inc., 1973–. Annual. $1040.
> Statistics published by all government agencies, congressional committees, and statistics-producing programs are indexed in this comprehensive, descriptive publication.

Business Periodicals Index.   New York: H. W. Wilson Company, 1958–. Monthly except August. Price varies.
> Overall subject coverage is included for selected periodicals in the following fields: accounting, advertising and public relations, automation, banking, communications, economics, finance and investments, labor, management, marketing, taxation, and specific businesses.

Predicasts F & S Index of United States.   Cleveland, Ohio: Predicasts, Inc., 1960–. Monthly. $700.
> Considered one of the best indexes for current information on companies and industries, *F & S Index* covers a wide selection of business, industrial, and financial periodicals, as well as a few brokerage house reports.

Wall Street Journal Index.   New York: Dow Jones and Company, 1958–. Monthly with annual cumulations. $550.
> Articles in the *Wall Street Journal* are indexed here, making this the single most important source for locating topical information in the *Journal.*

HANDBOOKS AND MANUALS

Dow Jones Investor's Handbook. Homewood, IL: Dow Jones-Irwin, 1966–. Annual. $9.95.

Daily closing Dow Jones averages for the most recent year, monthly closing averages, quarterly earnings, dividend yields, price-earnings ratios for over ten years, and the record for one current year are summarized.

Financial Analyst's Handbook. Sumner N. Levine, ed. Homewood, IL: Dow Jones-Irwin, 1975. $60.

Principles and procedures necessary for successful investment management are presented. Volume 1 covers "Methods, Theory, and Portfolio Management." Volume 2 covers an "Analysis by Industry."

Mutual Fund Fact Book. Washington, D.C.: Investment Company Institute. $4.

Comprised of basic statistics for the mutual fund industry, the *Fact Book* includes assets, total sales, redemption, etc., accompanied by a glossary of related terms.

BIOGRAPHICAL SOURCES

Who's Who in America. Chicago: Marquis Who's Who, 1899–. Biennial. $135.

Biographical data on approximately 75,000 prominent living Americans is provided.

Who's Who in Finance and Industry. Chicago: Marquis Who's Who, 1936–. Biennial. $105.

Career sketches are included of approximately 19,000 leading North American and international business professionals and others noteworthy in the fields of finance and industry.

DICTIONARIES AND ENCYCLOPEDIAS

Dictionary of Banking and Finance. Lewis E. Davids. Totowa, New Jersey: Littlefield, Adams and Company, 1979. $7.95.

Terms relevant to the banking and finance fields are defined, followed by a listing of agencies and organizations associated with banking and finance.

Thorndike Encyclopedia of Banking and Financial Tables. David Thorndike, ed. Boston, MA: Warren, Gorham, and Lamont, 1980. $78.

Tables for mortgage and real estate, compound interest and annuities, interest and savings, installment loans, leasing and rebates are among those presented in this comprehensive encyclopedia. A dictionary of financial words and phrases is also included.

Trade Names Dictionary. Donna Wood, ed. Detroit, MI: Gale Research Co., 1986. 2 vol. $270.

Entries for over 100,000 consumer product trade names, brand names, and product names, with addresses of their manufacturers, importers, marketers, and distributors, are included.

The Basic Business Library: Core Resources. Bernard S. Schlessinger. Phoenix, AZ: Oryx Press, 1983. $38.50.

Schlessinger provides annotated entries of essential business reference sources, with recommendations for libraries of various sizes. Essays are included in the second half of the book covering such topics as collection development, organization of materials, reference, and online services. (A revised second edition is due out in 1988.)

Business Information Sources. Lorna M. Daniells. Berkeley: University of California Press, 1985. $40.

Annotated entries for publications from all areas of the business field are arranged in chapters by subject. Sources covering such diverse topics as management, marketing, investments, and foreign statistics and economic trends make this a valuable tool for any business librarian.

PERIODICALS

Barron's. New York: Dow Jones and Company, 1921–. Weekly. $86.

Subtitled "National Business and Financial Weekly," *Barron's* includes quotes from Dow Jones averages and other financial indexes, foreign exchange rates, and basic economic financial indicators.

Best's Review. Life/Health Insurance Edition. Oldwick NJ: A.M. Best Company, 1899–. Monthly. $14.

Written for life/health insurance executives and agents, this periodical contains short, practical articles on timely topics in the life/health insurance field.

Best's Review. Property/Liability Insurance Edition.   Oldwick, NJ: A.M. Best Company, 1899–. Monthly. $14.
Concise articles of particular interest to property/liability insurance agents and executives are provided.

Business Month.   New York: Business Month, Inc., 1893–. Monthly. $32.
Formerly titled *Dun's Business Month,* this periodical analyzes current events in finance, business, and personal affairs.

Business Week.   New York: McGraw-Hill, 1929–. Weekly. $39.95.
This business news magazine provides succinct articles on new developments and trends of interest to executives in various business fields.

Commercial and Financial Chronicle.   New York: National Service, Inc., 1976–. Weekly. $140.
Daily high, low, and closing prices, quotations, dividends, and yearly ranges with a comprehensive index of several major financial markets are presented.

Earnings Forecaster.   New York: Standard and Poor's Corporation, 1966–. Weekly. $375.
Continuously updated listings are included of current corporate earnings estimates made by leading investment organizations. For each of the 1600 companies covered, the source and date of estimate, per share earnings for the past full year, estimate for the current year, and an estimate for the next year are given.

FE: The Magazine for Financial Executives.   Morristown, NJ: Financial Executives Institute, 1934–. Monthly. $40.
FE is published as an independent forum for authoritative views on the problems of business and financial management.

Financial Analysts Journal.   New York: Financial Analysts Federation, 1945–. Bi-monthly. $48.
Authoritative articles are provided, covering theoretical and practical problems concerning new developments in investment management, security analysis, and corporate finance in this journal written for the financial specialist.

Financial Post. Survey of Industrials.   Toronto, Ontario: Maclean-Hunter, 1927–. Weekly. $43.95.
Vital data on industrial securities are presented in this Canadian financial manual.

Financial Post. Survey of Mines and Energy Resources. Toronto, Ontario: Maclean-Hunter, 1927–. Weekly. $59.95.
Important financial and investment information regarding publicly owned Canadian crude oil, natural gas, and mining companies is reviewed.

Financial Times. London: Financial Times, Ltd. Daily. $365.
Worldwide coverage of business, finance, and economic news is provided.

Financial World. New York: Financial World Partners, 1902–. Biweekly. $44.95.
Designed for professional investors, this publication covers important trends and developments in the economy and stock market.

Forbes. New York: Forbes, Inc., 1917–. Biweekly. $45.
Consisting of articles of interest to business and financial executives and including prospects for industries and individual companies, this journal is a well-known source of current and longer term performance evaluations.

Fortune. New York: Time, Inc., 1930–. Biweekly. $44.50.
This prestigious business and management periodical includes thoroughly researched and well-written articles on topics of interest to business managers and investors.

Futures. Cedar Falls, Iowa: Penton Publishing Company, 1968–. Monthly. $34.
Activities and trends in futures trading are highlighted in regular columns and current articles focusing on commodities and options.

Industry Week. Cleveland: Penton Publishing Company, 1882–. Biweekly. $30.
Each issue of this popular trade journal covers current topics of general interest to business and management personnel.

Institutional Investor. New York: Institutional Investor, Inc., 1967–. Monthly. $165.
Providing useful articles of interest to money managers, such subjects as corporate financing, pension fund management, and investor relations are included with profiles of specific money managers.

Investment Dealer's Digest. New York: Institutional Investor, Inc., 1935–. Weekly. $195.
Written for financial and security brokers and dealers, topics include corpo-

rate and government financing, corporate earnings, research and development, and current financial news.

Journal of Business Strategy.   Boston: Warren, Gorham, and Lamont, Inc., 1980–. Quarterly. $72.
Articles useful for professional managers in the fields of marketing and technology are included.

Journal of Portfolio Management.   New York: Institutional Investor, Inc., 1974–. Quarterly. $145.
Authoritative discussions of risk and return by leading names in the field of portfolio management are presented.

Money.   New York: Time, Inc, 1972–. 13 times a year. $31.95.
Written for the general public, articles and topics cover various aspects of family and personal finance.

New York Times.   New York: New York Times Company, 1851–. Daily. $185.
All aspects of business, finance, and economics are treated with special emphasis given to advertising, banking, foreign trade, retailing, and securities markets.

Pension World.   Atlanta: Communications Channels, Inc., 1964–. Monthly. $41.
Written for plan sponsors and investment managers, topics include plan design, real estate, tax and other current issues in pension management and investment.

Pensions and Investment Age.   New York: Crain Communications, 1973–. Biweekly. $75.
Articles on investment and management topics written for corporate financial officers and investment professionals are presented.

Standard and Poor's Outlook.   New York: Standard and Poor's Corporation, 1937–. Weekly. $207.
Analysis and forecasts for business and stock market trends are included, with data on individual securities and purchase recommendations.

Wall Street Journal.   New York: Dow Jones and Company, 1889–. 5 times a week. $119.
Considered one of the most reliable sources for current business information, numerous topics such as taxes, government agency activities, port-

folios, consumer debt, and management are discussed, along with tables of corporate earnings, futures prices, mutual funds, foreign markets, and domestic markets.

Wall Street Transcript.   New York: Dow Jones and Company, 1963–. Weekly. $590.
> Texts are presented of several brokerage house reports on companies and industries, speeches of company officials, interviews with leading investment managers, and excerpts from corporate annual and interim reports.

GOVERNMENT DOCUMENTS

Business Conditions Digest.   Washington, D.C.: U.S. Bureau of Economic Analysis, U.S. Department of Commerce, 1961–. Monthly. $44.
> Charts and statistical tables are presented for the leading economic time series most useful to business analysts and forecasters, including cyclical indicators by economic process, national income and products, international comparisons, composite indexes and their components, and others.

Business Statistics.   Washington, D.C.: U.S. Department of Commerce, U.S. Government Printing Office, 1932–. Biennial. $13.
> Published as a supplement to *Survey of Current Business*, this document provides an historical account of the statistical series that appear currently in the *Survey.*

County and City Data Book.   Washington, D.C.: U.S. Bureau of the Census, U.S. Government Printing Office, 1949–. Irregular. $24.
> Information on cities, counties, states, and other geographical areas in the United States are included in a variety of lists. Results of censuses of the population and other statistical sources are used in determining sample data on education, labor force, income, etc.

Economic Report of the President. Transmitted to the Congress, February (each year); Together with the Annual Report of the Council of Economic Advisors.   Washington, D.C.: U.S. Council of Economic Advisors, U.S. Government Printing Office, 1947–. Annual. $8.50.
> A review is offered of the nation's economic condition, supported by vital statistics.

Federal Reserve Bulletin.   Washington, D.C.: U.S. Board of Governors of the Federal Reserve System, U.S. Government Printing Office, 1915–. Monthly. $20.
> Complete and accurate information, including statistics, on the financial

conditions of the United States is presented with reports on financial developments in other countries as well.

Producer Price Indexes. Washington, D.C.: U.S. Bureau of Labor Statistics, U.S. Department of Labor, U.S. Government Printing Office. Monthly. $29.

Text, tables, and technical notes covering producer price movements are presented.

SEC Monthly Statistical Review. Washington, D.C.: Securities and Exchange Commission, 1942–. Monthly. $22.

Monthly charts and graphs summarize statistical highlights in the stock market, options market, primary public offerings and registration. An index to statistical series not appearing monthly is included.

Statistical Abstract of the United States. Washington, D.C.: U.S. Bureau of the Census, U.S. Government Printing Office, 1879–. Annual. $27.

Considered one of the primary sources for statistical information of numerous varieties, data are provided on such topics as population, education, elections, finance, insurance, business enterprises, domestic trade and services, labor force, employment, and earnings.

Survey of Current Business. Washington, D.C.: U.S. Bureau of Economic Analysis, U.S. Department of Commerce, U.S. Government Printing Office, 1921–. Monthly. $50.

An overview is provided of business and economic activity in the United States, including articles, tables, and charts on industrial production, personal income, business and government expenditures, and other data relevant to business. Historical trends are kept current through the *Survey's* supplement, *Business Statistics.*

Treasury Bulletin. Washington, D.C.: U.S. Treasury Department, U.S. Government Printing Office. Quarterly. $20.

Up-to-date statistics are presented on federal fiscal operations, federal obligations, the U.S. Treasury, federal debt, public debt operations, U.S. Savings bonds, market quotations on Treasury securities, average yields on long-term bonds, and other government financial information.

U.S. Financial Data. St. Louis, MO: The Federal Reserve Bank of St. Louis. Weekly. Free to educational institutions.

Charts and graphs are presented weekly, showing levels and changes in adjusted monetary base, money stocks, money multiplier, total checkable deposits, and total time deposits.

United States Industrial Outlook. Washington, D.C.: U.S. Department of Commerce, U.S. Government Printing office, 1960–. Annual. $23.

Trends and forecasts for a number of U.S. industries are given with additional information on trends in world trade and the outlook for U.S. manufacturers, financial performance of U.S. manufacturing corporations, and industry highlights.

BIBLIOGRAPHY OF SUB-SAHARA AFRICAN LIBRARIANSHIP, 1988

Compiled by Glenn L. Sitzman

PREFACE

The present bibliography supplements the "Bibliography of African Librarianship" published in *African Libraries* (Scarecrow Press, 1988) and the "Bibliography of Sub-Sahara African Librarianship, 1986–1987" published in *Advances in Library Administration and Organization*, volume eight, 1989.

The search for new publications has again been focused on the three indexes, *Library Literature*, *Library and Information Science Abstracts*, and *Information Science Abstracts*. Examination of bibliographies in older publications continues to provide access to titles that were never indexed, as well as to information about ephemera and unpublished material. It also reveals that *much* African library material has remained unpublished and that many articles have never been indexed. For example, the lengthy bibliography appended to one article yielded twenty-seven retrospective titles new to this bibliography, with fourteen of them cited as unpublished. Incomplete citations taken from such bibliographies and bibliographical notes are entered here as they were cited in the compiler's sources.

Advances in Library Administration and Organization,
Volume 9, pages 199–227.
Copyright © 1991 by JAI Press, Inc.
All rights of reproduction in any form reserved.
ISBN: 1-55938-066-7

This supplement adds approximately three hundred titles to the growing bibliography. Roughly, about 45 percent of the titles included here were issued before 1980, with about 55 percent published 1980–1988. About one-third of the supplement deals with Africa more or less generally, one-third with Nigeria, and the other third with sixteen other Sub-Saharan countries. Titles added here for Nigeria include 34 pre-1980 items and 91 for the period 1980–1988. For the other sixteen countries represented here, 62 titles date from before 1980 and 109 after. For the Sub-Sahara in general the division is approximately half and half.

These statistics do not, of course, reflect accurately or completely on current library publication activities. Moreover, the date 1988 in the title indicates only the year in which the compiler's investigations occurred, and "current" in this context includes the period 1980–1988. One can, however, get some idea from these observations about past and current bibliographical activity with regard to particular countries. For example, thirty-seven retrospective titles were retrieved for Ghana, but only two current items. For Kenya there were nine retrospective titles and six current; for Liberia, seven pre-1980 and zero current; for Tanzania, six retrospective and five current. One must keep in mind that discovering retrospective material through older publications is often solely a matter of chance; and, apart from the indexes, the discovery of current material is sometimes also a matter of chance.

One important publication of 1987 that deserves special mention was Wilfred Plumbe's *Tropical Librarianship* (Scarecrow Press). In the volume Plumbe brings together all his short publications on librarianship in the Sub-Sahara and other areas of the Third World. Bringing this vast span of work together in one volume is an invaluable contribution to African librarianship and to international librarianship in general.

Another event of 1987 that deserves special mention was a conference in Zimbabwe devoted to Library Services to the Disadvantaged, the theme of the Annual General Meeting of the Zimbabwe Library Association, with papers subsequently published in the *Zimbabwe Librarian*. Overall, it appears to the compiler that, despite setbacks here and there, the library scene in the Sub-Sahara continues to be encouraging.

GUIDE TO ORGANIZATION OF BIBLIOGRAPHY

Africa in General

General and Peripheral
Bibliographies and Bibliography
Biographies of Librarians
Book Trade, Printing, and Publishing
Cataloging and Classification
Documentation and Information Science

Academic Libraries
Special Libraries

Africana

General
Africana Collections outside Black Africa

Inter-Regional and Regional

Inter-Regional
Central Africa
Eastern Africa
General
East African Library Association
Public Libraries
Southern Africa
West Africa

International Meetings

1963, Nairobi, Kenya, Conference on Education for Librarianship in East Africa
1970, Kampala, Uganda, Meeting of Experts on the National Planning of Documentation and Library Services in Africa
1978, Nairobi, Kenya, Standing Conference of Eastern, Central and Southern African Libraries

Bibliographies of Individual Countries

Botswana
Chad
Gambia
Ghana
General
Professional Associations
Academic Libraries
Public Libraries
School and Children's Library Services
Kenya
General
Public Libraries
School and Children's Library Services
Special Libraries
Liberia

Madagascar
Malawi
Mauritius
Namibia
Niger
Nigeria
  General
  Bibliographies and Bibliography
  Book Trade, Printing, and Publishing
  Cataloging and Classification
  Documentation and Information Science
  Librarians and Librarianship
  Library Education
    General
    Ahmadu Bello University
    Bayero University
    University of Ibadan
  Academic Libraries
    General
    Ahmadu Bello University
    Federal University of Technology, Makurdi
    University of Benin
    University of Ibadan
    University of Ilorin
    University of Jos
    University of Lagos
    University of Port Harcourt
  Children's Library Services
  National Library of Nigeria
  Public Libraries
    General
    Former Northern Region
    Kano State
    Lagos State
  School Libraries
  Special Libraries, Materials, and Services
    General
    Agriculture
    Law
    Medicine and Health Sciences
    Science and Technology
Seychelles
Sudan

Tanzania
    General
    Academic Libraries
    Public Libraries
    School and Children's Library Services
Zambia
Zimbabwe
    General
    School and Children's Library Services
    Special Libraries, Materials, and Services
        General
        Library Service to the Handicapped

Africa—General and Peripheral

Adewole, Segun. "Selecting Livestock Periodicals through Citation Analysis Technique." *Information Processing & Management.* 23(1987): 629–638.

Aithnard, K. M. "Bibliotheken in ontwikkelingslanden" (Libraries in Developing Countries). *Bibliotheek en Samenleving.* 16(1988): 51–53.

Andersen, Ida Marie. "Tid for 'Book-aid' mot bokhunger i Afrika" (Time for "Book Aid" against Book Hunger in Africa). *Bok og Bibloitek.* 54(1987): 28.

Archer, A. M. "The Overseas Book Centre: a Possible Outreach of Librarians to Developing Countries." *Canadian Libraries.* 22(1965): 149–151.

Brewster, Beverly J. *American Overseas Library Technical Assistance, 1940–1970.* Metuchen, NJ, Scarecrow Press, 1976. First presented as a master's thesis at the University of Pittsburgh, 1974, with the title "An Analysis of American Overseas Library Technical Assistance, 1940–1970."

Comparative and International Librarianship. Edited by P. S. Kawatra. Envoy Press, 1987.

Danset, Françoise, and Jean-Claude Le Dro. "Bibliothèques et développement en Afrique" (Libraries and Development in Africa). *Bulletin d'Informations de l'Association des Bibliothécaires Français.* 133(1986): 30.

Diop, Amadou. "Attitudes of Information Users in the Sahel." *Information Development.* 4(1988): 21–27.

Dua-Agyemang, H. "The African National Library Situation, Problems and Prospects." *Ghana Library Journal.* 3(1969): 25–33.

"Carnegie in Africa." *Times Education Supplement.* May 21, 1955, p. 54.

Fenton, Thomas P., and Mary J. Heffron. *Africa: a Directory of Resources.* Orbis Books, 1987.

Gardner, Frank Matthias. "The President's Page." *Library Association Record.* 12(1964): 585–587.

Gupta, Sushma. "The Role of the Library in the Life of an African Church." *Librarians' Christian Fellowship Newsletter*. 37(1987): 38–40.

Harris, G. "The Attempts of Library Associations to Assist Third World Librarianship." *IFLA Journal*. 12(1986): 291–295.

Hawkridge, D. "Distance Education and the World Bank." *British Journal of Education Technology*. 19(1988): 84–95.

Krieger, Milton. "African Policy Linking Education and Development: Standard Criticisms and a New Departure." *International Review of Education*. 34(1988): 293–311.

Mabomba, Rodrick S. "The Development of Librarianship in the Third World: a View from Africa." *INSPEL*. 21(1987): 181–207.

Ndiaye, A. Raphaël "Advancement of Librarianship in the Third World." *IFLA Journal*. 12(1986): 279.

_____. "Oral Culture and Libraries." *IFLA Journal*. 14(1988): 40–46.

Ofori, A. G. T. "The Cultural and Recreational Role of the Library." *Ghana Library Journal*. 4(1972): 513.

Plumbe, Wilfred J. "Education in Librarianship—to Long-suffering Library Assistants" [poem]. In his *Tropical Librarianship*, 158–159. Metuchen, N.J., Scarecrow Press, 1987. First published in *WALA News*. 3(March 1959).

_____. "Furniture and Equipment in Tropical Libraries." In his *Tropical Librarianship*, [29]–36. Metuchen, N.J., Scarecrow Press, 1987. First published in *UNESCO Bulletin for Libraries*. 15(Sept/Oct 1961).

_____. "Trends in Newly Developing Countries." In his *Tropical Librarianship*, [13]–17. Metuchen, N.J., Scarecrow Press, 1987. First published in *Library Trends*. 8(1959): 125–129.

_____. *Tropical Librarianship*. Metuchen, N.J.: Scarecrow Press, 1987.

Post, Mogens. "Afrikanske biblioteksglimmt" (Glimpses of African Libraries). *Bibliotek*. 70(1987): 372–374.

Rathgeber, Eva M. "A Tenuous Relationship: the African University and Development Policy Making in the 1980s." *Higher Education*. 17(1988): 397–410.

Sitzman, Glenn L. "African Librarianship, an Overview." Paper read March 25, 1976, to International Librarianship Class, Clarion State College.

_____. *African Libraries*. Metuchen, N.J., Scarecrow Press, 1988.

_____. "Libraries Around the World." [Videorecording of Lecture with transparencies given to School of Library and Information Science, Clarion State College] 1977. 2 videocassettes. black and white.

_____. "Selected Libraries of Africa." [Videorecording of lecture with color transparencies given April 14, 1982, to International Librarianship Class, Clarion State College] 1982. 1 videocassette. color.

Sloane, Ruth C. "Patterns of Library Service in Africa." *Library Trends*. 8(1959): 163–191.

Unesco. *Statistics on Libraries*. Paris, 1959.

Africa—Bibliographies and Bibliography

Aje, S. B. "The Role of National Libraries in Development and Problems of National Bibliography and Legal Deposit." *East African Library Association Bulletin*. 14(1974): 25–50.
Masanjika, Raphael. "Legal Deposit and a National Bibliography." *MALA Bulletin*. 4(1986): 22–29.
Mwalimu, Charles. "A Bibliographic Essay of Selected Secondary Sources on the Common Law and Customary Law of English-speaking Sub-Saharan Africa." *Law Library Journal*. 80(1988): 241–289.
Oluoch, A. R. "On Developing a National Bibliographic Agency." *MAKTABA*. 5(1979): 42–44. Also published in *The Development of Information: an African Approach*, edited by R. W. Thairu, 42–44. Nairobi, Kenya Library Association, 1979.
Zell, Hans. *Publishing and Book Development in Africa: a Bibliography*. Paris, Unesco, 1984.

Africa—Biographies of Librarians

Arthur-Aponsah, D. "In Memorian Kenneth Middlemast: Deputy Director of Library Services, Ghana." *West African Library Association News*. 3(1959): 81–83.

Africa—Book Trade, Printing, and Publishing

"African Books Collective." *Library Association Record*. 90(1988): 370.
Kgosidintsi, T. F. "Report on the African Book Exhibition Held in Montreal University: 28th April-3rd May, 1986." *Botswana Library Association Journal*. 8(1986): 40–44.
MacLam, Helen. " 'Food for Thought'—Relieving the African Book Famine." *Choice*. 25(1988): 1658–1659.
Mason, I. "Notes on Book Distribution: Books for Africa, 21st Jan., 1951." [citation from *International Handbook of Contemporary Developments in Librarianship*, 1981, p. 25]
Plumbe, Wilfred J. "Books and Writing in Africa and Asia before the Invention of Printing." In his *Tropical Librarianship*, 37–52. Metuchen, N.J., Scarecrow Press, 1987. First published in *Malayan Library Journal*. 2(1961): 41–50.
UNESCO. *Book Development in Africa: Problems and Perspectives*. Paris, Unesco, 1969.

Africa—Cataloging and Classification

Amankwe, Nwozo. "British and American Practice in Entering African Authors." Paper Read at the Seminar on Cataloguing and Classification of Africana, University of Ibadan, Institute of Librarianship, 1966.
———. *Classification of African Languages. 1. West Africa.* Nsukka, 1964. unpublished.
Armstrong, R. G. "Cataloguing (and Classification) of African Languages." Paper Read at the Seminar on Cataloguing and Classification of Africana, University of Ibadan, Institute of Librarianship, 1966.
Centre d'Analyse et de Recherche Documentaires pour l'Afrique Noire (CARDAN). Centre of African Studies. *Key-words Used by C.A.R.D.A.N. and C.A.S.: Correspondence between Indexing Systems.* Paris, CARDAN, 1966.
Dieneman, W. W. "The Cataloguing of Hausa Names. Followed by Appendices on 'Muslim Personal Names,' 'Nicknames,' 'Titles of District Heads,' (Issued by Commissioner of Police, Jos, on 1.7.30) and 'A Selection of Miscellaneous Titles'." *Northern Nigeria Library Notes.* 1(May 1964): 51–61.
Greenberg, J. H. *Languages of Africa: Studies in African Linguistic Classification.* 2d ed. The Hague, Mouton, 1966.
Hawkes, Arthur J. "An Extension and Revision of the Dewey's Africa Schedule." *The Librarian.* 3(1912/13): 242–245, 283–287.
Izard, Françoise. *Une expérience de traitement automatique de la documentation a partir de documents concernant l'Afrique au sud du Sahara.* Paris, Maison des Sciences de l'Homme (C.A.R.D.A.N.), 1962.
Johannesburg Public Library. *African Native Tribes: Rules for Classification of Works on African Ethnology in the Strange Collection of Africana, with an Index of Tribal Names and their Variations.* Johannesburg, 1956.
Mahmud, K. "Problems in Classifying Arabic Material." Paper Read at the Seminar on Cataloguing and Classification of Africana, University of Ibadan, Institute of Librarianship, 1966.
Nkwo, S. D. "Proposals for Modifying the Decimal Classification for Africana." Paper Read at the Seminar on Cataloguing and Classification of Africana, University of Ibadan, Institute of Librarianship, 1966.
Ogunsheye, F. A. "National Bibliographies: Arrangement and Suitable Modifications." Paper Read at the Seminar on Cataloguing and Classification of Africana, University of Ibadan, Institute of Librarianship, 1966.
Plumbe, Wilfred J. "Classification." *SCAUL Newsletter.* no. 4(April 1967): 181–186.
———. "Classification and Cataloguing of Africana." In his *Tropical Librarianship*, 142–157. Metuchen, N.J., Scarecrow Press, 1987. First read as a paper at the Commonwealth Foundation Conference of Librarians from Commonwealth Universities in Africa, held at the University of Zambia, Lusaka, August 1969.

Africa—Documentation and Information Science

Azubuike, Abraham A., and Jackson S. Umoh. "Computerized Information Storage and Retrieval Systems." *International Library Review.* 20(1988): 101–110.

Easterbrook, David L. "InfoTrac and Africa." *African Research & Documentation.* 44(1987): 12–15.

Hartevelt, J. H. W. van. "Advantages of CD-ROM for Local Access to Computerized Databases in Developing Countries, in Comparison with Traditional Bibliographic Services: Suggested Pilot Projects." *Quarterly Bulletin of the International Association of Agricultural Librarians and Documentalists.* 32(1987): 161–168.

Krissiamba Ouiminga, Ali. "Pour changer la situation documentaire au Sahel" (Changing the State of Documentation in the Sahel). *Documentalist.* 24 (1987): 230–235.

Ogwang-Ameny, Remy. "Information and Documentation as Modern Media of Research and Development." *International Forum on Information and Documentation.* 12(1987): 3–7.

Olden, Anthony. "Sub-Saharan Africa and the Paperless Society." *Journal of the American Society for Information Science.* 38(1987): 298–304.

Shayen, Mette. "Computerised Data Searching for the African Scholar." *African Research & Documentation.* 43(1987): 8–15.

Tiamiyu, Mutawakilu A., and Isola Y. Ajiferuke. "A Total Relevance and Document Interaction Effects Model for Evaluation of Information Retrieval Processes." *Information Processing and Management.* 24(1988): 391–404.

Africa—Academic Libraries

Bowen, Dorothy N. "Learning Style Based Bibliographic Instruction." *International Library Review.* 20(1988): 405–413.

Plumbe, Wilfred J. "Climate as a Factor in the Planning of University Library Buildings." In his *Tropical Librarianship*, [18]–28. Metuchen, N.J., Scarecrow Press, 1987. First published in *Unesco Bulletin for Libraries.* vol. 17, no. 6(1963).

_____. "Staff Education and Training in African University Libraries." In his *Tropical Librarianship*, 55–72. Metuchen, N.J., Scarecrow Press, 1987. First published in *Northern Nigeria Library Notes.* 2/3(1964–65): 131–148.

Africa—Special Libraries, Materials, and Services

Bellamy, Margot. "Bridging the Information Gap in African Agriculture: CABI's African Agricultural Literature Service." *Interlending & Document Supply.* 16(1988): 46–50.

Cooney, S., and D. N. Kaiyare, E. Lumande, S. S. Mbwana. "Information for Agricultural Development: the Role of Literature Services." *Quarterly Bulletin of the International Association of Agricultural Librarians and Documentalists*. 33(1988): 79–86.
Kaniki, Andrew M. "Agricultural Information Services in Less Developed Countries [Bibliographical Essay]". *International Library Review*. 20(1988): 321–336.
Mazikana, Peter C. "A Strategy for the Preservation of Audiovisual Materials." *Audiovisual Librarian*. 14(1988): 24–28.
Moss, W. W., and P. Mazikana. *Archives, Oral History and Oral Tradition: a RAMP Study*. Paris, Unesco, 1986.
Thomsen, P. "The Establishment of a Library Service to Visually Handicapped People in African Developing Countries." *IFLA Journal*. 11(1985): 36–42.

Africana—General

African Studies; Papers Presented at a Colloquium at the British Library, 7–9 January 1985. Edited by Ilse Sternberg and Patricia M. Larby. British Library, 1986.
Ajayi, J. F. A. "Factors that Have Influenced Scholarship and Research on Africa." Paper Read at the Seminar on Cataloguing and Classification of Africana, University of Ibadan, Institute of Librarianship, 1966.
Casada, Jim. "Armchair Adventures in Collecting Africana [Bibliographical Essay]." *AB Bookman's Weekly*. 81(June 13, 1988): 2505–2506+.
Kwafo-Akoto, Kate O. "Acquiring Unpublished Population Documents in Africa: a Personal Experience." *Aslib Proceedings*. 40(1988): 105–110.
Loh, Eudora I. "Africa, Asia, Europe, and Latin America [Government Publications, mid-1986 to mid-1987]." *Government Publications Review*. 14 (1987): 701–708.
Oliver, Eileen. "An Afrocentric Approach to Literature: Putting the Pieces back Together." *English Journal*. 77(1988): 49–53.
"SCOLMA Silver Jubilee Conference, London, 14–15 May 1987." *African Research & Documentation*. 44(1987): 23–26.
Sternberg, Ilse, and Patricia M. Larby, eds. *African Studies. Papers Presented at the Colloquiam at the British Library, 7–9 January 1985*. London, The British Library in association with SCOLMA, 1986.
Van Ausdall, Barbara Wass. "Images of Africa for American Students." *English Journal*. 77(1988): 37–39.
Zell, Hans, et al. *A New Reader's Guide to African Literature*. New York, Holmes and Meier, 1983.

Africana—Africana Collections outside Black Africa

Battle, T. C., and D. F. Joyce. "Resources for Scholars: Four Major Collections of Afro-Americana. Part 2: Two University Library Collections." *Library Quarterly*. 58(1988): 143–163.
Joyce, D. F., and H. Dodson. "Resources for Scholars: Four Major Collections of Afro-Americana. Part 1: Two Public Library Collections." *Library Quarterly*. 58(1988): 66–82.

Inter-Regional and Regional

Howse, F. G. "Problems and Prospects of the Library/Information Profession in the Eastern, Central and Southern African Region." *MALA Bulletin*. 4(1986): 4–16.

Inter-Regional and Regional—Central Africa

University College of Rhodesia. Dept. of African Studies. *Gazeteer of African Tribes in the Federation of Rhodesia and Nyasaland*. Salisbury, 1957. (mimeographed)

Inter-Regional and Regional—Eastern Africa—General

East African Literature Bureau. *Annual Reports, 1949–69*. Nairobi.
Huxley, E. *Literature for Africans: Report to the East African High Commission*. Nairobi, 1948.
Otike, J. N. "A Critical Analysis of the Legal Deposit Laws in East Africa." *International Cataloguing & Bibliographic Control*. 17(1988): 12–14.
Sitzman, Glenn L. "Libraries of East Africa." [Videorecording of Lecture with color transparencies given May 15, 1982, to International Librarianship Class, Clarion State College] 1982. 1 videocassette. color
Umbima, E. W., and C. M. Khamala. "The Library Scene in Kenya, Uganda and Tanzania." Paper prepared for the AFRO-NORDICC Conference in Helsinki, Finland, September 3–7, 1979.
Wise, M. C. "Library Cooperation in East Africa." *East African Library Association Bulletin*. 10(Oct 1968): 16–21.

Inter-Regional and Regional—Eastern Africa—East African Library Association

Musisi, J. S. "East African Conference: Sharp Conflicts Emerge." *Library Journal*. 95(Nov 15, 1970): 3864.

Inter-Regional and Regional—Eastern Africa—Public Libraries

Richards, C. G. "The Beginnings of Public Library Services in East Africa."
East African Library Association Bulletin. no. 4(June 1963): 4.

Inter-Regional and Regional—Southern Africa

Kamba, Angeline S., and Peter C. Mazikana. "Archive Repatriation in Southern
Africa." *Information Development*. 4(1988): 79–85.
Lor, Peter J. "The Southern African Interlending Scheme: Some Results of a
Comprehensive Survey." *Interlending & Document Supply*. 15(1987): 101–
107.
————. "The Volume and Distribution of Interlending within the Southern African Interlending Scheme." *South African Journal of Library and Information Science*. 55(1987): 81–93.
Thapisa, A. P. N. "Whither Human Being? Theories of Management as Applied
to Library Management in Southern Africa." *International Forum on Information and Documentation*. 12(1987): 14–20.

Inter-Regional and Regional—West Africa

Davies, Helen. *Libraries in West Africa: a Bibliography*. Munich, Zell, 1982.
NB. The 1974 ed. of the Davies bibliography is in *African Libraries*. p.
323.
Fayose, Philomena O. "Seminar Paper on New Directions in the Educational
Functions of West African Libraries." *Ghana Library Journal*. 3(1969): 16–
23.
Fraser, M. A. C. *Libraries in Africa: a Description of Various Aspects as Prac-
ticed in West and South Africa*. Washington, DC, Catholic University of
America, 1968.
Harris, John. "Co-operation between Universities in Printing and Publishing." In
*The West African Intellectual Community: Ibadan Papers . . . of an Inter-
national Seminar*, 289–313. Ibadan, University Press, 1962.
————. "Notes on Book Preservation in West Africa." *WALA News*. 2(1956):
102–105.
Kotei, S. I. A. "Further Concepts of Relevance in West African Librarianship."
Ghana Library Journal. 5(1973): 23–31.
Lancour, Harold. "Impressions of British West Africa." *ALA Bulletin*. 52(1958):
419–420.
"Library Service in British West Africa." *Fundamental Adult Education*. 3
(1951): 23–33.
"Library Statistics for West Africa." *WALA News*. 4(1961): 22–23.

Middlemast, Kennet. "Libraries and the West African Community." *WALA News*. 2(1955): 27–31.

Oddoye, E. Oko. "Seminar on Problems of Book Provision in West Africa— Working Paper on the Ghanaian Case." *Ghana Library Journal*. 5(1973): 40–47.

Ofori, A. G. T. "The Organization of the Library Profession in West Africa." In *The Organization of Library Profession Symposium Based on Contributions to the 37th Session of the IFLA General Session, Liverpool, 1971*, 77–84. Munich, Verlag Dokumentation, 1976.

Perry, Ruth. "Libraries in West Africa." *West African Review*. (Sept 1955): 827– 832.

Pitcher, G. M. "Donations of Books to Libraries in West Africa." *WALA News*. 2(1958): 164–165.

Thompson, J. S. T. E. "Postwar Development of Librarianship in Former British West Africa: a Historical Description of Library Development in Ghana, Nigeria, Sierra Leone and Gambia." Thesis, University College London, 1968/69.

International Meetings

1963 Nairobi, Kenya, Conference on Education for Librarianship in East Africa
"East African Library Association, Conference on Library Training for East Africa." *East African Library Association Bulletin*. no. 4(June 1963): 17– 18.

1970 Kampala, Uganda, Meeting of Experts on the National Planning of Documentation and Library Services in Africa
Unesco. *Meeting of Experts on the National Planning of Documentation and Library Services in Africa, Kampala, Uganda, Dec. 7–15, 1970. Final Report*. CCM/MD/18.

1978 Nairobi, Kenya, Standing Conference of Eastern, Central and Southern African Libraries
Kenya Library Association. "The Third International Standing Conference of ECSAL, 1978. Regulations." (Document No. 13)

Bibliographies of Individual Countries

Botswana

Boadi, B. Y. *Introduction to Librarianship and Documentation. Teaching and Learning Material for the Long Vacation Courses at the University of Botswana, 1984 to 1987*. 1987. ERIC. ED 288 546.

Gessesse, K. "Agricultural Library and Information Development in Botswana: a

Profile." *Quarterly Bulletin of the International Association of Agricultural Librarians and Documentalists*. 33(1988): 117–120.

Made, Stanley M. "Reading—Library Facilities in Botswana." F. L. A. thesis, University of Botswana, Lesotho, and Swaziland, 1977.

Mbaakanyi, D. M. "Educational Library Provision for the Blind in Botswana." *Information Development*. 3(1987): 220–225.

Monageng, Stella. "National Institute of Development Research and Documentation: Paper Presented at the Boleswa Research Institute's Workshop, 9–12 June 1986, Gabarone." *Botswana Library Association Journal*. 8(1986): 10–13.

Motlhatlhedi, L. M. "Development of a Fuel Control System for the Botswana Central Transport Organization." *Information Development*. 3(1988): 13–32.

Chad

Margarido, Alfredo, and Pierrette Ceccaldi. "Présentation du fichier ethnique du Centre d'Analyse et de Recherche Documentaires pour l'Afrique Noire (C.A.R.D.A.N.) et du projet de publication d l'inventaire provisoire des populations du Tchad" (Presentation of the Ethnic Card Catalog of the Center for Analysis and Documentary Research for Black Africa . . . and the Plan for Publication of the Provisional Inventory of the Populations of Tchad). *Africa*. 38(Apr 1968): 204–208.

Gambia

Harris, Gill. "Brikama: a Library in The Gambia." *Assistant Librarian*. 80 (1987): 150–152.

N'jie, S. P. C. "Collecting Policies and Preservation: The Gambia." (*IFLA Publications*, No. 40) In *Preservation of Library Materials. Proceedings of the Conference Held at the National Library of Austria, Vienna, April 1986, Volume I*, 24–30. New York, K. G. Saur, 1987.

Ghana—General

Agyemang, K. D. "The African Librarian and the African Revolution." *Ghana Library Journal*. 2(1965): 13–17.

Cornelius, David. "Possible Impact of Past, Present, and Future Developments of Library Services in Ghana." In *International Librarianship*, edited by G. Chandler, London, Library Association, 1972.

———. "The Role of Libraries in National Development." *Ghana Library Journal*. 5(1973): 32–39.

DeHeer, A. N., ed. *Workshop of International Standard Bibliographic Description (ISBD), Accra, July 1975*. Accra, Ghana Library Association, 1976.

Eedle, James. "The Ghana Book Club." *Ghana Teachers Journal*. 45(1965): 37–48.

Evans, Evelyn J. A. "Library News from the Gold Coast." *Unesco Bulletin for Libraries*. 6(1952): 137.

_____. "Library Services in Ghana." In *Library Work in Africa*, edited by Anna Britta Wallenius, 1–17. Uppsala, Scandinavian Institute of African Studies, 1966.

_____. "The Place of Ghana Libraries in World Institutions." *The Ghanaian*. 6(Oct 1958).

_____. "Preservation of Library Material in Tropical Countries." *Library Trends*. 8(1959): 291–306.

Ghana. Laws, Statutes, etc. *The Book and Newspaper Registration Act, 1961, No. 73 of 1961*. Accra, Government Printer, 1961.

_____. *The Book and Newspaper Registration (Amendment Act, 1961, No. 193 of 1961*. Accra, Government Printer, 1961.

_____. *Copyright Act, 1961, No. 85 of 1961*. Accra, Government Printer, 1961.

Ghana Library Association. "The Role of Books and Libraries in the Educational Systems of Ghana; Ghana Library Association Memorandum to the Education Review Committee Set up by the N. L. C. to Advise on National Education Policies." *Ghana Library Journal*. 2(1968): 46–51.

Griffen, Ella. *A Study of the Reading Habits of Adults in Ashanti, Southern Ghana and Trans Volta Togoland*. Accra, Bureau of Ghana Languages, 1959.

Harris, Philip. "Publishing in Ghana." *Ghana Trade Journal*. 33(1962): 26.

Johnson, P. H. "The Government and the People's Education." *Ghanaian Times*. (May 3, 1962): 7.

Kenworthy, L. S. "Library Progress in Ghana." *Wilson Library Bulletin*. 34(1969): 267–268.

Kimble, Helen. "A Reading Survey in Accra." *Universitas*. 3(1958): 77–81.

Kotei, S. I. A. "The Social Determinants of Library Development in Ghana, with Reference to the Influence of British Traditions." Master's thesis, University of London, 1972.

"List of Qualified Librarians and Archivists in Ghana, August, 1963." *Ghana Library Journal*. 1(1963): 22.

Nyarko, Kwame. "Kwame Nkrumah and the Growth of Libraries in Ghana." *Zambia Library Association Journal*. 4(1972): 30–32.

Ofori, Henry. "The Library and the Press." *Ghana Library Journal*. 3(1969): 7–9.

Ott, Albert. "Book Distribution in Ghana." *Ghana Trade Journal*. 33(1962): 24–25.

Scott, C. F. "Report on Ghana at Conference on the Acquisition of Material from Africa, University of Birmingham (25 April 1969)." *SCOLMA Newsletter*. (1969): 83–87.

Sitzman, Glenn L. "Libraries of Ghana." [Videorecording of Lecture with color transparencies given April 7, 1982, to International Librarianship Class, Clarion State College] 1982. 1 videocassette. color.

Storch, R. F. "Writing in Ghana." *Universitas*. 2(1957): 148–151.

Symposia on Problems of Communications between the Library and its Users, Accra, 10th–12th February, 1972. Accra, Ghana Library Association, 1977.

Tregido, P. S. "Reading for Pleasure." *Ghana Teacher's Journal*. 23(1969): 22–28.

Ghana—Professional Associations

Ghana Library Association. "Annual General Meeting." *Ghana Library Journal*. 1(1964): 31–33.

———. "2nd Annual Conference, Kumasi, September 1963." *Ghana Library Journal*. 1(1964): 27–31.

———. "Two-year Report of the Council for the Period 25th July 1965–28th August 1966 and 28th August 1966–30th July 1967." *Ghana Library Journal*. 2(1968): 68–73.

Oddoye, David Emmanuel Michael. "Presidential Address." *Ghana Library Journal*. 4(1970): 7–9.

Ofori, A. G. T. "Presidential Address." *Ghana Library Journal*. 2(1965): 2–3.

Ollennu, N. A. "Opening Address Delivered . . . on Saturday, August 27, 1966 at the Week-end Symposium of the Ghana Library Association . . . on the Theme 'The Library in Education'." *Ghana Library Journal*. 3(1969): 5–7.

Ghana—Academic Libraries

Agyei-Gyane, L. "The Development and Administration of the Africana Collection in the Balme Library, University of Ghana, Legon." *Libri*. 37(1987): 222–238.

Dean, John. "Library of Congress Modifications in the Balme Library, University of Ghana." Paper read at the Seminar on Cataloguing and Classification of Africana, University of Ibadan, Institute of Librarianship, 1966.

Morna, C. L. "Ghana's Universities Struggle to Cope with New Priorities." *Chronicle of Higher Education*. 35(1988): 43–44.

Ghana—Public Libraries

"Memorandum Presented to the Salaries Review Commission by the Director of Ghana Library Board." *Ghana Library Journal*. 2(1968): 55–68.

Ghana—School and Children's Library Services

Gold Coast Library Board. *An Investigation into the Reading Habits of Children in the Middle Schools in Towns in which Children's Libraries Have Been Opened*. Accra, The Board, 1956.

Okyne, R. R. "Some Common Causes of Backwardness in Reading in Middle Schools." *Ghana Teachers' Journal*. 22(1959): 3–11.

———. "Some Common Causes of Backwardness in Reading in Primary Schools." *Ghana Teachers' Journal*. 21(1959): 19–27.

Kenya—General

Keli, Ester. "A Preliminary Report on the Feasibility of Establishing District Documentation Centres. Prepared by the Subcommittee of an Interministerial Interagency Working Group. RSCTU.M/ECCA. Nairobi, August 1979." (mimeographed)

Kenya. *Law of Kenya: The Books and Newspapers Ordinance*. Chapter 3. 2d ed. Nairobi, Government Printer, 1962.

Kenya Library Association. "KLA Seminar on National Bibliographic Agency Held at KNLS on 18th March 1978, and Chaired by J. S. Musisi." (mimeographed)

———. "Report of the Education Sub-Committee, 1974." *MAKTABA*. 2(1975): 114–121.

Lieberman, Ronald. "Bookman's Safari: the Pursuit of Libraries in Kenya." *AB Bookman's Weekly*. 82(1988): 31–33.

Luckman, M. E. "Oldest Library in Kenya?" *East African Library Association Bulletin*. 9(1968): 18–20.

Musisi, J. S. "A New Library School Planned in Kenya." *COMLA Newsletter*. 55(Mar 1987): 2–3.

Kenya—Public Libraries

Kenya National Library Service Board. *Annual Report*. Nairobi.

Ng'ang'a, J. M. "The Development of Public Libraries in Kenya: Past, Present, and Future." Master's thesis, Loughborough University of Technology, 1979.

Opondo, R. G. "Public Libraries in Cosmopolitan African Cities, Nairobi: a Case Study." *MAKTABA*. 3(1976): 3–16.

Toweet, T. "Foreword to 1968–69 KNLS Annual Report." Nairobi, Kenya National Library Service Board, 1970.

Kenya—School and Children's Library Services

Otike, J. N. "Acquisition Problems in School Libraries: the Kenyan Situation."
    International Review of Children's Literature and Librarianship. 2(1987):
    181–190.
——. "The Role of a School Library: the Kenyan Experience." *International
    Library Review.* 19(1987): 413–421.
——. "Staffing Secondary School Libraries in Kenya." *Information Develop-
    ment.* 4(1988): 98–102.

Kenya—Special Libraries

Otike, J. N. "Special Libraries in Kenya." *International Library Review.*
    19(1987): 271–285.

Liberia

CARE-LIBERIA. "National Library Extension Program: The Library as a Com-
    plement to the Community School, 1972." (mimeographed)
Cornell University. "Cornell University at the University of Liberia. Final Re-
    port, May 28, 1962–July 31, 1968." (mimeographed)
Cuttington University College. *Annual Reports of the Librarian.* Monrovia.
Diggs, Osborne K. "International Book Year 1972 and Why Libraries."
    Monrovia, Liberia, 1972. (mimeographed)
Evans, E. J. *Liberia Libraries.* Paris, Unesco, 1967.
Institute of Librarianship. "Prospects of the Institute of Librarianship: a Two-year
    Program Study and Other Information." Monrovia, Liberia, 1975.
    (mimeographed)
Lancour, Harold. "The University of Liberia Library. Report of a Survey, 1960."
    (mimeographed)

Madagascar

Abraham, Raymond. *Classification decimale universelle de Madagascar.* Tan-
    ananrive, Bibliothèque Nationale, 1962.
Rakoto, R. "Razvitie bibliotechongo dela na Madagaskare" (Development of
    Librarianship in Madagascar). *Bibliotekovedenie i Bibliografia za Rubezhom.*
    108(1986): 16–18.

Malawi

Kadzamira, Z. D. "Opening of the 1985 Library Assistant Certificate Course
    under the Auspices of the Malawi Library Association, 9 April 1985."
    MALA Bulletin. 4(1986): 1–3.
Liyawo, B. B. "The Role of the Malawi Parliament Library to Members of

Parliament, Administrative Staff and Outside Users." *MALA Bulletin.* 4(1986): 17–21.

Macleod, R. "Library Orientation in an Academic Library in a Developing Country." *MALA Bulletin.* 4(1986): 44–62.

Msiska, Augustine W. "Malawian Librarianship Looks to Training for the Future." *Training and Education.* 5(1988): 44–48.

Mvula, H. S. T. "Interlibrary Loans in Malawi: the Case of University of Malawi Libraries—Situation and Proposals." *MALA Bulletin.* 4(1986): 30–36.

Nakahama, Michiko. "A Different Society and Culture: Thoughts on Working in a Library in Malawi." (In Japanese) *Toshokan Zasshi.* 81(1987): 194–195.

Plumbe, Wilfred J. "The University of Malawi Library." In his *Tropical Librarianship,* 111–121. Metuchen, N. J., Scarecrow Press, 1987. First published in *The Rhodesian Librarian.* 2(1970): 55–63.

Mauritius

"Children [from Olympia, Washington, Elementary School] Send Books to African School Library." *American Libraries.* 19(1988): 248.

Namibia

Mantel, Theresa. "Biblioteekfokus: Walvisbaai—diens aan die biblioteke" (Library Focus: Walvis Bay—Service to Libraries). *Cape Librarian.* 31(1987): 13–14.

Verbaan, M. "As Prospects for Namibia's Independence Improve, Territory's Education System Faces New Turmoil." *Chronicle of Higher Education.* 35(1988): A33.

Niger

Hukill, M. A. *Television Broadcasting for Rural Developoment in Niger.* 1986. ERIC. ED 285 576.

Nigeria—General

Harris, John. "Libraries and Librarianship in Nigeria at Mid-Century." *Nigerian Libraries.* 6(1970): 26–40. Also published as a pamphlet by the University of Ghana, Dept. of Library Studies, 1970.

Junaid, Muhammad Ibn, and Ian Lewis. "The Education of Minority Groups: Some Questions Raised by Consideration of the Nomadic Fulani of Nigeria." *Educational Review.* 40(1988): 219–226.

Lawal, O. "Professionalism in Nigerian Librarianship: an Evaluation of Factors in its Growth since 1948." *Dissertation Abstracts International.* 47(1986): 273.

"Library Advisory Committee of Nigeria." *WALA News.* 3(1959): 57.

Nigeria. *National Policy on Education*. Lagos, Federal Ministry of Education, 1977.

———. *Third National Development Plan, 1975–1980*. Lagos, Federal Ministry of Economic Development and Reconstruction, 1975.

Plumbe, Wilfred J. "International Librarianship." In his *Tropical Librarianship*, [3]–12. Metuchen, N. J., Scarecrow Press, 1987. First published in *Northern Nigeria Library Notes*. 1(May 1964).

———. "Libraries and the Economic Development of Nigeria." In his *Tropical Librarianship*, 73–83. Metuchen, N. J., Scarecrow Press, 1987. First published in *Nigerian Libraries*. v. 1, no. 4(1965).

Sitzman, Glenn L. "Libraries of Nigeria." [Videorecording of lectures with color transparencies given April 25, 1982, to International Librarianship Class, Clarion State College] 1982. 2 videocassettes. color.

Tashi, Leah, and Peter Havard-Williams. "Transfer of Information." *International Library Review*. 18(1986): 293–304.

Nigeria—Bibliograpies and Bibliography

Adeniran, O. R. "Bibliometrics of Computer Science Literature in Nigeria." *International Library Review*. 20(1988): 347–359.

Aina, Joseph O. "An Annotated List of Magazines Published in Nigeria." *Serials Librarian*. 14(1988): 145–156.

Afolabi, Michael. "The Literature on Librarianship in Nigeria, 1950–1973." *Nigerian Libraries*. 12(1976): 183–191.

Alegbeleye, G. O. "The Conservation Scene in Nigeria: a Panoramic View of the Condition of Bibliographic Resources." *Restaurator*. 9(1988): 14–26.

Nigeria—Book Trade, Printing, and Publishing

Oketunji, Ibidapo. "The Book Crisis in Nigeria: Implications and Possible Solutions." *Library Scientist*. 14(1987): 14–28.

Okojie, Victoria, and Abraham A. Azubuike. "Local Initiatives in the Nigerian Book Industry." *Information Development*. 4(1988): 28–32.

Publishing in Nigeria. Benin City, Ethiope Publishing Corp., 1972.

Nigeria—Cataloging and Classification

Aina, Joseph O. "Cataloguing and Classification of Nigerian Government Publications: Survey Report of the University of Ibadan and Obafemi Owolowo University Libraries." *Government Publications Review*. 15(1988): 137–145.

Amankwe, Nwozo. "Revision of Classification Schemes for Nigerian Needs." *Nigerian Libraries*. 1(1965): 165–173.

Greaves, M. A. "The Universal Decimal Classification and its Use in Nigeria." *International Forum on Information and Documentation.* 12(1987): 25–31.

Hoffman, Carl. "Hausa Personal Names and Traditional Titles." Paper Read at the Seminar on Cataloguing and Classification of Africana, University of Ibadan, Institute of Librarianship, 1966.

Igwe, G. E. "Personal Names and Traditional Titles in Nigeria: Igbo." Paper Read at the Seminar on Cataloguing and Classification of Africana, University of Ibadan, Institute of Librarianship, 1966.

Kirk-Greene, A. H. M. *A Preliminary Inquiry into Hausa Onomatology: Three Studies in the Origins of Personal, Title and Place Names.* Zaria, Institute of Administration, 1964.

Mahmud, K. "Arabic Names and Titles." Paper read at the Seminar on Cataloguing and Classification of Africana, University of Ibadan, Institute of Librarianship, 1966.

Okediji, F. Olu, and F. A. Okediji. "The Sociological Aspects of Names and Titles in Traditional Yoruba Society." Paper Read at the Seminar on Cataloguing and Classification of Africana, University of Ibadan, Institute of Librarianship, 1966.

Okeke, E. I. "African Names in the Catalogues of Nigerian Libraries." Paper Read at the Seminar on Cataloguing and Classification of Africana, University of Ibadan, Institute of Librarianship, 1966.

Peeler, Elizabeth H. "Nigerian Cataloguing and Classification Practice." *Nigerian Library Association, Eastern Division, Occasional Papers.* 3(April 1964): 1–12.

Tibbetts, G. R. "The Classification of Arabic Books." *Northern Nigeria Library Notes.* 2/3(1964/65): 91–117. First published in a slightly different form in *Library Quarterly.* 29(1959): 113–132.

Nigeria—Documentation and Information Science

Amadi, A. O. "Viewdata in the Office—User-friendly Page Identification." *Journal of Information Science: Principles & Practices.* 14(1988): 59–61.

Kehinde, L. O. "A Versatile Data Transmission Training Module." *IEEE Transactions on Education.* 31(1988): 132–136.

Nkereuwem, E. E. "Application of Information Technology in Nigeria: Problems and Prospects." *Information Services and Use.* 6(1986): 75–81.

Onuigbo, W. I. B. "Reprint Requests—a Tool for Documentation." *International Forum on Information and Documentation.* 10(1985): 7–9. Discussion: 11(1986): 40–41.

Nigeria—Librarians and Librarianship

Nzotta, Briggs C. "A Comparative Study of the Job Satisfaction of Nigerian Librarians." *International Library Review.* 19(1987): 161–173.

Nigeria—Library Education

Afolabi, Michael. "Careers in the Information Business." *Library Scientist.* 14(1987): 1–13.
Dean, John. "Professional Education in Nigeria." *Nigerian Libraries.* 2(1966): 67–74.
Nzotta, Briggs C. "Research and Education for Research in Nigerian Library Schools." *Education for Information.* 6(1988): 123–143.

Nigeria—Library Education—Ahmadu Bello University

Agada, John. "Occupational Choice and the Assertiveness of Librarians: a Comparison of beginning Students in Undergraduate Library, Law and Liberal Arts Schools in Nigeria." *Library & Information Science Research.* 9(1987): 305–325.
Ahmadu Bello University. Department of Library Science. *Annual Report.* Zaria.
Onadiran, G. Tunde. "Reactions of Past Students to the Bachelor of Library Science Degree of Ahmadu Bello University, Zaria, Nigeria." *Education for Information.* 6(1988): 39–59.

Nigeria—Library Education—Bayero University

Ibrahimah, M. Z. "The Teaching of Preservation and Conservation at Bayero University, Kano, Nigeria." *Restaurator.* 9(1988): 51–60.

Nigeria—Library Education—University of Ibadan

University of Ibadan. Department of Library Studies. *Annual Report.* Ibadan, Ibadan University Press.

Nigeria—Academic Libraries

Aboyade, B. O. "The University Library and Related Fields." In *In the University of Ibadan 1948–73*, edited by J. F. Ade Ajayi and T. N. Tamuno, Ibadan, University Press, 1973.
Bryce, J. "Nigerian Campuses in State of Turmoil." *Times Higher Education Supplement.* 828(Sep 16, 1988): 11.
———. "Nigerian Government Orders Re-opening of Campuses." *Times Higher Education Supplement.* 823(Aug 12, 1988).
Ehikhamenor, F. A. "Perceived State of Science in Nigerian Universities." *Scientometrics.* 13(1988): 225–238.

Fadiran, Dokun. "Classification and Shelving of Periodicals in Academic Libraries in Nigeria." *Serials Librarian.* 13(1987): 107–111.

Fafunwa, A. Babs. *A History of Nigerian Higher Education.* Lagos, Macmillan, 1971.

Ike, V. C. *University Development in Africa: the Nigerian Experience.* Ibadan, Oxford University Press, 1976.

Nigeria. Commission on Post-School Certificate and Higher Education in Nigeria. *Investment in Education: Report of the Commission.* Lagos, Ministry of Education, 1960.

Nigeria. National Universities Commission. *University Development in Nigeria.* Lagos, National Universities Commission, 1963.

Okafor, Nduka. *The Development of Universities in Nigeria.* London, Longman, 1971.

Ozowa, V. N. "Planning University Library Buildings in Nigeria." *International Library Review.* 20(1988): 375–386.

Nigeria—Academic Libraries—Ahmadu Bello University

Onadiran, G. T., and R. W. Onadiran. "Nigerian University Library Services: Students Opinion." *Journal of Library and Information Science* (India) 11(1986): 45–60.

Plumbe, Wilfred J. "Ahmadu Bello University Library: the First Three Years." In his *Tropical Librarianship,* 84–106. Metuchen, N. J., Scarecrow Press, 1987. First published in *Northern Nigeria Library Notes.* 4(Oct 1965: Also published in *Nigerian Libraries.* 3(1967): 46–62.

Woakes, Harriet, and Grace Toni Gandu. "The Development of an Index to Pictorial Materials in the Kashim Ibrahim Library, Ahmadu Bello University." *Audiovisual Librarian.* 13(1987): 209–214.

Nigeria—Academic Libraries—Federal University of Technology, Makurdi

Plumbe, Wilfred J. "Federal University of Technology, Makurdi [Brief to the Architects for the University Library Building on the Permanent Site, June 1983]." In his *Tropical Librarianship,* [122]–141. Metuchen, N. J., Scarecrow Press, 1987.

Nigeria—Academic Libraries—University of Benin

Sanni, Grace A. "Some Management Issues of Subject Specialisation with Reference to the University of Benin Library." *Library Scientist.* 14(1987): 44–56.

Nigeria—Academic Libraries—University of Ibadan

Aina, L. O. "Newspaper as a Tool in Educational Research in Nigeria." *INSPEL*. 21(1987): 163–167.

Nigeria—Academic Libraries—University of Ilorin

Olorunsola, Richard. "Crimes in Academic Libraries: University of Ilorin Library Experience." *Library Scientist*. 14(1987): 29–43.

Nigeria—Academic Libraries—University of Jos

Nwafor, B. U. "Adaptations of Buildings to University Library Use: a View from the Third World." In *Adaptations of Buildings to Library Use* . . . edited by Michael Dewe, 190–198. Saur, 1987.

Nigeria—Academic Libraries—University of Lagos

Udoh, D. J. E., and M. R. Aderibigbe. "The Problems of Development, Maintenance, and Automation of Authority Files in Nigeria." *Cataloging & Classification Quarterly*. 8(1987): 93–103.

Nigeria—Academic Libraries—University of Port Harcourt

Ahiakwo, Okechukwu N. "Forecasting Techniques and Library Circulation Operations: Implications for Management." *Library and Information Science Research*. 10(1988): 195–210.
Ahiakwo, O. N., and N. P. Obokoh. "Attitudinal Dimension in Library Overdues among Faculty Members—a Case Study." *Library and Information Science Research*. 9(1987): 293–304.
Obiagwu, Marcel C. "Scope and Methods of Long-essay Projects in Education: the Nigerian Horizon." *Education Libraries Bulletin*. 31(1988): 24–38.
Osiobe, Stephen A. "Information Seeking Behaviour [among Undergraduates]." *International Library Review*. 20(1988): 337–346.
———. "Use and Relevance of Information on the Card Catalogue to Undergraduate Students." *Library Review*. 36(1987): 261–267.

Nigeria—Bibliographies and Bibliography

Afolabi, Michael. *Library Literature on Nigeria, 1910–1978*. Zaria, Nigeria, Ahmadu Bello University, 1979.

Nigeria—Children's Library Services

Greene, Brenda M. "A Cross-cultural Approach to Literacy: the Immigrant Experience." *English Journal.* 77(1988): 45–48.
Osa, Osayimwense. "Buchi Emecheta's *The Bride's Price*: a Nondidactic Nigerian Youth Novel." *Children's Literature in Education.* 19(1988): 170–175.
Segun, Mabel D. "Illustrating for Children in a Developing Country: the First Illustrators' Training Workshop in Nigeria." *Phaedrus.* 12(1986–87): 61–62.

Nigeria—National Library of Nigeria

Aje, S. B. "National Library of Nigeria." *Nigerian Libraries.* 4(1968): 79–83.
Nzotta, Briggs Chinkata. "The National Library of Nigeria." In *Comparative and International Librarianship*, edited by P. S. Kawatra, 30–47. Envoy Press, 1987.

Nigeria—Public Libraries

Nzotta, Briggs C. "Fiction in Nigerian Public Libraries." *Collection Management.* 9(1987): 103–116.

Nigeria—Public Libraries—Former Northern Region

Faseyi, J. A. "Public Library Service in the Former Northern Nigeria." *Nigerian Libraries.* 4(1968): 68–69.
Plumbe, Wilfred J. "Samaru Gets a Public Library." In his *Tropical Librarianship*, 107–110. Metuchen, N. J., Scarecrow Press, 1987. First published in *Library Review.* no. 149(1964): 332–334.

Nigeria—Public Libraries—Lagos State

Lieberman, Irving. *A Survey of the Lagos City Library: Complete Report.* Lagos, City Council, 1964.
Olden, Anthony. "Alan Burns, the Lagos Library, and the Commencement of Carnegie Support for Library Development in British West Africa." *Journal of Library History, Philosophy & Comparative Librarianship.* 22(1987): 397–408.

Nigeria—School Libraries

Elaturoti, David F. "The School Librarian as Intermediary to Knowledge: What Future in Nigerian Schools?" In *The School Library: Gateway to Knowl-*

edge; Proceedings, compiled and edited by Sigrún Klara Hannesdóttir, 248–252. Kalamazoo, MI, International Association of School Librarianship, 1988.

Fadero, J. O. "The Federal School Library Service." *Nigerian Libraries*. 4(1968): 63–68.

Ibe-Bassey, G. S. "How Nigerian Teachers Select Instructional Materials." *British Journal of Educational Technology*. 19(1988): 17–27.

Obi, Dorothy S. "Promoting School Libraries in Eastern Nigeria." *COMLA Newsletter*. 60(June 1988): 8–9, 15.

Nigeria—Special Libraries, Materials and Services

Akinyemi, K. "Nigeria: Low Cost Educational Technology Promoted by Exhibitions." *Media in Education and Development*. 20(1987): 134–139.

Nwakoby, Martina A. "Portrait of a Newspaper Library in a Developing Country [Library and Documentation Centre of Star Printing and Publishing Company Limited, Enugu, Nigeria]." *Serials Librarian*. 14(1988): 121–128.

Olanigan, S. A. "Information Needs of the Consultant to Business Enterprises." *International Library Review*. 19(1987): 345–357.

Nigeria—Special Libraries—Agriculture

Adedigba, Yakub A. "Budgeting in the Agricultural Libraries and Documentation Centers in Nigeria." *International Library Review*. 20(1988): 215–226.

Aina, L. O. "The Use of Government Documents by Researchers in Agricultural Economics and Agricultural Extension in Nigeria: a Research Note." *Government Publications Review*. 15(1988): 61–64.

Akhibge, Funmi O. "Kolanut: the Characteristics and Growth of its Literature in Nigeria." *Quarterly Bulletin of the International Association of Agricultural Librarians and Documentalists*. 33(1988): 47–52.

Ibekwe, G. O. "The Present Constraints to the Realization of the Role of Nigerian Agricultural Libraries in Food Production and Prospects for Fulfillment." *Quarterly Bulletin of the International Association of Agricultural Librarians and Documentalists*. 33(1988): 121–134.

Nigeria—Special Libraries—Law.

Ifebuzor, Christopher C. "Wanted: Standards for Academic Law Libraries in Nigeria." *Law Librarian*. 18(1987): 81–86.

Okewusi, Peter Agboola. "Law Libraries in the Western Region/State of Nigeria." *International Library Review*. 20(1988): 227–232.

Nigeria—Special Libraries—Medicine and Health Sciences

Ikpaahindi, L. H. "The Relationship between the Needs for Achievement, Affiliation and Power and Frequency of Use of Information Sources and Scientific Productivity among Nigerian Veterinary Surgeons." *Dissertation Abstracts International.* 47(1986): 1518-A.

Iroka, Luke A. "Hospital Libraries in Patient's Education." *International Library Review.* 20(1988): 111–114.

Nigeria—Special Libraries—Science and Technology

Nkereuwem, Edet E. "A Conceptual Framework for the Use of Scientific and Technical Information in National Development in Nigeria." *Information Services & Use.* 5(1985): 323–330.

Seychelles

Benoit, Marie Consuelo. "The Seychelles, Libraries in." In *Encyclopedia of Library and Information Science*, v. 41, suppl. 6, p. 321–332. Dekker, 1986.

Jackson, Flavie. "Library Services in the Seychelles: the National Library and its Auxiliary." *COMLA Newsletter.* no. 55(Mar 1987): 8–9.

Sudan

Rosenberg, Diana, and Brigid O'Connor. "Training at the Grassroots: an Integrated Approach to Training Library Assistants in Southern Sudan." *Information Development.* 4(1988): 14–20.

Tanzania—General

Askin, S. "2 African Countries Adopt Policies Emphasizing Pre-college Education." *Chronicle of Higher Education.* 34(1988): A31.

Bourne, Charles. *Planning for a National Research Information Center. United Republic of Tanzania.* Paris, Unesco, 1975.

Kaungamno, E. E. *Mass Media and Youth.* Dar es Salaam, Tanzania Library Service, 1977.

Nawe, Julita. "The Impact of a Dwindling Budget on Library Services in Tanzania." *Library Review.* 37(1988): 27–32.

Ndamagi, C. "The Tanzania Government Household Budget Survey System." *Information Development.* 2(1987): 337–346.

Tanzania Library Service. *Occasional Papers.* Dar es Salaam.

226 GLENN L. SITZMAN

Tanzania—Academic Libraries

Chiduo, V. "Problems of Librarians in the Third World: the Experience of the University of Dar es Salaam." *Botswana Library Association Journal.* 8(1986): 14–18.

Tanzania—Public Libraries

Nyerere, J. K. "Speech at the Official Opening of the National Central Library, Dar es Salaam, December 9, 1967."

Tanzania—School and Children's Library Services

Kaungamno, E. E. "School Libraries as a Basic Tool for Teaching." *Tanzania Education Journal.* 3(May 1974): 38–40.
_____. "Teachers College Library Development." *Someni.* 1(1968): 4–7.
Saunders, Murray. "Managing the 'Practical Curriculum': Headteacher Responses in Tanzania and Britain." *Educational Review.* 40(1988): 203–209.

Zambia

Kelly, M. J. F. "Computer Utilisation and Staffing in Zambia: a Survey Conducted in Late 1986." *Information Development.* 2(1987): 283–292.
Khapwale, G. K. "An Experimental Provision of Patent and Non-patent Documents to R&D Projects in the Scientific Research Council in Zambia." *World Patent Information.* 10(1988): 175–180.
Shitima, M. N. "Information Technology in Government: the Zambian Grade VII Examination System." *Information Development.* 3(1988): 33–39.

Zimbabwe—General

Barnshaw, A. E. "The Influence of Information Technology on the Availability and Use of Information in the Future." *Mousaion.* 5(1987): 76–88.
MacKenzie, Clayton G. "Zimbabwe's Educational Miracle and the Problems it Has Created." *International Review of Education.* 34(1988): 337–353.
Patte, G., and A. Geradts. "Home Libraries in Zimbabwe." *IFLA Journal.* 11(1985): 223–227.
Zwangobani, E., and H. Mayo. "Zimbabwe Voters' Registration System." *Information Development.* 3(1988): 77–100.

Zimbabwe—School and Children's Library Services

Roller, Cathy M. "Transfer of Cognitive Academic Competence and L2 Reading in a Rural Zimbabwean Primary School." *TESOL Quarterly*. 22(1988): 303–318.

Zimbabwe—Special Libraries, Materials, and Services

Bourdillon, Jane. "The Photographic Collection of the National Archives of Zimbabwe." *African Research & Documentation*. 43(1987): 23–27.

Zimbabwe—Special Libraries—Handicapped

Addison, Joan. "Academic Library Services and the Disadvantaged: the Needs of Visually-handicapped-learners." *Zimbabwe Librarian*. 19(1987): 5, 7–8, 11.
Doust, Robin. "Library Services for the Disadvantaged." *Zimbabwe Librarian*. 19(1987): 13–15.
"Library Services for the Disadvantaged: 1987 A. G. M. and Conference of the Zimbabwe Library Association." *Zimbabwe Librarian*. 19(1987): 4–19.
Madzima, J., and Bilha Pfukani. "Library Services for the Blind and Deaf: the Jairos Jiri Association for the Rehabilitation of the Disabled and Blind." *Zimbabwe Librarian*. 19(1987): 17–19.

THE I. T. LITTLETON
THIRD ANNUAL SEMINAR

INTRODUCTION

Cynthia R. Levine

INTRODUCTION

The I. T. Littleton Seminar series was established in 1987 on the occasion of the retirement of Dr. I. T. Littleton as Director of D. H. Hill Library at North Carolina State University. The seminar was intended as a staff development event that would allow librarians and support staff to attend a high-quality, informative program without the necessity of travel to distant locations. The seminar is also open to any interested individuals from outside the library, and publicity is distributed nationwide. Each year, a small committee selects the seminar topics, invites speakers, and organizes the program.

On October 27, 1989, the third annual seminar was held. The topic was the distribution of information to researchers in agriculture. This particular topic was selected in order to commemorate the centennial year of North Carolina State University, an institution that has a long history of contributions to agricultural research. We entitled the program, *Agricultural Inquiry: A New Century*. Within this framework, we hoped to provide a forum in which to explore the importance of agricultural information to society, and to provide an opportunity for attendees to learn about the university's support for agricultural research. From presenta-

Advances in Library Administration and Organization,
Volume 9, pages 231–232.
Copyright © 1991 by JAI Press, Inc.
All rights of reproduction in any form reserved.
ISBN: 1-55938-066-7

tions given by researchers, we hoped to learn more about the perceived needs of agricultural researchers and to explore ways in which libraries can work to meet these needs. An additional goal of the Seminar was to provide a forum for addressing the topic of technological innovation as it applies to agricultural information.

The first half of the program consisted of several presentations by NCSU faculty members. Dr. Durward Bateman, Dean of the College of Agricultural and Life Sciences, set the stage by giving an overview of the College as well as analysis of agricultural trends in the state of North Carolina. Dr. Jim Riviere, professor from the NCSU College of Veterinary Medicine, shed light on the research publication process and the information retrieval needs of researchers. These papers are presented in their entirety below.

After a mid-afternoon break, attendees heard about new technologies that have the potential to help libraries deliver information. Joseph Howard, Director of the National Agricultural Library, spoke of his belief that libraries must continue to preserve and service existing collections as well as participate in today's technological revolution, and that library personnel will assume the role of information intermediaries. Howard stressed the necessity of cooperation between the private and public sectors, and between federal, state, and local agencies. Examples of what can be accomplished through cooperation include the U.S. Agricultural Network, the AGRICOLA database, computer-assisted training for cataloging staff, the Forest Service laser disc, the Aquaculture disc, and the Digitized Text Transmission Project, a joint project of NAL and the NCSU Libraries.

The final presentation was given by Dr. Henry Schaffer, Associate Provost for Academic Computing at NCSU. He discussed in more detail the Digitized Text Transmission Project and shared insights on the use of technology for researchers. This paper is also presented in its entirety.

THE COLLEGE OF AGRICULTURE
AND LIFE SCIENCES: AGRICULTURE
AND THE FUTURE

D. F. Bateman

I am very pleased to have this opportunity to meet with the library staff on the occasion of the Littleton Seminar. I am also pleased that you will be considering the information needs of the College of Agriculture and Life Sciences.

As the person who tries to meet the insatiable needs of the faculty in this College of Agriculture and Life Sciences for space, laboratory equipment, and computers, etc., I am in sympathy for those of you who are trying to satisfy their appetite for information. I expect that they gobble up everything you can provide and remain hungry for more.

Yet information is the real life blood of every university. It is essential to our students as they pursue their educational goals, and it is crucial to our faculty as they contribute to the frontiers of their sciences and transmit information to clientele across the State. Our students and faculty are no different from students and faculty in other colleges—they want all the information they can get on just about every subject.

Advances in Library Administration and Organization,
Volume 9, pages 233–238.
Copyright © 1991 by JAI Press, Inc.
All rights of reproduction in any form reserved.
ISBN: 1-55938-066-7

The librarians probably know better than anyone on campus that the bounds of the subjects of interest to the College of Agriculture and Life Sciences are extremely broad and they are expanding almost daily.

To set the stage for looking at the information needs of the College, let's look briefly at North Carolina, its agriculture and resource base, and then take a brief overview of the College, its missions and responsibilities to students, the sciences, to agriculture and to the people of the North Carolina.

SOME FACTS ABOUT NORTH CAROLINA

North Carolina is the tenth most populous state. We are also the most rural State in terms of the ratio of non-urban to urban population. We rank tenth among the states the farm value of our agriculture. Agriculture, including the production, processing, manufacturing and distribution sectors, is by far the largest industry in our State and accounts for almost one-third of all private sector employment. The highly technical, scientifically based agriculture in North Carolina that engages less than 3 percent of our population in farming, but furnishes a great deal of employment through the input industries, processing, manufacturing and distribution of agricultural products.

North Carolina currently has the largest and most diversified agriculture in its history. Only California and Florida exceed us in diversity. Today, some 70 commodities make up the commercial base of our agriculture. Our College has been a major factor in promoting this diversity over the past 40 years.

THE COLLEGE OF AGRICULTURE
AND LIFE SCIENCES

CALS is the largest and most diverse College at North Carolina State University. It is made up of 22 departments, 10 University Research Units, 15 Outlying Research Stations, and 100 county extension programs. We have 3,700 students on the campus and 3,200 employees on the campus and across the State.

The College is organized along functional lines—Research, Academic Affairs, and Extension. The Dean, Assistant Dean and three Associate Deans and Directors serve as the administrative team for the College.

The research division, the North Carolina Agricultural Research Service, links directly with 19 of the 22 departments of the College. It also operates the 10 University Research Units and, jointly with the North Carolina Department of Agriculture, the 15 Outlying Research Stations. Its responsibilities are statewide.

The Academic Affairs division offers degrees in 19 of the 22 departments; it functions primarily on campus. Programs of study are offered at the Associate Degree level in some 9 majors within the Agricultural Institute. The Bachelor of

Science Degree is offered in 46 specializations that span the agricultural and biological sciences. Degrees at the graduate level, M.S. and Ph.D., are offered in 26 specializations. The scope of the educational opportunities in the College is unique on our campus.

The third division, the North Carolina Agricultural Extension Service, has some 200 faculty in 18 of the 22 departments of the College. There are about 560 extension agents plus support staff stationed in the 100 countries and on the Cherokee Reservation. The Extension Service is the major link of North Carolina State University with the people of the state. It conducts programs not only in agriculture, but also in community and resource development, home economics and 4-H.

MISSION OF THE COLLEGE

Our mission is spelled out in three pieces of legislation: the Morrill Act of 1862, the Hatch Act of 1887, and the Smith-Lever Act of 1914. I don't intend to review these acts, but merely to indicate that our responsibility is to provide educational opportunities for the sons and daughters of North Carolina, including those of the working classes. Through research in the sciences we are developing new technologies to undergird agriculture, and through extension programs we are transferring technology and information to the citizens of the State which will aid them in their life pursuits. Traditionally the focus of our programs related to production agriculture and the rural sector. Today, our focus includes a much larger sector of society, i.e. agribusiness, communities, youth, etc.

CALS is the home of the basic biological sciences at NCSU. Thus, its mission also includes the teaching and advancement of the biological sciences on this campus. The bringing together of the agricultural and biological sciences into one college provides a synergism that strengthens both. Our structure facilitates the building of bridges between accomplishments in science and their application for the benefit of society. It also provides a unique environment in which to educate future scientists as well as others who will play leadership roles in our society.

We take seriously, our mission to be the "People's University." Because of our structure and state-wide presence, CALS is in the best position of any of the Colleges at NCSU or within the UNC System to fulfill the ideal of the Land Grant philosophy.

CHANGES IN THE CONCEPT OF AGRICULTURE IMPLICATIONS FOR THE FUTURE

Over the years this College and its programs have been catalysts for the diversification of North Carolina agriculture and for many other changes that have improved the welfare of North Carolinians. In the future the role of this college will be even more important.

I want to share with you some thoughts on the changes taking place in agriculture. These relate to our constantly growing need for rapid access to an ever-expanding store of information and knowledge.

The first point I want to make is that agriculture is much more than farming. While it is certainly true that "farming is agriculture," the reverse is not true. The relationship of agriculture to society and the welfare of man is vital to continued human progress. The way in which we view agriculture and the disciplines and specializations related to agriculture have changed enormously during this century. We have seen a gradual evolution from agriculture being equated with farming, to systems for producing food and fiber, to the interface that involves all of the elements between human and natural systems. As we move into the twenty-first century, this interface concept, elaborated by Dahlberg,[1] becomes more and more the necessary model for agriculture in a finite world with fragile limited natural resources.

It is widely recognized that without a stable food supply there can be neither peace nor human progress. Further, we now recognize that with the number of humans on this earth, and the number projected in the future, the science of agriculture must involve our understanding and proper use of the geosphere, the hydrosphere, the atmosphere and the biosphere—i.e., all of nature.

Sir Eric Ashby, one of England's greatest educational leaders, predicts that for "the rest of man's history on earth, he will have to live with problems of population, of resources, and pollution."[2] Since agriculture must be sustainable if man is to survive, all of the issues that concern the relationships between humans and the environment become agricultural issues.

If you examine the subject matter of the 22 departments within CALS you will see that the subjects of study and research do indeed span the realm between natural and human systems. It was not by chance that the twenty-second department added to CALS in July of 1989 was the Department of Toxicology. The matter of toxic substances used throughout our society has taken on great importance, and, if CALS is to meet its responsibility to North Carolina, this area must receive greater emphasis in our research, teaching and extension programs.

A second point I would like to make has to do with the specificity of agriculture and the need for research under local conditions. For some sciences and technologies, the social and environmental context makes very little difference. Chemistry, for instance, or electronics, can be practiced in Japan or Brazil or North Carolina without much adaptation. Agricultural systems, however, are much more closely tied to their social and environmental settings.

And even though agricultural scientists are concerned about *global* problems of food production and environmental pollution, the solutions they propose will have to succeed under very *local* conditions.

Consider for a moment, the development of new varieties of crop plants. At the minimum, a successful variety needs to be appropriate for day length, soil type, weather, and length of growing season. It should be able to tolerate at least some of the attacks by insects and diseases, and be able to withstand some competition from weeds. It must fit into a needed rotation cycle with other crops. It needs to be harvestable with available labor or equipment. It must process well into a product that consumers will purchase. It must meet consumer requirements for taste, appearance, and nutritional value. And it must yield well enough under all these constraints to bring a profit to the producer.

Almost all of these factors require very localized knowledge of the conditions that will prevail in any particular agricultural production system. North Carolina produces about 70 different commodities in commercial quantities. The College of Agriculture and Life Sciences conducts research on all of them. This kind of work at the intersection of environmental systems and social systems requires access to a tremendous supporting literature.

My final point concerns the reintegration of agricultural sciences into the mainstream of intellectual life. Fifteen years ago, it was possible for the Mayers to write a paper called "Agriculture, the Island Empire," in which they complained that the so-called "agricultural" sciences had become isolated from the rest of the university over the past hundred years.[3] They pointed out that almost every discipline reflected this separation. Agricultural economists, rural sociologists, and crop scientists, for instance, have professional societies and professional journals independent of general economics, sociology, and plant sciences societies.

The authors traced this isolation to the structure of the land grant colleges which established agricultural research stations in 1887 and extension programs in 1914 to meet the needs of farm and rural clientele. There is, I believe, some validity to these observations. But times have changed. And that is my last point today. If there has been a time of isolation of agricultural disciplines within the sciences, that time has ended.

The revolution in the biological and environmental sciences has brought the sciences that undergird agriculture back to a central place in the mainstream. The isolation of agricultural science has vanished as land-grant scientists have become full participants in the basic discoveries in genetics, molecular biology, plant sciences, and every other field in which we work.

For example, ten years ago animal science might fairly have been called an "applied" science. The greatest number of journal articles published by our faculty members appeared in the Journal of Animal Science and the Journal of Dairy Science.

In 1988, approximately the same number of faculty members published twice as many articles in professional journals, and they published in more than twice as many journals. The new entries are mostly in more specialized journals— *Gastroenterology* and *Reproductive Fertility*—for example. These are mainstream science journals—not specifically agricultural journals. This is not an isolated phenomenon. In 1988, the Crop Science faculty published articles in 17 journals that did not appear in their report for 1979.

At the same time, scientists outside of the land-grant universities are finding out that some of the most interesting challenges in science are in agriculture. These days very basic discoveries are turning out to have almost immediate application, and scientists in other institutions and private industries are flocking into subjects like animal vaccines or pesticide degradation or nitrogen fixation that we used to consider "our territory." This means that the number of scientists publishing "agricultural" literature has expanded greatly over the past decade.

This ferment and competition is good for scientists in colleges of agriculture— but it is no doubt hard on librarians and taxing for library resources. However, if our scientists are going to be able to work at the frontiers of basic science, their information needs are going to reflect the tremendous proliferation of information sources.

I am afraid that I can hold out no hope for you that the information needs of the faculty in the College of Agriculture and Life Sciences will diminish. On the contrary, I believe that these needs will continue to increase. Perhaps all I can do at this time is to thank you for your help in working with us, and assure you that I believe our faculty and students are concentrating their energies on some of the most important problems facing North Carolina and the world today.

NOTES

1. Dahlberg, Kenneth A. 1979. Beyond the Green Revolution. Plenum Press.
2. Ashby, Sir Eric. 1977. Reconciling Man with the Environment. Stanford University Press.
3. Mayer, André and Mayer, Jean. 1976. Agriculture the Island Empire. Daedalus 103:83–95.

PERSPECTIVES ON THE INFORMATION NEEDS OF THE AGRICULTURAL RESEARCHER OF THE 21ST CENTURY

J. Edmond Riviere

On the occasion of the centennial anniversary of the Libraries of North Carolina State University (NCSU), I appreciate this opportunity to comment on my perspectives on the informational needs of the agricultural researcher and how this interfaces with the functioning of a research library in the twenty-first century. This will be in the format of a personal editorial based on how as an individual, I have interacted with the library during my career at NCSU. First and foremost, it is from the perspective of a faculty researcher who avidly reads the literature and contributes to it. Secondly, it is as an author of the United States Department of Agriculture (USDA) supported national Food Animal Residue Avoidance Databank (FARAD), a computer based system designed to provide information relevant to avoiding chemical residues in the edible tissues and products of food animals (Riviere et al., 1986). Thirdly, it is from the perspective of being an

Advances in Library Administration and Organization,
Volume 9, pages 239–248.
Copyright © 1991 by JAI Press, Inc.
All rights of reproduction in any form reserved.
ISBN: 1-55938-066-7

editor of the *Journal of Veterinary Pharmacology and Therapeutics*, an international journal focussed on publishing research articles on the action and disposition of drugs in animals of veterinary importance. Finally, it is as a teacher of professional veterinary and graduate students who use the library as their primary source of keeping abreast of developments in their fields. Because most of my professional experience is in the fields of veterinary medicine, pharmacology and toxicology, this perspective is largely based on the biomedical literature of these fields.

Common to all disciplines, there are certain widely accepted factors which complicate access to today's published scientific literature. The first is the information explosion and the dawn of the information age. Mastery of information is a hallmark of survival as society enters what Alvin Toffler calls civilization's "Third Wave" (Toffler, 1980). John Naisbitt similarly characterized modern civilization in a transition between an "industrial society" and an "information society" whose economy is increasingly being based on self-generating information resources (Naisbitt, 1982) rather than on exhaustible energy resources. Naisbitt's portrait of the magnitude of this information explosion illustrates the problems facing the library of the twenty-first century. He estimates that currently between 6,000 and 7,000 scientific articles are written each day. This translates to a doubling of the total published scientific literature every 5.5 years which he predicts will shortly reach a doubling period of every two years. The Association of Research Libraries has estimated that there are approximately 28,000 serials in circulation today. These statistics of such a rapidly increasing volume of information attest to the difficulty that a modern scientist faces when an attempt is made to "search" the published literature.

One might question why such an information explosion has occurred. It may partially be blamed on the often cited "publish or perish" phenomenon operative in academia where tenure and promotion is based on the number of publications in one's resume. This has led to the practice of fragmenting research results into papers of diminishing length, the so-called "least publishable unit" (Broad, 1981). Another practice that contributes to this growth is the premature publication of studies still in progress which occurs in an effort to avoid being "scooped." One can often see a series of papers from one research group which range over time from "preliminary findings" to the "definitive report." However, with some of todays complicated long term studies which may take years to plan, implement and finally analyze all data, it is understandable that promising preliminary results be reported, especially if they have a direct positive benefit on human health. There are other explanations to this phenomenon. More than ever before, science is a multidisciplinary endeavor. The days of journal articles being written by a single author are limited if not already past since collaborative research is the normal way of doing science. Eugene Garfield, founder of the Institute for Scientific Information (ISI) (Garfield, 1988), has attributed this growth of the scientific literature to the fact that there are more scientists alive today than ever lived before and publication in journals is the primary mechanism of disseminating their research findings. Similarly, the fractionation of knowledge which occurs with specialization results in the establishment of new journals where these specialists can communicate with like-minded colleagues.

Complicating this picture even more is the fact that research data is published in many formats other than the relatively easily accessible "journal." These include books, monographs, proceedings of meetings, conferences, congresses and symposia, abstracts, industry periodicals, professional newsletters and government reports. Not all of these sources are accessed or searched by a single computer-based system. A paradox facing the library of today is that many avid users never actually enter the library and few workers ever see the journal in which an article is published. Instead, after identifying a relevant article from a literature search, reprints are often obtained directly from the author by mail. An even more common situation is to obtain a "photocopy" of the article which I venture to guess is the primary method most active scientists employ in reading the literature. Because of the sheer volume of journals in circulation, very few are ever read "cover to cover." Rather a few selected general coverage serials and a few journals in the researcher's specialized areas are all that the professional scientist could ever hope to thoroughly scan. Information scientists have estimated that for the great majority of scientists in any field, there are not more than 25 journals that contain the significant publications relevant to their specialty (Garfield, 1988).

WHAT IS A SCIENTIFIC ARTICLE?

In order to shed additional light on why such an information explosion has occurred, it is informative to classify the types of research articles that may be written. This will serve as a useful basis for describing the type of research that is conducted. The primary purpose for publishing a scientific article is to report on new discoveries and disseminate new information. These articles are generally findings based on the use of the experimental method. They may announce a novel biological effect, a new mechanism of action, a new therapeutic drug or agricultural compound, or document a new approach to treat a disease or increase the yield of an agricultural product. These articles may report on breakthroughs in fields such as molecular biology or analytical chemistry and include the pivotal papers which create new fields. In previous centuries, these often were published in books. In modern science, these seminal works, although often initially ignored, are usually published in prestigious journals widely read by their peers (Mayer, 1982). It is this classification of select papers which often results in the growth of new "themata" or paradigms in science (Holton, 1988). Of course, very few of these works are truly revolutionary. However, it is generally this type of paper which generates the greatest impact in most scientific disciplines. This category is also what most people consider the primary purpose for publishing. However, they probably account for a small fraction of the total number of articles published. An extension of this classification are the plethora of subsequent articles which either support or refute the original findings.

A second type of article is that which postulates new theories. It may present a hypothesis which offers a new explanation for already published data. Others may be purely theoretical papers not based on laboratory experimentation. A third type of paper is one which documents or validates a specific experimental method. It can be a source of information which standardizes a specific analytical assay or describes a surgical technique. The theory and documentation behind computer software is often published in this format. This class of publication often eliminates the need to duplicate an experimental technique in the body of a research manuscript. It allows the article to be published in a journal specializing in the science of the technique, which may not be the same field where the method is being applied.

A fourth type of paper is what I refer to as archival. This may consist of data collected under defined conditions in a specific field which characterize a specific phenomenon. For example, a paper may document the efficacy of a pesticide against a number of insects or describe the toxicity of a chemical in different animal species. A great body of descriptive research also falls in this category, such as comparative anatomy or physiological studies. Some may not consider such publications as "dynamic" when compared to the earlier categories, however, in many circumstances they form the foundation of scientific knowledge and may be the most important to have continuous access to. Additionally, by surveying this literature, one can often gain an appreciation of the evolution of a scientific discipline. What was once a novel finding may now serve as an accepted technique applied to many different fields.

A fifth type of paper is the case report or field trial. In medicine, these are composed of individual or cohorts of clinical cases describing a specific disease syndrome. In agriculture, they may consist of reports of the results of a field trial of a new product or management methodology. Many epidemiological studies would also fall into this category.

The final category is best classified as review. The overviewed published literature is either in a general field or a focussed area and organized from the perspective of a single individual. It may be published in a typical research journal, as a supplement issue, as a monograph, in a "review" journal or as a chapter in an edited textbook. These are a primary mechanism by which the relevance of research results are judged and intellectual synthesis occurs. Because of the previously mentioned growth of the scientific literature, reviews in active areas need constant updating to reflect new information and concepts. Thus, these secondary articles tend to have a shorter "life" than the primary sources. However, they are the best source for reviewing progress in a field or for introducing "outsiders" to a new area. Consistent with this function, they also are a primary source for continuing education. Writing these articles requires a great deal of effort from the author and demands that the literature be thoroughly searched. They often are written as a by-product of the literature review required for most grant applications. Finally, review articles can serve the function of identifying key papers in a field and are often used as a first step in searching the literature. They obviously are a major source material for supplementing textbooks in classroom teaching.

WHERE ARE ARTICLES PUBLISHED?

Now that one can classify an article based on its contents, what journal would it be most likely published in? To take an example in agriculture, I surveyed the literature to determine where one would most likely find an article on a specific pesticide. Many pivotal articles are published in the general scientific literature (e.g., *Science, Nature, Life Sci.*). A common source is in journals dedicated to pesticides (e.g., *Adv. Pest Control Res., Pesticide Biochem. Physiol.*) or entomology (e.g., *Bull. Entomol. Res., J. Econ. Entomol., Ann. Rev. Entomol., J. Insect Physiol.*). Alternatively, papers dealing with pesticide interactions with non-target species such as plants and animals may be found in agricultural research (e.g., *J. Agr. Food Chem., J. Anim. Sci., Can. J. Zool.*) or veterinary journals (*Am. J. vet. Res., Vet. Human Toxicol., J. Am. Vet. Med. Assoc.*). Publications dealing with human effects may be found in various general medical (*J. Am. Med. Assoc., Lancet, Ann. Int. Med.*) or specialty journals (*J. Invest. Dermatol., Endocrinology, Brain Res.*). Pesticide articles may be found in pharmacology (*J. Pharmacol. Exp. Therap., J. Clin. Pharmacol., J. Pharm. Sci.*), toxicology (*Toxicol. Appl. Pharmacol., Bull. Environ. Contamin. Toxicol., Fundam. Appl. Toxicol.*) or pathology (*Am. J. Pathol.*) serials. Many articles dealing with pesticide chemistry or metabolism are published in biochemistry journals (*Biochemistry, J. Chem. Soc., J. Biochem., J. Assoc. Offic. Anal. Chem.*). Because of the health hazards involved with pesticide exposure, additional papers may be found in risk-assessment (*Environment, Arch. Environ. Health*) or agricultural policy publications (*Environ. Mgmt., Fed. Reg.*). Finally, much valuable safety information is printed in manufacturer's Material Safety Data Sheets (MSDS). Based on this far from exhaustive search, articles on pesticides could be found in 37 different sources, a number easily tripled if all sources were listed.

   Why then does an investigator select a specific journal for publishing an article? I believe that the major criterion is the journal's reputation, judged by its circulation, review policy, makeup of its editorial board, and citation history. Journals affiliated with specific professional societies often are selected so that members of a discipline impacted by the work will find and read the article without doing exhaustive literature searching. By looking at the relative citation rates of journals in a field, the leading ones can easily be identified and often are

Table 1.   Classification of a Journal's
Subject Matter

Compound studied: pesticide, antibiotic

Species utilized: microbe, insect, plant, farm animal, man

Biological response seen: enzyme inhibition, neurological
activity

Methods: analytical technique, synthetic method

Adverse reactions: toxicology, risk assessment

Mathematical complexity: kinetic analysis, molecular modelling

Organ system: skin, brain, liver

Novel effect of compound: carcinogenesis, mutagenesis,
molecular probe

---

the official publications of major professional associations. Often a journal is selected because the subject matter is compatible, even if the journal is not the official publication of one's association. Research may take on a different slant due to novel findings or techniques utilized that force publication in a journal whose readership is outside of the primary field of an investigator. Often, a journal is selected purely because the worker wants the research to reach a different audience then would normally be reached if published where most of his or her other research was presented. Finally, most workers want their findings published in a peer-reviewed journal so that it has credibility in the field.

As can be seen from the pesticide example above, there are a number of reasons why a journal's subject matter and review board may be appropriate for a specific article. These are outlined in Table 1. Based on this analysis, one can begin to appreciate why the scientific literature is so complex and realize the futility in hoping that it will become more simplified in the decades ahead. The challenge facing both the researcher and information specialist is how to optimally manage this interweaving matrix to meet their everchanging needs.

SEARCHING THE LITERATURE

This complexity of modern science makes the searching of the available literature a daunting task. From a personal perspective, the primary methods I use to keep abreast of the literature are (1) computerized literature searches to identify promising articles, (2) read review papers or recent textbooks, (3) access databanks which provide summary information, and (4) scan publications such as ISI's Current Contents which publish the Table of Contents from the primary journals in different scientific areas.

By far, computerized searching of the literature (e.g., MEDLINE, AGRICOLA) is the major method used to identify articles in the biological sciences. In general, these do an excellent job of identifying articles published in the open scientific literature if proper key words are selected. However, not accessible by these searches are articles published in proceedings, chapters in textbooks, or government documents. For the latter, independent sources (e.g., National Technical Information Service, Defense Technical Information Center) often have to be consulted. The advent of computer scannable strips of abstracts in an issue of a journal may improve the efficiency of this process. This was recently adopted for the *Journal of the American Veterinary Medical Association* (*JAVMA*, 1989, 195:429–430). However the utility of such a system would only be optimized if it were universally adopted.

A very efficient method of searching the literature is the "Citation Searching" service ASCA provided by the ISI. This weekly service identifies articles which quote a user-identified author in their bibliographies. Standard keyword searches are also performed. If one knows the active researchers in a specific field, then any article which references this person's work in their bibliography can be identified. This is very effective in identifying journal articles relevant to one's area that are published in different fields.

The advent of electronic databanks is also a recent development designed to facilitate extracting information from the literature. A databank is defined as a source of information in contrast to a bibliographic database which only identifies the literature where specific information can be found. A good listing of databases and databanks available in animal health can be found in Ostroff (1982). Databanks are thus computerized systems which contain information relevant to a specific field for which the literature has already been searched and abstracted. Such databanks may serve as depositories of specific information such as protein or nucleotide sequences, chemical structures or toxicologic data (e.g., Toxicology Data Bank). The source of the information is usually linked to the relevant literature citation. Therefore, when an individual searches such a databank, specific scientific information will be located rather than just a citation to where that information could be found. The advantages to such an approach are obvious. An interesting problem arising from their use is that often when this data is utilized in a subsequent publication, the databank rather than the original citation is quoted as the source (Hodgson, 1987).

In order to give the reader a better flavor of what a databank is, I will briefly overview the structure of the Food Animal Residue Avoidance databank (FARAD) for which this author was a primary architect (Riviere, 1986). FARAD is a USDA supported national comprehensive computerized databank of regulatory and pharmacologic information useful for mitigating drug and chemical residue problems in food producing animals. This was done in collaboration with the University of Florida at Gainesville and the University of California at Davis. The National Agriculture Library through the D. H. Hill Library at North Carolina State University provided document delivery services.

The purpose of FARAD was to identify, extract, assemble, evaluate and distribute relevant data to reduce the incidence of violative chemical and drug residues in the edible tissues (meat) and products (milk, eggs) of food producing animals. FARAD allows information about residue avoidance from all sources to be instantaneously available at one point for interpretation and dissemination to impacted producers and veterinarians. The sources of data in FARAD include (1) information on drugs registered for use in food producing animals by the Food and Drug Administration (FDA) indexed by manufacturer's products, (2) physiochemical data on drug and chemical entities, (3) regulatory data from the FDA and USDA on tissue tolerances of these compounds, and (4) pharmacokinetic data extracted from the open literature and government reports describing the disposition and metabolism of these compounds in food animals. The chemicals included are those approved as therapeutic or growth promoting compounds in the United States or chemicals which may inadvertently contaminate the food supply. All individual data are referenced to source. The drug registration data was obtained from FDA files and cross checked with the relevant manufacturers for accuracy.

The generation of the pharmacokinetic data involved searching the literature to identify articles which may contain information on the concentration of a drug or chemical in an animal's tissue as a function of time. The data may have been obtained from publications in analytical chemistry or animal science journals which had never analyzed this information in a manner that would allow residue predictions. Thus, these data had to be individually entered into a pharmacokinetic computer program in my laboratory and analyzed according to accepted models so that the relevant parameters could be generated. This pharmacokinetic file currently contains over 10,000 records.

The advantages of a system such as FARAD are obvious. When a producer has a potential residue problem, the relevant data in the proper format is immediately available for use. The user of this information thus has had the literature searching, extraction, and analysis already done for them. An electronic databank such as this can be constantly updated to reflect new research and the most current federal regulations governing drug use. As we enter the twenty-first century, and as computer technology gets more powerful and economical, databanks should proliferate in most fields. The logical "keepers" of these systems will be the information specialists employed by libraries.

THE FUTURE

As can be appreciated from what I have already presented, science will continue to grow in complexity and computers will continue to become tools essential for managing this ever increasing body of data. As is already happening, individual researchers will do their own "on-line" or "CD-ROM" literature searches using systems available in their library systems. Libraries must provide training in search strategies and maintain both current and archival files. Also, they must be aware of what researchers in their universities are doing so that new relevant computer databases and databanks are always available. One can argue that this is the researcher's responsibility. However, most scientists are not in the position to sort through and evaluate new products without help from professional information specialists.

I also see many exciting developments in the nature of scientific publishing on the horizon. The integration of video technology with digital computers should facilitate the development of "electronic" journals. With the rapid advances being made in "FAX" communications, I could easily imagine FAX-based publishing becoming a reality. Obviously, this technology would greatly expedite the submission and review process in journal publication. However, it would also be possible for individual subscribers or libraries to receive their journals electronically. Storage would thus be on an electronic medium with hardcopy being produced by the enduser's laser printer. Such a system would give new meaning to "camera-ready" and "rapid publication" journals.

The complexity and efficiency of databanks will also increase as more artificial intelligence (AI)-based expert systems are developed. Major problems with these are providing adequate peer-review and copy right protection. Who pays for their development and maintenance? Future literature searching software will employ more integrative searching algorithms (e.g., neural networks, topological systems, hypertext). These will all demand that libraries have on staff information specialists very familiar with specific research fields to help their scientists explore the total literature base and identify the optimal electronic databank for their needs.

One can easily appreciate that future libraries will have to focus greater resources on literature searching and maintenance of databanks. Journals must be either physically available in the library or rapid and economical access provided articles identified in searches. Finally, integrated databases must be established which cover all classifications of publications, not just journals.

In conclusion, as agricultural science continues to contribute to and borrow from other scientific disciplines, the rapid access to information will become more important. The strength of a research university is inextricably linked to the quality of its library system. As we enter the "Information Age," immediate access to and efficient utilization of available data will determine the success of a research program.

ACKNOWLEDGMENTS

I would like to thank Drs. N. A. Monteiro and P. L. Williams for their critical reading of this manuscript.

REFERENCES

Broad, W. J. "The Publishing Game: Getting More for Less," *Science* 211: 1137–1139, 1981.

Garfield, E. "Too Many Journals? Nonsense," *The Scientist*, 2 (5): 11, 1988.

Hodgson, J. "Citation Inadequacy Via Databanks" *The Scientist* 1 (9):14, 1987.

Holton, G. *Thematic Origins of Scientific Thought* Cambridge, Harvard University Press, 1988.

Mayer, E. *The Growth of Biological Thought*, Cambridge, Belknap Press, 1982.

Naisbitt, J. *Megatrends: Ten New Directions Transforming Our Lives*, New York, Warner Books, 1982.

Ostroff, J. *International Directory of Animal Health and Disease Databanks* National Agricultural Library Misc. Publ. Number 1423, 1982.

Riviere, J. E. "Food Animal Residue Avoidance Databank (FARAD): An Automated Pharmacologic Databank for Drug and Chemical Residue Avoidance" *Journal of Food Protection* 49:826–830, 1986.

Toffler, A. *The Third Wave*, New York, Bantam Books, 1980.

COMPUTING TECHNOLOGY AND LIBRARIES

Henry E. Schaffer

Libraries existed very early in the history of civilization. The scholar takes the existence of the library for granted, and the use of the library has been continuous. But from the point of view of a person interested in technology, there has been a marked change as technology has been incorporated in the library. The early history of application of technology was in the production of the collection, i.e., the production of books, journals, etc.. The remarkable technological advances such as the printing press and moveable type had a major effect on the library by making printed items more available, but left the library functioning in an essentially unchanged manner.

Even though the books, etc., were printed, the library still carried out its function of acquisition, and then organized, preserved, and provided access to the collection. These functions were provided in similar manners over time, with technology gradually creeping into the library. The improvements of typing or printing catalog cards instead of writing them them out by hand are examples of improvement which had little effect on the functioning as seen by the patron. The use of the computer to keep and process records of orders, payments, binding, etc. also were very helpful to the library but hidden from the patron. The more

Advances in Library Administration and Organization,
Volume 9, pages 249–253.
ISBN: 1-55938-066-7

recent use of computer data files, leading to on-line catalogs have been more visible to the patron, but all of these technological advances ended up with the patron obtaining the book or journal which was then used in the same way it has been used since time immemorial.

Since this Seminar is in honor of I. T. Littleton, Director Emeritus of the D. H. Hill Libraries, I would like to add an historical note. I. T. Littleton saw the need for technology early in the development of computer applications to libraries. He started working to provide the basis for the incorporation of technology in library applications at NSCU. His vision was broader than just our campus, and his efforts have been expressed in the state and regional cooperative programs which we now have. He hired the late Bill Horner who laid the groundwork for our more recent efforts, and then, after Bill's retirement, he hired our current leader in library systems, John Ulmschneider. These activities and accomplishments set the stage for the appearance of our current Director of the D. H. Hill Libraries, Susan Nutter, who has already made a major impact on using the application of technology to enhance library capabilities.

After many centuries of gradual addition of technological improvements, mainly in the production of the library collection and in enhancement of "back room" library operations, we have come to a time in which technology is changing the way in which we, the patrons of the library, will use the library collection. One of the traditional library responsibilities has been to provide access to the collection. The use of technology to extend access will be recognized, as the quality and pervasiveness of this application increases, as a revolution in the library-patron relationship. In an overly simplistic view, it appears that searching of the library collection will be improved by automating the card catalog. That appears to be a convenience, not a fundamental change. Its revolutionary implications come from the unstated requirement that the ability to search the collection implies that the collection must be organized in such a way as to facilitate searching. This is another traditional responsibility of the library, but now the responsibility must encompass the collection as a whole, transcending the individual units (volumes) which comprise it.

The collection must be viewed as a "database" in which all the contents are linked and accessible through a searching mechanism. Volumes, individual articles in journals and less traditional media must all be encompassed. The newer media such as hypertext and hypermedia gracefully are included in this view of the collection. The Patron Interface (usually called the "user interface" in the computing world) must incorporate both searching and display capabilities. In this context, even the "full text" view of the collection is not sufficient. Rather we must have a "full collection" view. The patron has requirements for non-text information, and the Patron Interface (and the underlying organization of the collection) must therefore include full graphical capabilities so that that the entire collection can be searched and retrieved. While the collection may mainly be textual, there also are pictures/graphics, in both black and white, and color.

Some parts of the collection are animated graphics (e.g., movies, video tapes,) and that leads to the inclusion of sound and multimedia. Our goal is a unified view of the collection.

Once the patron's window into the organized collection is the screen of a computing workstation, then the location of this workstation becomes important. Perhaps it would be better to say that it is important that the location be unimportant! With proper data communications support, the workstation can be anywhere and still provide the patron with the same high quality services. The same data communications infrastructure which is developing in the academic world, and which is spreading into the commercial, industrial and governmental environments, starting with the research institutions, will also serve the library patron.

The expertise needed to bring about this enhanced state of library services is found both in the library and the computing center. The expertise which these two organizations bring to bear is not the same. There is some overlap, but there are so many differences that both are needed. Since my audience consists mainly of librarians, it is clear that the library's knowledge of, and experience in, acquisition, organization and access is a critically important part of producing a solution. The computing center's knowledge of, and experience in, computing technology, including hardware and software, data communications systems, and user interfaces is equally important. This brings me to my usual sermon on the importance of having these two organizations work in full cooperation. They are different in their methods, culture and goals. These differences justify having two separate organizations. However the two overlap in a number of essential areas which are needed to provide a modern full spectrum of services to the library patron. Remote access is what will allow the phrase "library patron" to include all people who could benefit from the library, instead of just the chosen few who live or work in the vicinity of the research library (which everyone here takes for granted.)

I could elaborate further, but will instead just restate my point. We need both computing centers and libraries, and they have sufficient differences so that doing away with either one, or merging them into one single organization, will leave some portions of our constituency poorly served. However, because the two organizations each provide components which are essential in the provision of services to our patrons, neither can we afford to have these two working in an uncoordinated fashion. The joint planning and cooperative implementation of projects by the two organizations will provide the broad solutions needed to use modern technology to provide the most powerful intellectual tools in order to serve the patron of the library.

The problems we must face are not only technological, but include working with the patrons so that they can make good use of this new technology. In addition, there are problems of cost of the technology and of the information itself. The computers used to be such a major cost item that they dominated all discussion of the costs involved. Now that the costs of computing have decreased sharply, we can see that the information in the library collection is going to be a significant portion of the cost in these new modes of functioning. We are starting to see that the vendors (publishers, etc.) of information see this as a business opportunity and stand read to charge for every new and innovative use of the information which they provide. I do not mean to imply that there is anything improper with compensating them for the information and services they provide, but I am very concerned that an overly greedy approach on their part could easily inhibit or deter progress towards providing the truly organized and accessible library collection.

As an application of some of the technology providing remote access, NCSU has been working with the National Agricultural Library (NAL) on a project to transmit and utilize digitized scientific publications which are useful in agricultural research. This ties in with an NAL project which has led them into the preparation of digitized representations of publication and storage of this information. This allows text, formulas, diagrams and photographs to be included. In the NCSU-NAL project, the digitized information is sent from the NAL, upon request of NCSU, via the Internet. The Internet is the major digital communications research network in the country. It is composed of connected computer networks using the TCP/IP protocol suite, with the primary constituent being the NSFnet including its regional mid-level networks. The southeastern mid-level network is SURAnet, which serves both NCSU and the NAL. The connectivity is such that exactly the same technology being used in this project can be used without change to serve any library connected to the Internet, and so the benefits of this project will be able to be widely applied.

Once the information has been transmitted by the NAL and received at NCSU, it is stored and then can be printed, or re-transmitted to a research lab on campus where they can print it, or perhaps use the information in some format on one of their computers. This flexibility illustrates a major difference between this computer based digitized storage and transmission and the common use of facsimile. Because the digitized information is stored on a computer, the printing can be done on a printer of whatever quality is desired, and can be redone if the quality is not sufficient. Additionally, the research worker has the capability of reusing the data, since it already is on a computer, and the same computer system which is used for other purposes, including electronic mail, can be used in this context since it already has the required communications connectivity.

This digital data communications connectivity will be getting much more common, and will be available in every laboratory and at the desk-top of each scientist. It will be an end-to-end method of communications for the research worker. The same methodology that will provide the ability to receive the digitized data will also provide the capability to interact with other on-line services of the modern library.

It is the use of computing technology which will make these services available to the patron of the library, and it is the cooperative collaboration of the library and the computing center which will make it possible for the computing technology to be applied to provide these services. At NCSU these two organizations have been working in such a cooperative relationship, which demonstrates that this cooperation is well within the traditions and culture of each of the organizations.

*   *   *

This article is based on a talk given at the I. T. Littleton Seminar on October 27, 1989.

BIOGRAPHICAL SKETCHES
OF THE CONTRIBUTORS

Durwood E. Bateman is Dean of the College of Agriculture and Life Sciences, North Carolina State University. He has written more than seventy scientific papers, lectured throughout the world, and participated in numerous international symposia.

Rashelle S. Karp is Associate Professor of Library Science, College of Communications and Computer Science, Clarion University of Pennsylvania.

Serena McGuire is Director of Extension Services for the Stanly County Public Library, Albemarle, North Carolina. Formerly, she was a graduate student at the University of North Carolina, Chapel Hill, where she earned her master's degree in Library Science.

George Messmer is an Associate in Library Services in the State Library of New York. He serves as an automation consultant and coordinator of the New York State Interlibrary Loan Telecommunications Network.

Nahla Natour is a Librarian at the Ministry of Planning, Amman, Jordan. A former graduate student in Library Science at Clarion University of Pennsylvania, she has authored another paper in ALAO, Volume 7.

Lori Rader is a Librarian on the staff of the University of Delaware. She earned her degree at Texas Woman's University.

Elizabeth Molnar Rajec is Chief of Acquisitions at the Cohen Library, City College of New York. She has compiled bibliographies on literary onomastics, and has compiled a two volume bibliography on the playwright Ferenc Molnar.

Jim E. Riviere is Professor of Pharmacology and Toxicology, College of Veterinary Medicine, North Carolina State University. He directs the NCSU-Batelle Cutaneous Pharmacology and Toxicology Program.

Kris Sandefur is Head Librarian of the reference library of the Fort Worth Star-Telegram. Her master's degree in Library Science was earned at Texas Woman's University.

Henry E. Schaffer is Associate Provost for Academic Computing, North Carolina State University. He has been a visiting scholar at Duke University. He is the author of numerous books and articles.

Bernard S. Schlessinger is Professor and Associate Dean, School of Library and Information Studies, Texas Women's University.

Glenn L. Sitzman is a former Librarian from the Carlson Library, Clarion University of Pennsylvania. He has worked in African libraries.

Alice G. Smith is Professor Emeritus, University of South Florida, School of Library and Information Science. She is an authority on and teacher of the subject of Bibliotherapy.

Frederick E. Smith is an Associate in Library Services in the State Library of New York. He is a former director of the library at Westminster College, New Wilmington, Pennsylvania.

Annabel K. Stephens is an Assistant Professor in the Graduate School of Library Service, University of Alabama. She was Director of the Union County Library, Mississippi, and a former branch head for the Memphis and Shelby County Public Library and Information Center, Tennessee.

Allen B. Veaner is Principal, Allen B. Veaner Associates, a private firm consulting to libraries, information-related businesses and government agencies. His writings on the profession of librarianship are well known.

Sohair Wastawy-Elbaz is an Information Researcher at the Center for the Study of Ethics in the Professions at the Illinois Institute of Technology, Chicago. She has written on other subjects in the field of librarianship.

INDEX

Advances in Library Administration and Organization

Edited by **Gerard B. McCabe**, *Director of Libraries, Clarion University of Pennsylvania* and **Bernard Kreissman**, *University Librarian Emeritus, University of California, Davis*

REVIEWS: "Special librarians and library managers in academic institutions should be aware of this volume and the series it initiates. Library schools and university libraries should purchase it."

— *Special Libraries*

"... library schools and large academic libraries should include this volume in their collection because the articles draw upon practical situations to illustrate administrative principles."

— *Journal of Academic Librarianship*

Volume 7, 1988, 287 pp. $63.50
ISBN 0-89232-817-7

CONTENTS: Introduction, *Gerard B. McCabe.* **A Comparative Study of the Management Styles and Career Progression Patterns of Recently Appointed Male and Female Public Library Administrators (1983-1987)**, *Joy M. Greiner, University of Southern Mississippi.* **Library Services for Adult Higher Education in the United Kingdom**, *Raymond K. Fisher, University of Birmingham, England.* **Chinese Theories on Collection Development**, *Priscilla C. Yu, University of Illinois Library.* **An Overview of the State of Research in the School Library Media Field, with a Selected Annotated Bibliography**, *P. Diane Snyder, Clarion University of Pennsylvania's College of Library Science.* **A Comparison of Content, Promptness, and Coverage of New Fiction Titles in Library Journal and Booklist, 1964-1984,** *Judith L. Palmer, North Texas State University and Irving Texas Public Library.* **Librarians as Teachers: A Study of Compensation and Status Issues,** *Barbara I. Dewey and J. Louise Malcomb, Indiana University.* **Academic Library Buildings: Their Evolution and Prospects,** *David Kaser, Indiana University.* **Accreditation and the Process of Change in Academic Libraries,** *Delmus E. Williams, University of Alabama, Huntsville.* **College and University Libraries: Traditions, Trends, and Technology,** *Eugene R. Hanson, Shippensburg University of Pennsylvania.* **A Reference Core Collection for a Petroleum Library,** *Nancy Mitchell-Tapping, Texas Woman's University, Valerie Lepus, Rashelle S. Karp, Clarion University of Pennsylvania, and Bernard S. Schlessinger, Texas Women's University.* **Private Institutions and Computer Utilization in Community Service and Education: The Case of the Abdul-Hamid Shoman Foundation,** *As'ad Abdul Rahman, Abdul-*

Hamid Shoman Foundation. Abdul-Hameed Shoman Public Library, Nahla Natour, Ministry of Planning, Amman, Jordan. **Bibliographical Sketches of the Contributors. Index.**

Volume 8, 1989, 302 pp. $63.50
ISBN 0-89232-967-X

CONTENTS: Introduction, *Bernard Kreissman.* **Quality in Bibliographic Databases: An Analysis of Member-Contributed Cataloging in OCLC and RLIN,** *Sheila S. Intner, Simmons College.* **The Library Leadership Project: A Test of Leadership Effectiveness in Academic Libraries,** *Eugene S. Mitchell, William Paterson College.* **Applying Strategic Planning to the Library: A Model for Public Services,** *Larry J. Ostler, Brigham Young University.* **Management Issues in Selection, Development, and Implementation of Integrated or Linked Systems for Academic Libraries,** *Elaine Lois Day, Hollins College.* **Acquisitions Management: The Infringing Roles of Acquisitions Librarians and Subject Specialists-An Historial Perspective,** *Barbara J. Henn, Indiana University.* **Development and Use of Theatre Databases,** *Helen K. Bolton, Clarion University of Pennsylvania.* **The Academic Library and the Liberal Arts Education of Young Adults: Reviewing the Relevance of the Library-College in the 1980s,** *Peter V. Deekle, Susquehanna University.* **College Libraries: The Colonial Period to the Twentieth Century,** *Eugene R. Hanson, Shippensburg University of Pennsylvania.* **Library Administrators' Attitudes Toward Continuing Professional Education Activities,** *John A. McCrossan, University of South Florida.* **A Core Reference Theatre Arts Collection for Research,** *Sharon Lynn Schofield, Ector Community Library, Odessa, Texas, Helen K. Bolton, Rashelle S. Karp, Clarion University of Pennsylvania, and Bernard S. Schlessinger, Texas Woman's University.* **The Library Buildings Award Program of the American Institute of Architects and the American Library Association,** *Roscoe Rouse, Jr., Oklahoma State University.* **Bibliography of Sub-Sahara African Librarianship, 1986-1987,** *Glenn L. Sitzman, Clairon University of Pennsylvania Libraries.* **Bibliographical Sketches of the Contributors. Index.**

Also Available:
Volumes 1-6 (1982-1987) $63.50 each

JAI PRESS INC.
55 Old Post Road - No. 2
P.O. Box 1678
Greenwich, Connecticut 06836-1678
Tel: 203-661-7602